The Scepter Shall Not Depart from Judah

RELIGION, POLITICS, AND SOCIETY IN THE NEW MILLENNIUM

Series Editors: Michael Novak, American Enterprise Institute, and Brian C. Anderson, Manhattan Institute

For nearly five centuries, it was widely believed that moral questions could be resolved through reason. The Enlightenment once gave us answers to these perennial questions, but the answers no longer seem adequate. It has become apparent that reason alone is not enough to answer the questions that define and shape our existence. Many now believe that we have come to the edge of the Enlightenment and are stepping forth into a new era, one that may be the most religious we have experienced in five hundred years. This series of books will explore this new historical condition, publishing important works of scholarship in various disciplines that help us to understand the trends in thought and belief we have come from and to define the ones toward which we are heading.

Political Memoirs
by Aurel Kolnai, edited by Francesca Murphy

Challenging the Modern World: Karol Wojtyla/John Paul II and the Development of Catholic Social Teaching
by Samuel Gregg

The Scepter Shall Not Depart from Judah: Perspectives on the Persistence of the Political in Judaism
by Alan L. Mittleman

An Uncommon Pontificate
by Macej Zieba (forthcoming)

Society as a Department Store
by Ryszard Legutko (forthcoming)

The Scepter Shall Not Depart from Judah

Perspectives on the Persistence of the Political in Judaism

Alan L. Mittleman

LEXINGTON BOOKS
Lanham • Boulder • New York • Oxford

LEXINGTON BOOKS

Published in the United States of America
by Lexington Books
4720 Boston Way, Lanham, Maryland 20706

12 Hid's Copse Road
Cumnor Hill, Oxford OX2 9JJ, England

British Library Cataloguing in Publication Information Available

Library of Congress Cataloging-in-Publication Data

Mittleman, Alan.
    The scepter shall not depart from Judah : perspectives on the persistence of the
political in Judaism / Alan L. Mittleman.
        p.   cm. – (Religion, politics, and society in the new millennium)
    Includes bibliographical references and index.
    IBSN 0-7391-0096-3 (cloth : alk. paper) – ISBN 0-7391-0097-1 (paper : alk. paper)
        1. Judaism and politics. 2. Judaism and state. 3. Covenants—Religious aspects—
Judaism. 4. Leadership—Religious aspects—Judaism. 5. Political science—
Philosophy—History. I. Title. II. Series.

BM645.P64 M58 2000
296'.3'82—dc21   99-053428

Printed in the United States of America

⊖™ The paper used in this publication meets the minimum requirements of American
National Standard for Information Sciences—Permanence of Paper for Printed Library
Materials, ANSI/NISO Z39.48–1992.

The scepter shall not depart from Judah, nor the ruler's staff from between his feet.

Genesis 49:10

"The scepter shall not depart from Judah" — these are the exilarchs in Babylon who rule over Israel with a scepter. "Nor the ruler's staff from between his feet" — these are the sons of the sons of Hillel, who teach Torah in the public domain.

B. Sanhedrin 5a

Contents

Acknowledgments

It has been my good fortune this past decade to have joined in the work of the Jerusalem Center for Public Affairs and to have participated in its annual Summer Workshops on the Jewish Political Tradition. Some of the essays in this volume were first presented at those workshops. I gratefully acknowledge my scholarly debt to friends and colleagues in those sessions, too numerous to mention, whose comments and criticisms helped to refine my views. I single out for special acknowledgment the late Prof. Daniel J. Elazar, founding president of the Jerusalem Center. Prof. Elazar has been a guiding light in my search for Jewish political thought. My debt to him is immeasurable. I also want to thank Dr. Robert Licht, whose knowledge of political theory has contributed to my education in these matters. I thank my wife, Patricia Mittleman, and my children, Ari and Joel, for their patience during my annual sojourns in Jerusalem. Finally, I dedicate this book, with love and gratitude, to my mother, Shirley L. Mittleman, whose spirit of voluntarism has taught me many things about both individuality and community.

Introduction

The title of this volume is drawn from Jacob's blessing to his children and grandchildren. His blessing to Judah contains the promise that Judah will become a royal house. Kings will issue, perhaps forever, from his loins. Kings, of course, ceased in Israel, but politics did not. Regime replaced regime. National independence was compromised and lost, regained and lost again. Yet, as the citation from the Talmud indicates, attention to political things—to matters of authority, organization, division of power, legitimacy, and so on— was not lost. Old texts were applied to new political realities. Political awareness and thought, constantly transformed and adapted to new historical exigencies, persisted among the Jews.[1]

Contemporary scholarship has been able to discern this persistence of political currents. Although scholars differ over whether essential political values persisted among Jews, the presence of political institutions and thought per se is not in doubt.[2] It is, therefore, not the task of this volume to prove that traditions of Jewish political life and thought continued to exist after the loss of ancient statehood. I regard that as already established. Rather, the essays in this volume examine some of the key concepts of politics through a Jewish lens. By *concepts of politics*, I refer to such matters as authority and its legitimacy, consent, obligation, regime types, and myths of political founding. By *Jewish*, I mean primarily the "normative" tradition of rabbinic literature, although I have drawn from the philosophical and theological expressions of that Judaism as well. I consider also texts of modern and contemporary Jewish scholarship that seek to reconstruct the contents of Judaism in a secular context. Our concern here is at once both historical, in the sense of the history of ideas, and philosophical. That is, the aim is both to look at the political ideas of the past and to articulate the enduring value that I believe they have for the present and

1

future. The agenda therefore is both descriptive and normative. Historically oriented study is intended to serve a philosophical interest.

This book might best be described as an apologia for traditional Jewish political values. Apologetics, as Franz Rosenzweig pointed out many years ago, is decidedly out of fashion. The apologetic profession par excellence, Rosenzweig noted, was lawyering. Both the apologist and the lawyer make their living, so to speak, from lying.[3] But Rosenzweig was quick to add that defense can be one of the "noblest of human pursuits." Indeed, the burden of his essay on apologetics is to argue that *most* of Jewish thought has fallen into this genre. Unlike Christian thought, which could express itself in a highly systematic and dogmatic architecture, as in Thomas's *Summa*, Jewish thought could never transcend the give and take of argument and defense. That is to say, Jewish thought did not often evade its political condition. It could not simply be in dialogue with itself. It had to articulate itself in dialogue with its cultured and not so cultured detractors, non-Jew and Jew alike. Consequently, in Rosenzweig's view, Jewish thought lacks the calm dispassion of the philosopher who treats his object as an *explicandum*: the Jewish thinker does not think *about* Judaism. Rather, the Jewish thinker thinks *within* Judaism, while turning out from it toward the tense intellectual field of the outside world. Thus both rooted and dialogic, Jewish thought exemplifies, for Rosenzweig, apologetics at its best. It is a paradigmatic case of what he elsewhere calls "new thinking."[4]

Rosenzweig's model of apologetics is especially well suited to a study of political theory. The Western tradition of political theory, like Jewish thought, developed in conjunction with an ongoing, often catastrophe-prone social experience. Political theory is generally polemical, engaged, tactical. Articulated in the midst of social crisis, it has, despite its often abstract tone, practical import. It is apologetic, in Rosenzweig's sense. Its vision is a vision of the human political condition.[5]

Jewish thought cannot evade its political condition. The contemporary Jew has what Leo Strauss called a "theological-political predicament."[6] This predicament, or problem, refers to the spiritual dependence of modern Jews on the political system in which their Judaism nestles. For most modern Jews, that political system is liberal democracy. Under liberal democracy, Judaism evolved into a "religion" from its earlier condition of being an all-encompassing milieu. Religion, on the Enlightenment terms assumed by liberal democracy, is basically a private matter. Jews purchased their admission into Western states and societies at the cost of repudiating the public, political dimensions of their Jewish reality. They ceased to be (at least complete) outsiders, tolerated members of a separate nation, and became citizens. They endlessly adapted their Judaism to fit into the social and cultural framework demanded by this transformation.

The problematic aspects of this theological-political nexus are many. As confidence in liberal democracy, progress, the Enlightenment and so on, weakens, as it surely did in the Weimar Republic of Strauss's day, Jewish faith, to the extent that it is has been tightly tied to the civic framework, also weakens. With weakened faith, Jews qua Jews cannot survive. As one student of Leo Strauss puts it, the theological-political problem is "the condition in which the contemporary Jew is no longer able to believe what his ancestors believed and has lost his faith in the possibility of a solution, and especially a liberal solution to the Jewish Problem. Yet the modern Jew is no longer prepared to accept Jewish suffering. He asks: 'Why should I, or any Jew, suffer anything for being a Jew?'"[7] The ancestors, unacquainted with liberal democracy, were no strangers to suffering and did not lack the religious resources to accept it, however bitterly. In the grip of a theological-political problem, predicament, or crisis, the religious horizon is conditioned and constrained by the political one. The imagination of the one runs no further than the *Weltbild* of the other. One of the purposes of this book is to come to appreciate the theological-political conceptions of Jews whose outlooks were shaped by other forms of politics. To what extent can those very different theological-political visions speak to those of us in liberal democracies? To what extent can the crisis of liberal democracy be ameliorated by exposure to those visions?

American Jews face the theological-political problem in a different way than do Israeli Jews. In America, owing to liberal democracy, Jews have found an unprecedented level of social acceptance. That is not due to human beings' having suddenly become more virtuous. Rather, it has to do with the growth of an increasingly open, commercial culture in which meritocratic advance in the marketplace has replaced traditional, stratified distinctions. The principal support for traditional distinctions, religious difference, has become increasingly irrelevant to political and economic life. The political and economic success of the commercial republic, best represented by the United States, has assured Jews a secure place as citizens of free societies. Unlike Strauss's Germany, the consequence of the theological-political nexus is not weakened resolve in the face of suffering. The American Jewish problem is that Jewish group consciousness and identity are attenuating, if not disappearing altogether among some segments of the population. How are Jews to survive as a self-conscious, distinctive group in the contemporary free society? To put it glibly, why be Jewish? Absent the entrenched discrimination and attendant self-consciousness that marked Jewish life in most European societies before World War II, it is unclear on what basis American Jews will, qua Jews, persist. The problem, in political terms, is this: how can the modern principle of political obligation be reconciled with the traditional, and still persisting, Jewish principle of obligation? How can covenantal duty speak for and defend itself in a culture of rights and individualism? The articulation and defense of covenantalism and its duties is a constant theme of these essays.

In Israel, by contrast, the problem is not one of loss of distinctiveness brought on by an overly Americanized, liberal democratic faith. Nonetheless, Israeli Judaism is also in the grip of a theological-political problem. Israel's settlement of religion and politics, "church and state" in Western terms, has begun to unravel. For various political and social reasons, religious sectors of Israeli society, ranging from moderate and extreme nationalists to extreme anti-nationalists, are no longer marginal. The secular sectors, which dominated society from the pre-state period to the present, no longer have a coherent, confident, and Jewishly credible ideology. Zionism, in all its varieties, was an ideological program for organizing Jewish masses, conducting settlement and diplomatic activities, in short, for founding a new Jewish society and a state. It no longer serves as an ideology for a rapidly maturing, "normalizing" society. The best the secular sectors can offer is the vision of a society drawn from the modern, democratic West: the free, egalitarian, human-rights-respecting, commercial republic. The problem with this is that such a society, envisioned and prophesied by Jewish heretics such as Spinoza, has an acutely controversial relationship with Jewish tradition. How are Judaism and democracy to be reconciled? Can they be? This is no abstract question. In Israeli society the problem is made all the more acute by institutional arrangements (such as established orthodox religion), political culture (a proportional representation system that ensures disproportionate power for religious parties), and historic antagonisms. There is a fundamental need for recalling the covenantal and consensual basis on which Jewish peoplehood rests. The essays in this book, although not explicitly directed at Israel's current problem of religious-secular dissensus, try to repair to fundamental issues in such a way as to throw light on the current problem.

Situating this book in the genre of apologetic literature and enunciating some of its generative problems ought to clarify for the reader what to expect. Nonetheless, since books of this kind are always open to a host of methodological objections from scholarly readers, I would like to try to further clarify some recurrent terms. Specifically, let us consider what Jewish philosophy means in this context. Let us also consider the relationship between philosophizing and using history.

Scholars are divided on what constitutes the category "Jewish philosophy." Is Jewish philosophy (or literature or art) simply philosophy written by Jews? That would be far too broad. Is Jewish philosophy philosophy written by Jews that takes an interest in Jewish things and is directed toward a Jewish audience? That might be narrow enough, but would it not violate philosophy's historic aspiration to universality? After all, we no longer admit such distorted ideas as "Jewish mathematics"; why should we allow "Jewish philosophy"? Medieval Jewish philosophers such as Maimonides certainly "took an interest" in Jewish things and wrote for (a highly specific) Jewish audience, but they also thought that they were addressing universal problems in a universal way. And when they were truly universal, were they in any significant way Jewish? Leo Strauss and his followers might well say that philosophy entails a stance and a conviction so dramatically at odds with biblical faith and the belief in divine revelation that Jews qua Jews cannot be philosophers. Those texts that we might casually call "Jewish philosophy" are really Jewish theology.

If we admit Jewish philosophy as philosophy written by Jews that takes an interest in Jewish things, this definition can also be seen to suffer from too much inclusiveness. It fails to draw a distinction between Jewish philosophy and Jewish thought as such. Although we cannot draw a hard and fast distinction between Jewish philosophy and Jewish thought, we ought to draw some distinction. Jewish thought includes, for example, Zionism. While Zionism can be thought of as a political ideology with significant philosophical influences and implications, it is not philosophy in an academic sense. We should not press this distinction too far, for example by artificially isolating the mystical tradition from the philosophical one, but we should admit it to the extent that it is useful. How then can we constitute Jewish philosophy?

One recent attempt to stipulate a necessary and sufficient criterion for Jewish philosophy is that of Steven Schwarzschild. Schwarzschild argued that what distinguishes Jewish philosophical inquiry is its ethical interest.[8] It is essential to Jewish philosophy to seek an ethical moment. Schwarzschild's judgment has the ironic consequence that not all philosophy written by Jews is Jewish philosophy, but that at least some philosophy written by non-Jews is Jewish philosophy.

Quite arguably, however, the question "What is Jewish philosophy?"— that is, what constitutes the essence of Jewish philosophy—is misguided. Contemporary scholars are highly suspicious, if not outright dismissive, of inquiries into essence. Daniel Frank argues that Jewish philosophy in the sense of a distinct body of texts and a distinct tradition of praxis does not in fact exist. It is a construct of nineteenth-century German Jewish academicians. In their search for social integration, they canonized a diverse set of rationalistically oriented Jewish cultural products and invented a tradition. "Indeed," Frank writes, "if I am right there was no Jewish philosophy and there were no Jewish philosophers before the nineteenth-century historians of Jewish philosophy invented the subject."[9] Frank believes that philosophers such as Maimonides believed that they were writing philosophy, not "Jewish philosophy." Furthermore, philosophy per se had a completely different character and self-understanding in the age of Maimonides. In this sense, it is hypostatic in the extreme to posit both a Jewish philosophy and a set of perennial problems that such a putative tradition must address. There is no tradition stretching from, say, Philo to Rosenzweig, nor are there common problems that all Jewish philosophers must treat. Philosophers indeed there are, but "Jewish philosophy" is our heuristic idea, not theirs.

Frank is reacting to the residue of German idealism that influenced modern Jewish studies during its birth in nineteenth-century Germany and still apparently taints it to this day. Idealism saw history as a rational process or at least as a process animated by the evolution and realization of ideas. Every epoch had its leading idea, every people its characteristic intellectual *Wesen*. As Judaism was transformed by integrationist and reform-minded modernizers from a covenant people's comprehensive way of life to a religion in the modern sense, Jewish uniqueness, a continuing Jewish raison d'etre, was sought in unique ideas rather than in an unwieldy field of historic particularities. All streams of emerging nineteenth-century Judaism posited their own version of what constituted the "essence of Judaism."[10] The last great expression of essentialism, as applied to Jewish philosophy, was Julius Guttmann's *Die Philosophie des Judentums*. Here, Judaism was essentially religious experience, was constituted by specific experiences of the divine. Shaped by the thought of Schleiermacher and Otto, Guttmann had a phenomenological orientation: irreducible religious experience lay at the heart of religion. This is religion's essence. Judaism is a religion. Jewish philosophy is a type of philosophy of religion. It is this essentialism that contemporaries such as Frank reject.

Frank's position has merit but seems in some ways an overreaction. For one thing, it is predicated on the notion of the death of the tradition. The modern is left with history, the premodern with an authoritative tradition. For the modern, history has undercut the authority of tradition by revealing its genesis and temporality.[11] The modern cannot participate unselfconsciously in the world of tradition and must, as historian, practice a self-imposed alienation from the tradition. This is actually liberating, not in the familiar progressivist sense of liberation from the "dead hand of tradition," but liberating for the tradition. That is, once we realize the insurmountable otherness of the past we can refrain from imposing our problems and preoccupations upon it. We liberate it from our needs and let it speak for itself.

But are matters necessarily so? In the social sciences, the stark distinction between traditional societies and modern ones has broken down. Traditional societies have been revealed as dynamic rather than static entities. The persistence of tradition in even radically modernizing societies such as Soviet Russia or revolutionary France has been demonstrated. It seems precipitous to uncritically assume the death of tradition, of tradition's withdrawal into a bygone and lost world. Without dismissing Frank's insightful account of the construction of the category "Jewish philosophy" in the nineteenth century, we can modify it to account for a more generous role for tradition as an abiding category of human social life.

Contemporary Jewish philosophy, no less than prior Jewish philosophy, is not so much philosophizing about a tradition as philosophizing (as noted above) within a tradition. To philosophize within a tradition means to be both in constant conversation with the traditions of philosophy in the non-Jewish world and in constant critical dialogue with the diverse and often conflicting voices within Jewish tradition.[12] It is not uncommon today to argue that all philosophizing is situated, conditioned by a traditional horizon. Jewish philosophizing is self-consciously and intentionally situated. It has the virtue of its necessity. Any philosopher, the Jewish philosopher included, makes use of the history of philosophy relevant to his or her subject. In addition, the Jewish philosopher must discover how the concepts relevant to his or her inquiry appear in previous Jewish thought. Thus, contemporary Jewish philosophy has, inevitably, a historical orientation. It ranges over the accumulated endowment of Jewish intellectual culture in order to situate itself. Without having given a definition of Jewish philosophy, we have at least described, in a preliminary way, some of what Jewish philosophy does.

How then does this not-quite-defined Jewish philosophy relate to Jewish history? The aims of the Jewish historian, especially the historian of Jewish philosophy, and the Jewish philosopher are both overlapping and divergent. Historians want to give the most defensible account possible of what the past was like and why it was as it was. Philosophers want, broadly speaking, to clarify concepts and evaluate beliefs.[13] Let us focus on the first goal, the clarification of concepts. Political philosophy, for example, is concerned to clarify concepts such as obligation, rights, sovereignty, power, authority, freedom, justice, and consent. By analyzing these concepts into their component parts and reconstructing the logical relationships between them, the political philosopher can give a more solid account of what they mean than the man in the street can, or so it is hoped. Yet however much political philosophy improves upon the understanding of citizens as such, its clarifications ought to ring true to them. Political philosophy is inconceivable without political life. It grows out of it, but always refers and returns back to it. Political institutions and practices themselves, Michael Sandel tells us, embody philosophical theories.[14] Political philosophy is both a "model of" and a "model for," a reflection of and a blueprint for political life.[15]

So too, Jewish political philosophy is concerned to clarify key concepts as they have appeared in previous expressions of Jewish thought, whether biblical, rabbinic, medieval, or modern, and as they are embodied in relevant institutions. Jewish political philosophy is nourished by Jewish political experience and by the primary forms of reflection upon it. It turns to both the textual sources of political thought and the institutional arrangements of political life. At this point, the interest in clarification cannot proceed without historical research. The aims of the historian and the political philosopher converge.

What is the point of clarifying concepts? Why should we want to know what Jewish thinkers in various eras thought about the general ideas of politics?

If our interest is strictly historical, then the question need not even be raised. It is interesting and valuable to know these things in and of themselves. The philosopher's interest in the clarification of concepts has, however, not been an end in itself. Rather, it has served the correlated purpose of evaluating beliefs. Political philosophy, for example, has classically been interested not only in "what does justice mean?" but in "what is the most just regime?" Political philosophy took upon itself the task not only of clarifying what people believe, but of evaluating what people believe about the public sphere and of recommending certain beliefs and discouraging others. Political philosophers were situated in their own society's traditions of political life and used those traditions to seek a wisdom able to respond to the crises of their times.

Some political philosophers in the twentieth century rejected this second, traditional aim of evaluation, believing that analyzing the logic of political concepts marks the limits of philosophy's competence. This predilection for a meta-ethical stance is based on the assumption that clarification per se is a non-evaluative or value-neutral activity similar to research in the hard sciences. This view finds few supporters today, whether because of John Rawls's pathbreaking return to normative moral and political theory or, for another community of philosophers, because of Leo Strauss's return to classical political rationalism or because science's claim to value neutrality has been attacked by a host of critics. However this may be, the Jewish philosopher, by contrast, was never much inclined to the luxuries of meta-ethics. To be situated also means to have taken a stand. Jewish philosophizing is not only about a "what" but about a "whither." Jewish philosophers want both to clarify relevant concepts within their tradition and to evaluate the significant beliefs that have been held about them in light of present theological-political exigencies. That is to say, they want to do their work with reference to the present situation in which the Jewish people finds itself.

There is a common charge leveled against books that seek to present Jewish views on political or moral topics. It is the charge of tendentiousness: the author has selected only those views exemplified in the traditional literature which reflect his or her own tendency. The concern here is that Jewish sources are so vast and variegated, so polyphonic that it is simply an intellectual swindle to imply that Judaism says anything simple and definite about anything, indeed, that there is a simple and definite Judaism that *can* say anything. Related to this is the charge of essentialism: that some ahistorical "Essence of Judaism" floats Platonically above all historical conditions. To talk about "the rabbis" as if Hillel and Samson Raphael Hirsch belong to the same universe of discourse is to be guilty of essentialism. The first of these errors betrays an apologetic motive held to be unworthy of serious scholarship. Yet if Rosenzweig is correct, then apologetics is redeemable, less as a mode of scholarship than as a mode of constructive thought. The second charge, essentialism, derives arguably from a misguided attempt by philosophy to trump history. Philosophers are impatient with the endless particularities of history. They seek more deductive, ideal-typical patterns that historians abjure.

There may be something to be said for metaphysical essentialism. Essence implies that without which something cannot be or cannot be conceived.[16] It is difficult to conceive, for example, of a Jewish philosophy that is not concerned with clarifying the concepts of "the people Israel" or "the God of Israel." Jewish philosophers may differ with one another to the greatest extent imaginable about the meaning and significance of these terms, but can they wholly ignore them and still be held to be Jewish philosophers? At the end of the day, however, essence may still require too much. Perhaps a weaker version of essence, Wittgenstein's "family resemblance," could help. Wittgenstein introduced this term to account for the usage of general concepts such as that of the game. Rather than posit some invariant essence that characterizes all games, Wittgenstein analyzed the concept of a game in terms of overlapping properties. Thus, while all board games have something in common (the board), this feature is not shared by card games or by ball games. Card games and board games, however, do have some overlapping properties, such as being played on tables, which ball games do not necessarily have. The point is to see the concept of a game not as characterized in every case by a single definable property, or by a set of definite properties, but by patterns of resemblance such as one might find, expressed to greater or lesser degrees, in a photograph of an extended family. The members retain their unique traits while also sharing elusive but nonetheless real physiognomic characteristics.[17]

Examples of Jewish philosophical thinking across the centuries may be said to have family resemblances with each other. This is true of Jewish political philosophy as well. While no single essence can be said to define the dizzying array of Jewish political thinkers from Philo to the Bundists or Jewish political institutions from kingship to the Jewish Agency, significant overlapping nonetheless exists. For one thing, Jewish political experience can be said to derive some unifying patterns of resemblance by what it has persistently excluded. That experience, and the thought that grew out of it, excluded divinized emperors, absolutized states, and cosmologically ordered caste systems. These exclusions were all based on the moral and political legacy of the Bible. The Bible, in particular the Pentateuch, has so shaped and saturated all recognizable "Judaisms" that it remains a persistent, if highly mutable, source of Jewish political thought. By treating a biblical text, a midrash, and a medieval commentary at the same level of discourse, however, I do not mean to imply that there are no significant differences among them either as texts or as documents of social worlds. I do mean to call attention to the persistence of controlling metaphors and symbols (such as "covenant") across a broad range of Jewish thought.

If this answers, at least in a preliminary way, the charge of essentialism, it does not yet address the charge of tendentiousness. How does one know whether the texts one has chosen are representative of large, significant patterns? The texts commented on in this book lend themselves to political readings. There are innumerable other texts that do so as well. While it would be foolish to claim comprehensiveness, I nonetheless believe that I have chosen and employed materials that are representative of Jewish political thought, or that, minimally, I can show awareness of the ways in which they fail to be representative. I can try to indicate the alternatives. But what if the problem of tendentiousness has less to do with the representativeness of the texts one selects than with the inherent problem of interpreting *any* text? Oliver Leaman argues that there is a fundamental tension between religious texts and the philosophical interpretations of those texts. Jewish texts are underdetermined. Stories, as well as legal dicta, can be read in numerous, equally plausible ways. This underdetermination of meaning is, in fact, essential to their effectiveness as religious texts. Philosophical interpretation, by contrast, constrains the range of the text. It traps it into supporting the philosopher's purpose. Another philosopher, with a different theory, could probably exploit the open-texturedness of the text for his or her purpose with equal facility. On one level, Leaman argues that all philosophical readings are tendentious. The implication of this goes beyond the problem of tendentiousness, however. Leaman questions whether a Jewish practical philosophy is possible in the first place.

Leaman indicts the philosopher's most fundamental instinct in approaching a religious text: "We tend to think that if we wish to show that particular philosophical views are representative of a tradition, then what we need to do is demonstrate some degree of agreement between the forms of the tradition and those views. I have argued . . . that it is too easy to do this for it to be worth doing."[18] For Leaman, the world of the religious text and the discourse of the philosopher are incommensurable. The text is indiscriminately exposed to the depredations of the theorizer. What can constrain this arbitrariness? Apparently only a general theory of translation from a religious idiom into a philosophical idiom: "To relate a tradition to a philosophical theory in more than a casual manner is viable only if we have a theory that possesses rules capable of transforming the language of the tradition into philosophical language. Until we have such a theory, we should be very careful about the ways in which we link together religious with philosophical statements."[19]

What would such a theory look like? Leaman gives no indication of the possible shape of a contemporary theory, but he does hint at the theory that guided some medieval philosophical exegetes: the theory of double truth. Religious language expresses in rhetorical, politically efficacious language the same truth that philosophers express demonstratively for their own circle. Philosophical language expresses the kernel of truth resident in religious language with precision and transparent conformity to the norms of universal reason. Such a general theory would find few adherents today. We would be uncomfortable with the hubris implicit in such a view. Nonetheless, the theory has its own kernel of truth, for it is roughly equivalent to the role of philosophy noted above, namely, the clarification of concepts. To the extent that philosophy can clarify the system of concepts actually at work in a segment of religious tradition, it does express, at a higher order of abstraction, the thought of the tradition. Philosophical analysis does not, of course, demonstrate the truth of that thought. It merely displays it. Here it parts company with the medieval theory.

But is a modern theory truly necessary? I don't see how it could be. I don't see how we could ever reach any consensus on a theory of religious language, let alone an agreed-upon method for translating religious language into philosophical discourse. Certainly, what is required is a keen awareness of the typical pitfalls Leaman exposes for us. But any exegete, philosophically oriented or not, should be constantly open to the possibility that his or her interpretation fails to persuade. A rational interpretation of a text is an interpretation that gives sound reasons for itself. If it ultimately manages, in the face of alternative texts and counterinterpretations, to persuade a readership, then it may be thought the most coherent interpretation under the circumstances. Shared conversation about the plausibility of interpretation seems to me to provide better insurance of fidelity to the text than would the application of a longed-for theory.

Practical philosophy, including political philosophy, comes out of and contributes to, after all, a community that must both speak and act. The community, if it aspires to some rationality in its affairs, must constantly reflect upon and discuss its own practices and values in light of its current situation. Philosophy is the thin end of the wedge of this public discourse. It is at once its most sharply incisive and fragile part. Jewish texts, the Jewish tradition in the round, form the subject matter of this discourse for tradition-oriented Jews. The current situation, both historical, political and epistemic, forms the framework in which texts must become intelligible. The work of clarifying those practices and values resident in the Jewish tradition that we call political cannot be postponed. It is ongoing as well as integral to the community's aspirations for good governance and moral conduct. It cannot be put on hold until a theory is refined. The community devises its practices of interpretation as it goes, refining and discarding them as its intergenerational dialogue proceeds. What will count as the best possible interpretation will be contingent upon not only an elemental affinity with the text, but a conformity with the prevailing canons of reason and value. How well interpretations suit the social needs of the community of interpreters will also be a crucial factor.

The interpretation of the classic texts is not an end in itself. Concepts are clarified so that the community can subject its beliefs to ongoing criticism and evaluation. Leaders and ordinary citizens will constantly be asking questions such as: "How much public criticism of policy is optimal?" The liberal democratic tradition puts the threshhold for criticism and dissent quite high. How high would (should) the Jewish tradition set it? Presumably, those Jews, philosophers included, who would read the relevant texts to support a straightforward libertarian view would merit Leaman's criticism. (And rightly so.) But the weakness of Leaman's position is that the political articulation of any view, as well as of higher-order theoretical constructs, is also suspect. But legitimate questions, such as the one above, require thoughtful, reasoned answers. It is intolerable that practical philosophy should be allowed to speak within other civil traditions yet be silent among the Jews because they have Scriptures and commentaries! Precisely because Jews have Scriptures and commentaries, and indigenous traditions of philosophical reasoning about those texts, practical philosophy has a clear role to play among them. This is part of what it means to philosophize within a tradition.

It is the province of historians of Jewish thought or law to answer such questions as: "How high would the Jewish tradition . . .?" They can explore the relevant texts and make judgments about how Jewish thinkers and decisors responded to this problem in the past. Jewish philosophers speak to the question of "How high should . . .?" The philosopher needs to attend not just to a body of laws and cases, but to a large-scale comparison of the ethos of Jewish tradition with the ethos of, for example, the modern liberal tradition.[20] To evoke something as nebulous as an ethos is necessarily a risky and speculative theoretical exercise. But it need not (and must not) be arbitrary. Identifying the typical patterns of concepts, the representative resemblances across the tradition, such as covenant or divine kingship, fleshes out the tradition's logic and discovers principles for organizing its dicta. A society that understands itself in terms of covenant will draw the parameters of individual liberty somewhat differently from a society with a purely contractual, natural, or hierarchical self-understanding. The philosopher would then go on to ask comparative questions about how liberty, for example, looks to persons in these different sorts of societies. Is one society's version of liberty genuine and another's spurious? How much elasticity is there in the concept of liberty? What criteria must a Jewish concept of liberty meet to count as a genuine concept of liberty? To count as a Jewish concept? What is it best for Jews to believe about liberty?

Assuming that these queries could be answered by a Jewish theory of liberty, how would we know that the theory is "authentically" Jewish? Leaman's point, after all, is not that practical philosophy is not possible, but that Jewish practical philosophy may not be possible. The difficulty is in what, if anything, authenticates a practical philosophy as Jewish. This is a persistent anxiety. There is little doubt that, say, halakhic productivity by traditional decisors is an authentically Jewish activity, but outside of that domain we seem to be either worried or perplexed about whether or if certain cultural products ought to count as Jewish. Schwarzschild's insightful way of answering the question of what constitutes the Jewishness of a philosophical project allays the anxiety, at least for a moment. Such an anxiety resembles the nineteenth century's "Bibel und Babel" controversy. To what extent was the biblical literature unique? To what extent was it a revised version of Mesopotamian myth and law? Was it authentically Israelite? What does it mean to call something authentically Israelite?

Expanding the scope of knowledge, in this case knowledge about the history of religion, necessarily problematizes the identity of those who situate themselves within the religion. The problem is not just one of assimilating new facts or accepting a new paradigm, that is, it is not just a cognitive problem. It is an ontic problem. The issue of what constitutes the Jewish authenticity of an intellectual practice is not only an intellectual matter. It does not permit of an intellectual solution. Or better: it does not permit of only an intellectual solution. One cannot give a list of necessary and sufficient conditions that a cultural expression must meet in order to be considered Jewish. As an ontic problem, its symptom is anxiety, not simply perplexity. The alleviation of anxiety is not a psychological matter. It is a matter of a Jew achieving an overall integration of personal existence; of being able to live objectively within the covenant traditions of the Jewish people with inner confidence that his or her personal path belongs. It is a matter of a Jew knowing before Whom he or she stands and being able to give a reasoned account and defense of a life. The question of what is authentically Jewish can become a postmodern parlor game, but at its deepest level it represents the anxiety of the defendant before the judge: the anxiety of judgment.

If the Jewishness or Jewish authenticity of a project cannot be ascertained in advance of living the project or living with the project in community, then Leaman's question cannot be definitively answered. We cannot know in advance whether an "authentic" Jewish practical philosophy is possible. Claimants for this distinction are actual, so of course they are possible. But we cannot certify that they are authentic. That, I suggest, can only be settled in the conscience of the theorist and the historic life of the community. At any rate, practical philosophy is not only philosophy of practice, it is also a practice itself. It arises in the context of the life of the community or polity and contributes to its thought about itself.

In the following essays, I try to consider the Jewish people as a polity and Judaism as a body of thought attuned to the problems of politics. My warrant for doing so is twofold. First, it seems clear to me that, rivers of nineteenth-century ink notwithstanding, the Jews are a nation. Granted, they are not a "normal" nation on the modern model. Despite a century of Zionism, the Jews remain a most peculiar nation. But they are, nonetheless, a nation. Attempts to render the Jews a non-nation, a mere confession, or a fully modernized secular nation always seem to founder, whether on the shoals of hostile antisemitic incredulity or on the Jews' own longing for the restoration of cosmic purpose.

Jewish nationhood was attained in antiquity and cannot be disentangled from the divine covenant that constitutes its founding. Insofar as the Jews are a nation, their law and literature have always had a scope that far exceeds the limited domain circumscribed by Christian and Enlightenment notions of "religion." The Jewish loyalty to Judaism, furthermore, is not captured solely by categories such as "faith." Jewish piety seems often (perhaps always) to entail a dimension of self-sacrifice to the covenant community, to the nation. Judaism is not constituted simply by an ontology of beliefs and correlated practices. It is constituted by a thick web of obligatory associations reaching backward and forward in time. Jewish faith, I would argue, is analogous to the obligation Socrates felt toward Athens, as reported in the *Crito*, or to the civic republicanism the American Founders sought to instill in the citizen. That is to say, the uniquely theological-political thing that Judaism is can be brought to greater clarity through a framework of analysis attuned to political theory.

Second, we seem to be at a historic juncture in which the intellectual confidence and syntheses of the Enlightenment no longer command the loyalty of the enlightened. Perhaps the owl of Minerva has taken flight. This juncture is marked by the idea of postmodernism. At the end of this sad and violent century, we are no longer convinced that tradition, religious or otherwise, is a bar to rational progress or that society can be redesigned on strictly rational lines by ardent, competent humanists. Modernity began, in political theory at least, with an assault on the basis (or what was taken to be the basis) of governing tradition: Scripture and revelation. The early modern theorists, such as Hobbes, Locke, and Spinoza, attacked the view that Scripture, as interpreted by Christian religious elites, held political wisdom and conferred political legitimacy.[21] Yet, was it the case, as Leo Strauss argued, that these moderns never really disproved revelation but only damaged its plausibility through mockery? In postmodernity, the laughter has died down. Although without a firm faith in its revelation or its divinity, even secular political scientists have found in the Bible the stuff of Spinoza's nightmares. The Bible is read once again as a source for political insight and instruction. These essays are situated in that ironic movement of return.

The first chapter of this book looks at how the Jews distanced themselves from a political self-understanding in early modern times. In line with Christian and Enlightenment norms, Jews transformed their complex heritage into a religion, denaturing their nationhood and shedding the overtly political elements of their communal life. After describing those political elements in historic communal life, and the process of their decline, I turn to a twentieth-century text: Hermann Cohen's critique of Heinrich Graetz's programmatic statement on the nature of Jewish history. In Cohen's attack on Graetz's eminently political concept of the "essence of Judaism," one can see the completion of a long process of obscuring and negating the political character of Judaism and the Jews.

In chapter 2, I focus on one dimension of the recovery of the political character of Judaism by looking at a treatment of the concept of covenant. The emphasis is on Max Weber, an upstart figure in the world of early twentieth-century biblical scholarship. Weber was a bridge between the classic of critical scholarship, Julius Wellhausen, and the later scholars of the twentieth century. Weber's importance for our study rests, as Arnaldo Momiliagno has observed, on being the first to restore the full political salience of the covenant idea.[22]

Chapter 3 begins to move the focus away from historiographical concerns toward more philosophical ones. It explores a variety of rabbinic texts and investigates how biblical ideas about covenant were reinterpreted by the early rabbis. I argue that the seeds of the modern movement away from a truly political Jewish self-understanding were already to be found in early rabbinic Judaism. The philosophical point here is this: by redefining biblical ideas of covenant, the rabbis shifted the ground of obligation to the covenant community from an explicitly political act (individual consent) to series of tacit gestures (such as circumcision), thereby problematizing consent as a basis for political obligation. I consider whether there are affinities therefore between rabbis and others, such as David Hume, who also problematized the concept of consent.

Chapter 4 continues to examine the nexus of political obligation and consent through the lens of rabbinic commentary, both midrashic and medieval, on the biblical story of Nimrod. Nimrod, I argue, gives the rabbis an occasion to think about the origins of political association and the ideal values that political society ought to embody. Nimrod provides a myth of origin, similar in function to social contract theory in Locke or conquest in Machiavelli, through which fundamental political values are refracted. The chapter raises the problem of the grounds of legitimate authority. Does rabbinic Judaism require that public authority derive in some sense from God?

Chapter 5 continues this inquiry by exploring the concept of rights. Modern thought has made rights the centerpiece of modern republicanism. Rights seem to presuppose a concept of personhood unencumbered by social or religious distinctions, indeed by any attributes judged to be irrelevant. Personhood, shorn of the *imago dei*, becomes the ground of rights. This presupposes an essentially secular view of the world and of the origins of public authority. The chapter explores Jewish critiques of rights. As theonomists, the Jewish critics assail the secular concept of personhood. One of the features of that concept is its stress on autonomy. The conflict between theonomy and autonomy throws into relief the contrast between the ancient tradition of the virtuous republic, still alive in Judaism, and the modern democratic and commercial republic.

In chapter 6, I continue this thrust by contrasting the situated, or metaphysically encumbered, self of Judaism with the rational, liberal self envisioned by modern political theorists. What are the consequences for political obligation of this more ancient understanding of selfhood?   How   is the proper relationship between the pursuit of personal life-projects and public duty to be constituted?

In chapter 7, I continue to look at the problem of individual freedom versus commitment to the common good. How should individual interests be aligned with the general welfare? The subject matter is a Talmudic discussion of the claims of the community upon the individual. I try to show the ways in which the contemporary American variant of the civic republican tradition (communitarianism) resembles rabbinic thinking and how it differs from it.

Chapter 8 looks at the fundamental contrasts between the ideal-typical Jewish polity and the modern, democratic one through an exploration of the thought of an Orthodox traditionalist, Shimon Federbush. Federbush, in the 1950s, produced a systematic treatise on Jewish law and modern politics. He sought to guide the public institutions of the nascent State of Israel into conformity with halakha without (*mirabile dictu!*) loss of either democracy or halakhic legitimacy. I consider specifically Federbush's balancing of halakha with popular sovereignty. Federbush's thought crystallizes all of the contrasts mentioned above between ancient and medieval, and modern possibilities of a Jewish politics.

Earlier versions of chapters 2 and 4 through 8 have appeared in the *Jewish Political Studies Review, First Things,* and *S'VARA.* I thank the editors of these journals for their permission to revise and expand these articles.

Notes

1. The text from which this book takes its title, Genesis 49:10, has itself been the topic of extensive political exegesis. Insofar as it was taken by Christians to predict the demise of Jewish power and the messianic dominion of Christ (that is, the scepter shall not depart from Judah *until* Shiloh (= Christ) comes), Jews had to interpret the verse to show that, first, "Shiloh" does not mean Christ and, second, that Jewish dominion has not been permanently suspended. Jewish exegetes took various tacks. For some, real Jewish political life has been suspended until the messiah comes. For others, Jewish political life has been transformed and persists. For a full accounting of Jewish, Christian, and even Muslim exegeses, see Adolf Posnanski, *Schiloh: Ein Beitrag zur Geschichte der Messiaslehre,* Vol. I (Leipzig: J. C. Hinrichs, 1904). For an apparent denial of the persistence of Jewish political life in the context of a Jewish-Christian disputation, see Nachmanides' Barcelona disputation in Hyam Maccoby, *Judaism on Trial* (London: Littman Library of Jewish Civilization, 1982), 105-108.

2. An interest in Jewish political life and institutions was coeval with the birth of modern Jewish scholarship per se. So eminent a *Wissenschaftler* as Zechariah Frankel published a lengthy article on Jewish communal institutions in the second issue of his *Monatsschrift.* Similarly, two great twentieth-century scholars, Salo Baron and Louis Finkelstein, published significant studies of medieval Jewish political thought and

practice. Nonetheless, the uncritical but typically modern assumption that politics refers only to events at the level of nation-states impeded all of these authors from recognizing the full political content of their studies. The category of the "social" seemed more comprehensive and accurate to them than the "political." More recently, however, historians such as David Biale and Ismar Schorsch, and political scientists such as Daniel Elazar, Stuart Cohen, and Ella Belfer, taking advantage of expanded, late-twentieth- century definitions of politics, have shown that it is fully appropriate to speak of Jewish political traditions persisting over the centuries. They differ, of course, on the content and character of these traditions. For a review of the issues, see Alan L. Mittleman, *The Politics of Torah: The Jewish Political Tradition and the Founding of Agudat Israel* (Albany: State University of New York Press, 1996), 29-42.

3. "Apologetisches Denken," in Franz Rosenzweig, *Kleinere Schriften* (Berlin: Schocken Verlag, 1937), 41.

4. Rosenzweig, *Kleinere Schriften*, 373ff.

5. On the relationship of political theory to political institutions and the crises they confront, see Sheldon Wolin, *Politics and Vision* (Boston: Little, Brown, 1960), 6-11.

6. Leo Strauss, *Jewish Philosophy and the Crisis of Modernity*, Kenneth Hart Green, ed. and trans. (Albany: State University of New York Press, 1997), 137.

7. Martin Plax, Review of Leo Strauss, *Jewish Philosophy and the Crisis of Modernity*, *Jewish Political Studies Review*, vol. 10, nos. 3 and 4 (Fall 1998), 118.

8. See, for example, Steven Schwarzschild's "Modern Jewish Philosophy," reprinted in Menachem Kellner, ed. *The Pursuit of the Ideal: Jewish Writings of Steven Schwarzschild* (Albany: State University of New York Press, 1990), 229.

9. Daniel Frank and Oliver Leaman, eds. *History of Jewish Philosophy*, Routledge *History of World Philosophies*, vol. II (London: Routledge, 1997), 5.

10. For a study of the polemical uses to which the concept "essence of Judaism" was put, see Uriel Tal, "Theologische Debatte um das Wesen des Judentums" in Werner Mosse, ed., *Juden in Wilhelminischen Deutschland 1870-1914* (Tübingen: J.C.B. Mohr, 1976), 599-632.

11. Frank and Leaman, *History of Jewish Philosophy*, 7.

12. Rosenzweig also noted the temptation of the apologist to simplify his own tradition and neglect its discordant voices. Cf. Rosenzweig, *Kleinere Schriften*, 40.

13. This formulation of the aims of political philosophy is taken from D. D. Raphael, *Problems of Political Philosophy* (New York: Praeger, 1970). Raphael's formulation assigns philosophy a dialectical rather than a demonstrative role. That is, philosophy does not claim to work from necessarily true universal premises to necessarily true conclusions. It works rather with premises embedded in particular intellectual contexts and subjects them to rigorous, if often inconclusive, analysis. Insofar as we are dealing with practical philosophy, whose subject matter is drawn from traditions of political and moral life, a dialectical construal of philosophy is more appropriate than a demonstrative one. See Oliver Leaman, "Is a Jewish Practical Philosophy Possible?" in Daniel H. Frank, ed. *Commandment and Community: New Essays in Jewish Legal and Political Philosophy* (Albany: State University of New York Press, 1995), 57.

14. Michael J. Sandel, *Democracy's Discontent: America in Search of a Public Philosophy* (Cambridge, Mass.: Belknap Press of Harvard University Press, 1996), ix.

15. On the concept of the model as a way of explaining culture, see Clifford Geertz, *The Interpretation of Cultures* (New York: Basic Books, 1973), ch. 4.

16. See Spinoza's definition of essence at *Ethics*, Part II, Definition II.

17. Ludwig Wittgenstein, *Philosophical Investigations*, G. E. M. Anscombe, ed. (New York: Macmillan, 1968), pt. I, para. 67.

18. Leaman, "Is a Practical Jewish Philosophy Possible?" 68.

19. Ibid.

20. By implying a division of labor between historians and philosophers, I certainly do not mean to imply that rabbinic legal decisors (*poskim*) have no role to play in Jewish political thought or life. Indeed, some movements in Jewish Orthodoxy, such as Agudat Israel, invest significant political decision-making power in contemporary rabbinic sages. (For the theory underlying this move, see Alan Mittleman, *The Politics of Torah.*) The emergence of rabbis as key political authorities is an important piece of the history of Orthodoxy in the last two centuries. I am, however, basically agreeing with Menachem Kellner that certain matters are typically "meta-halakhic." The sort of political philosophical questions addressed here, while nourished by halakhic sources, call for other than strictly halakhic responses. For an argument carving out a meta-halakhic sphere in theological matters, see Menachem Kellner, *Must a Jew Believe Anything?* (London: Littman Library of Jewish Civilization, 1999), 90-92.

21. I do not mean to imply that all of the early modern political thinkers were hostile to the Bible as a source of political teaching. Machiavelli, for example, for all of his criticism of the Roman papacy, found wisdom in the Mosaic polity, as did Hobbes. For an overview, see Douglas Kries, ed., *Piety and Humanity: Essays on Religion and Early Modern Political Philosophy* (Lanham, Md.: Rowman & Littlefield, 1997) and Ronald Biener, "Machiavelli, Hobbes, and Rousseau on Civil Religion," *Review of Politics* 55 (Fall 1993), 617-38.

22. Arnaldo Momigliano, *Essays on Ancient and Modern Judaism*, Silvia Berti, ed. (Chicago: University of Chicago Press, 1994), 177.

Chapter One

Paradigm Lost: The Decline of the Jews As a Polity

At the dawn of the modern era, Jewish communal autonomy—the limited right of self-rule or self-administration granted by European Christians to the Jews in their midst—declined. The exercise of that right (or more properly that *privilege*) had enabled Jews to imagine that they enjoyed some shreds of continuity with their former state of national sovereignty. Although they knew themselves to be a conquered and exiled people, they also knew themselves to be a political people, that is, a people who could still govern some aspects of its common life according to its own traditions and values.[1] The decline of communal autonomy changed that perception. As early as the fifteenth century, European rulers began to limit or curtail self-rule privileges.[2] Centralizing states with expanding bureaucracies interfered in the administrative and electoral procedures of Jewish communities (*kehillot*). Jews themselves often sought to escape the burdens of belonging, seeking to pay taxes directly to the gentile state and avoid the assessments of Jewish communal leaders. Jews defected from Jewish courts and Jewish law, taking their disputes before the state courts. Communal autonomy was caught between two pincers. It declined as the gentile state chiseled it away piece by piece. Its decline was also abetted by Jews seeking relief from its often oligarchic structures and procedures, thus further encouraging the state to view the *kehillot* as expendable rather than as assets. By the eighteenth century, this internal Jewish movement against communal autonomy received a full-fledged philosophical articulation—in the name of religious liberty—from Moses Mendelssohn.[3] With this,

19

Enlightenment, liberal notions of religion as the personal creed of individuals began to overcome inherited ideas of Judaism as the covenantal political-juridical order of a people. The confessionalization of Judaism, its recasting as a modern "religion," had begun.[4]

In this chapter, we consider the decline of Jewish communal autonomy and its conceptual consequences. Our concern is less with the social and institutional history of communal decline and Jewish integration than with the impact of that history on self-representation, on how the Jews imagined themselves. In the first part of the chapter, I discuss the constitution of public authority in the Jewish political tradition, as well as its erosion in early modern times. This sets the stage for the second part of the chapter, a translated text, with commentary, from the early–twentieth-century philosopher Hermann Cohen. In this text, Cohen criticizes the popular nineteenth-century Jewish historian Heinrich Graetz. Graetz argued, in his first programmatic writing on Jewish history, that Israel began as a political people, that Israel's religious consciousness was inextricably linked to her political self-understanding. Graetz sought to restore the balance between political and religious elements of Jewish self-representation. Cohen wished no such restoration. By rejecting Graetz, Cohen, an heir of Mendelssohn in this respect, privileges the religious dimension and suppresses the political. In Cohen's denial that the Jews are a political people, we see an intricate philosophical effort to take the scepter away from Judah forever.

Public Authority and Its Discontents

It has often been remarked that while Christianity developed in the cities of the Roman Empire, Judaism came upon the stage of history in the Sinai wilderness. Christianity grew in a world of settled legal and political institutions and could therefore articulate itself as a faith, a way of salvation, taking the political constitution of society for granted. Judaism, by contrast, had to devise its own legal and political institutions. It had to start from scratch, as it were.[5] Needless to say, this generalization is a caricature. But it does get at a basic difference between the two heirs of the biblical world. Judaism continued to develop the civil, criminal, and public law of the Bible as an integral aspect of its historic civilization. Christianity was content to claim the Ten Commandments as binding moral law and shed what remained of biblical law, both civil and cultic, as irrelevant to its new dispensation. (It was never that simple, of course. Christianity did have to develop social forms and political institutions adequate to its moral and salvific vision. Furthermore, Jewish law continued to exert a tremendous pull on many Christians, both in its more purely ritualistic dimensions and as a source for political guidance. "Judaizing," that is, return to Jewish religious usages, represented a continuing problem for Christian authorities. In the Reformation period and afterwards, biblical law was also appropriated as the positive law of Christian commonwealths by Puritans and others.)

The Jewish bent toward extensive legislation, toward remaking the whole of the world under the sovereignty of God, meant that the political ordering of a righteous community could not be neglected. The Bible attests to the struggles of ancient Israel to achieve a political order commensurate with both the demands of a righteous God and the hard realities of national survival. Within the two millennia of biblical history, Israel experimented with at least four types of regime: that of the charismatic prophet, the anarchic confederacy, kingship, and, at the end of the biblical period, a custodial regime of limited self-government under various imperial umbrellas.

Political authority in the Bible flows from God to humans. Initially all authority is God's. He delegates it to those whom he chooses. He gives them a right to rule, which is to say a right to expect the consent of those whom they rule. That consent is not guaranteed, but must be secured by formal acts of acceptance. Despite the prominence of human intermediaries, for example, Moses, his successor, Joshua, and the Judges, Israel's government could be characterized, as Spinoza observed, as a theocracy. God was, if we take the texts at their word, Israel's true ruler. The charismatic human rulers were in constant living relationship with the divine ruler. No settled rational system of administration and decision had evolved. Nor could public authority be justified in an immanent or pragmatic way. Yet the Torah anticipates a time (the critic would say retrojects a time) when Israel will grow restive under God's direct rule and clamor for a king. Israel will seek a more proximate ruler. It will seek to rule itself by designating one of its own as ruler. In Deuteronomy 17:14-20, we read:

> If, when you have entered the land that the LORD your God has given you, and occupied it and settled in it, you decide, "I will set a king over me, as do all the nations about me," you shall be free to set a king over yourself, one chosen by the LORD your God. Be sure to set as king over yourself one of your own people; you must not set a foreigner over you, one who is not your kinsman. Moreover, he shall not keep many horses or send people back to Egypt to add to his horses, since the LORD has warned you, "You must not go back that way again." And he shall not have many wives, lest his heart go astray; nor shall he amass silver and gold to excess. When he is seated on his royal throne, he shall have a copy of this Teaching written for him by the levitical priests. Let it remain with him and let him read in it all his life, so that he may learn to revere the LORD his God, to observe faithfully every word of this Teaching as well as these laws. Thus he will not act haughtily toward his fellows or deviate from the Instruction to the right or to the left, to the end that he and his descendants may reign long in the midst of Israel.

The immediate import of this text is to constrain the institution of human rule so that it does not alienate itself from divine authority. Human public authority must remain dependent on God's will and God's law. The text reflects deep-seated ambivalence about the potential of kingship. The ambiguous wording at the beginning of this biblical passage ("if. . .when. . .you decide") gives rise to a Talmudic discussion about whether kingship is commanded or merely permitted. Is kingship an intrinsic good or a tolerated but necessary evil? Debate on this point reverberated over the centuries.[6] In a sense, it has never been settled. Despite the ambivalence, it is clear, however, that the Jewish tradition endorsed forms of decision-making authority that are relatively independent of the law of the Torah. We do not yet know what the king, anticipated in Deuteronomy, may legitimately do. We only know what he may not do. We also know that he is to have a Torah scroll by his side and that he should be instructed in it so that his as yet unspecified power may be conditioned by the Torah's principles of justice and reverence. The king is to be a constitutional ruler. He is to be constrained by the Torah, yet he is to have a certain legitimate discretion to frame his own law and policy as well.

With the development of kingship during the time of Samuel, God's unmediated rule is increasingly displaced by a more "rational" form of human agency.[7] The question of what this agency may permissibly do becomes acute. Ancient Israel attempted in various ways, such as rebellion and prophetic opposition, to check the natural increase of the power of the king. What concerns us here is rabbinic Judaism's understanding of the range of the king's power or, more broadly, of human public authority. The rabbis' approach is based on the Talmud's reading of the key text from Samuel that narrates the transition from the rule of judges to the rule of kings:

> This will be the practice of the king (*mishpat ha-melekh*) who will rule over you: he will take your sons and appoint them as his charioteers and horsemen, and they will serve as outrunners for his chariots. He will appoint them as his chiefs of thousands and of fifties; or they will have to plow his fields, reap his harvest, and make his weapons and the equipment for his chariots. He will take your daughters as perfumers, cooks, and bakers. He will seize your choice fields, vineyards, and olive groves, and give them to his courtiers. He will take a tenth part of your grain and vintage and give it to his eunuchs and courtiers. He will take your male and female slaves, your choice young men, and your asses, and put them to work for him. He will take a tenth part of your flocks, and you shall become his slaves. (I Sam. 8:11-17)

The Talmud finds in the idea of *mishpat ha-melekh*, of the king's law, a category of legislation outside of the legislation given by God at Sinai through Moses. For the first time, Israel, through its authorized political representatives, is empowered to apply practical reason to public affairs. Yet what is the extent of this public authority? Is Samuel warning the people of what a king might do so as to discourage them from making the fateful choice? Or is he delineating the legitimate powers of the king? The Talmudic sages are divided on this point, as they are divided on the propriety of kingship per se.[8] The general conclusion was that kings had extensive executive, legislative, and judicial powers. These powers not only included immediate matters of politics and economics such as war and taxation, but criminal matters as well. Kings could execute rebels and criminals whose execution might otherwise be prohibited by halakha.[9]

Ancient Judaism showed remarkable flexibility in accommodating different forms of regime. Despite a strong initial bias for direct divine rule mediated by charismatic leaders, both people and God came to accept human kingship. Yet the experience of kingship was hardly happy. It began tragically with Saul. The upstart son of Jesse who replaced him, the idealized model for all future righteous rulers, was himself subject to searing prophetic critique. Most of the kings of Judah and Israel were evil in the Bible's judgment. The old yearning for God's direct, theocratic rule continued in some dissident groups such as the Rechabites. Nonetheless, ancient Israel came not only to accept but to idealize kingship. "I have installed My king on Zion, My holy mountain!" (Ps. 2:6) A righteous king, following ancient Near Eastern practice, was known as God's son: "You are my son, I have fathered you this day" (Ps. 2:7; cf. II Sam. 7:14). The prophetic critics of the kings did not seek to undo kingship per se, but to render it righteous through fidelity to God's way or, as we would say, through constitutional limitation. Similarly, although some of the rabbis and traditional commentators sought to negate kingship altogether, these discussions were, in a sense, beside the point since all traditional authorities accepted the necessity for *rational and responsible public authority* in the Jewish polity. As kingship fell into desuetude, the interpreters of Torah sought to endow subsequent regime forms with the halo of legitimacy anciently acquired by kingship. *Mishpat ha-melekh* was the device for permitting duly authorized political representatives to cope with the continuous vicissitudes of history.[10]

Jewish political theorists differ over the degree to which *mishpat ha-melekh*, the discretionary sphere of public authority, was independent (at any rate, qualifiedly independent) of halakha. Some advocates of *mishpat ha-melekh*, such as R. Shimon Federbush, as we will see in more detail in chapter 8, invest this sphere with very broad powers. Federbush bases himself on authorities such as Maimonides and R. Nissim Gerondi, who massively expanded the role of "discretionary power" in their schemes of political governance.[11] Others, such as Isaac Breuer, subordinate the discretion of political leaders entirely to halakha and its intepreters. Indeed, this becomes a central problem in Jewish political history and theory. As independent, self-governing communities become the normal form of Jewish polity in Europe from the tenth century on, the grounds of their political authority and the relation of that authority to the halakha become controversial.

To a limited degree, the legitimacy of public authority in the *kehillot* was based on the precedent of *mishpat ha-melekh*. It is not clear whether Jewish communal rulers were empowered by halakhic authorities or whether, ex post facto, halakhic authorities appealed to devices such as *mishpat ha-melekh* to justify existing conditions of lay authority. The Talmudic citation at the beginning of this book equating the exilarch, the head of the Babylonian Jewish community, with the kings of Judah is an example of rabbinic legitimating of lay rule on the basis of *mishpat ha-melekh*.[12] But perhaps this identification of exilarch and king was already the self-representation of the Jewish ruling elite itself. One cannot know. At any rate, the situation of the exilarchs was quite different from that of the councils who governed the *kehillot* of medieval Europe. The exilarchs traced their biological descent from King David and were also invested with the trappings of royal office by the Persian and later Islamic rulers.[13] The heads of *kehillot*, initially rabbis then later prominent men who were not necessarily scholars, had no such pretensions. What then was the basis for their authority?

From the mid-tenth century on, the sources strongly affirm the authority of the community over its members.[14] These sources were based on a Babylonian (i.e., Gaonic) responsum of R. Hananiah Gaon, head of the academy of Pumbedita during the years 938-943. R. Hananiah was responding to a crisis. A town had been pillaged and the members of the community had all lost their marriage contracts. Hananiah ruled that the elders of the city should determine how much each contract was worth based on their assessment of each citizen's wealth. Anyone who disagreed with their assignation could be excommunicated. In articulating this judgment, Hananiah offered some principles for the legitimation of the elders' authority:

> And thus it is for any occurrence which may occur to (i.e. any enactment which may be enacted for) the members of a city, [as long as] they are all equal in it, and it is beneficial for them, and they need it. The concurrence of the elders is operative for them, and all the members of the city come under their jurisdiction, as it states: "Whoever will not come in three days, as is the counsel of the princes and elders, all his property shall be forfeit, and he shall be cut off from the congregation of the captivity." (Ezra 10:8) And our rabbis have said: "The townspeople are at liberty to fix weights and measures, prices, and wages, and to inflict penalties for the infringement of their rules," and this is all with the assembly of the elders. From these verses and rabbinic statements we learn that the elders of the city have the authority to pass enactments for the members of their city, and to coerce them to abide by what they have enacted.[15]

Hananiah formulates three principles that must be met for a communal enactment to be valid: It must be equally applicable to all. It must be beneficial to the community. It must provide something for which there is a need. We will consider this Jewish version of the concept of the "common good" in greater detail below.[16] Here I want to focus on Hananiah's hermeneutically based argument for the authority of the elders per se. Hananiah offers two texts, one biblical, the other rabbinic, as grounds for the authority of the community over its members. The biblical text, from the Book of Ezra, recalls an early enactment, made by the officers and elders of the "congregation of the returning exiles" (*kahal ha-golah*). Ezra, alerted by the officers (*sarim*), realizes that the people are in violation of God's covenant by having intermarried with the people of the land (Ezra 9). As Ezra fasts and prays to God for forgiveness, he is surrounded by a great crowd of Judeans who apparently realize for the first time that their behavior violated God's law. A Judean leader proposes to Ezra that the people make a new covenant with God to expel their foreign wives and their offspring (Ezra 10:1-4). Ezra, in response, makes the leaders and the people take an oath that they will comply with this intention. While Ezra returned to his place before the ruined Temple to fast and intercede, the leaders issued a proclamation that all the returnees must assemble within three days for the covenant renewal ceremony or else their property will be expropriated by the officers and the elders.

In part, this is a story about covenant: about a people pledging themselves before God to undertake a course of consensual action. It derives some of its energy from the well-established prior biblical practice of covenant making and covenant renewal. As we will be discussing the political and historical dimensions of covenantalism in the next two chapters, I will not explore this dimension further here. The only point I wish to make is that, significantly, for the rabbis the covenantal dimension of this story is not prominent.[17] Indeed, Hananiah, following the Talmud, reads the Ezra episode as the basis for an important practice of rabbinic courts: *hefker bet din hefker*, the power of the court to expropriate property despite biblical prohibitions to the contrary.[18] *Hefker bet din hefker* becomes an expansive category in Jewish law, allowing a court to overturn or circumvent both biblical and prior rabbinic halakha. As such, it came to be one of the principal ways that communal enactments (*takkanot ha-kahal*) were justified by rabbinic authority, particularly when they were in tension with or contradicted Talmudic law. *Hefker bet din*, however, implies quite literally that the agency empowered to expropriate or, in general, to enact new law as conditions require is the court (*bet din*). Thus begins the conceptual move of construing public authority on the model of the authority of the court.

R. Hananiah, however, introduced a second line of argument that works in the other direction. He bases himself on a Talmudic passage (B. Baba Batra 8b) to the effect that the townspeople may fix certain economic conditions pertinent to their welfare and enforce them on one another. This rabbinic text implies that the community is a free association of its members, a partnership, rather than a court. On this model, the covenantal dynamic is somewhat more prominent. Jewish political theory never settled definitively on one model or the other. The court model of community was sometimes preferred insofar as courts had far greater power for independent action under Jewish law than did partnerships. A halakhist seeking to legitimate the power of communities to innovate and enforce policies was more likely to ground that power on the likeness of the community to a court than on its being a partnership of all its members. Thus, a leading Spanish decisor, R. Solomon b. Abraham Adret (Rashba) asserted: "The majority in each town is to each of the townspeople as the High Court is to the entire Jewish people."[19] He also likened the public authorities to the leading rabbis of Babylonia: "Every local community is considered as if it possessed the authority of the Geonim, whose enactments bound the whole of Israel."[20] Rashba endorsed the power of the community to enforce sanctions not validated by rabbinic law, including fines, and corporal as well as capital punishment, based on the extraordinary power of the court.[21]

The court's power of *hefker bet din hefker* also determined the Ashkenazi halakhists' understanding of the grounds of communal authority. R. Meshullam ben Kalonymus in the tenth century, and Rabbenu Gershom at the beginning of the eleventh century, ruled that the community council's enactments can overrule positive talmudic law insofar as the council functions as if it were a *bet din* with the power of declaring someone's property *hefker*, that is, of expropriating it for a suitable public purpose.[22] Rabbenu Gershom's successors built on this principle and invested the community, now understood to be constituted by a majority of its members and not necessarily by its "elders," with wide-ranging coercive powers. Insofar as courts operated on the basis of majority decision, communities construed as courts were also held to make their decisions on that basis.

A public authority articulated in the will of the majority naturally raised questions of the limits of the majority's power. Halakhists asked the following questions, in Menachem Elon's words:

> Must a communal enactment be adopted by all the people and in their presence, or can it be adopted in the name of the public by the public's delegated representatives? Can a majority of the people impose their view on the minority, or must an enactment be adopted unanimously, obligating only those who accept it from the outset? How and on what basis can an enactment obligate someone who at the time of its adoption is not a member of the community but joins it only later, or someone who is born after the enactment was adopted?[23]

Political theorists will recognize these questions as typical of the problems of consent theory. Thus, although the theoretical basis of public authority favored the court model more than the partnership model, the problems of consent foundational to any covenantal society could not be suppressed.

The will of the majority was legitimate, but the will of the majority could not be the sole source of legitimacy. The Jewish polity should be based, so to speak, more on Rousseau's "general will" than on the "will of all." How can majority rule be prevented from descending into majoritarian tyranny? The true interests of the community (the general will) had to be distinguished from numerically superior opinion (the will of all). We recall that R. Hananiah, in his path breaking responsum on public authority, had laid down three criteria for determining whether a proposed enactment represented the true interests of the people. The enactment had to be equally applicable to all, i.e., equitable. It had to be beneficial. And it had to be necessary. These criteria were expanded over the course of centuries. An enactment, for example, could not be blatantly unjust. That is to say, the majority's decision on a putatively beneficial policy must not violate traditional norms of justice. But what are traditional norms of justice? These might refer to highly concrete matters such as "strongly traditional, deeply entrenched tax regulations and commercial prerogatives."[24] And who is to decide which traditional norms are binding and which can be overcome? The bias in rabbinic societies was toward leadership elites, whether of rabbis or of laymen subject to their review. The leaders represent the community. Their interests are closest to the real interests of the members, that is, to the interests the members *should* have.[25]

Lay leaders of Jewish communities were, for the most part, elected by their members throughout the Middle Ages.[26] When gentile authorities curtailed electoral processes and appointed communal leaders, communities resisted and rejected their authority. The *kehilla*, despite its theoretical reliance on the *bet din*, was, in constitutional terms, a republic. Although citizenship was not developed as a theoretical concept, in practice a role was given to the consensual participation of the people (that is, of the propertied males) in forming the regime. The consent given by the majority to an elected leadership (*parnasim*, "providers" or *tovei ha-ir*, "good men of the city") sufficed to validate the leadership's subsequent policies. In the course of the Middle Ages, governance shifted from *parnasim* who were rabbis to *parnasim* who were not. With the enlargement of lay governance, rabbis were called upon to give approval to policies devised through lay political means. Rabbis and *parnasim* depended upon one another, sometimes supporting one another's authority, sometimes competing for it.[27] Thus the nature of public authority was relatively fluid. Majorities expressed themselves through electoral procedures, but then were bound by the decisions of those whom they elected. The leaders, however, knew that they could not pass ordinances that the people would not obey. Rabbis possessed a right of judicial review or a power of halakhic approval. But rabbis could also not go too far against the wishes of their communities. Leaders were supposed to represent the "true interests" of the people. Yet leaders had to remain somewhat responsible to the people. Despite the umbrella of *mishpat ha-melekh* under which they worked, they were not kings. They could not, unlike some of the despotic kings of ancient Israel, rule unchecked.

The decline of the medieval *kehilla* came, as suggested at the outset, from two interlocked movements. Externally, the development of royal absolutism and centralization of power eroded the autonomy of the *kehilla* and other medieval corporate structures such as communes, universities, and estates. Since the *kehilla* was always a creature of royal power, its autonomy a product of grant and privilege, and since the Jews had no power base other than royal favor, they could provide little resistance to the absolute ruler. Internally, a rising Jewish middle class with an emancipationist orientation was only too willing to abandon the corporate status of the community for the promise of integration.

After the Thirty Years War, especially in the German states, stronger centralized governments arose to reconstruct war-ravaged societies. In the new era of strong government, independent Jewish communities made little sense. A seventeenth-century Christian jurisprudentialist put it this way:

> Jews should not be permitted secular jurisdiction and their exercise of judicial authority in resolving disputes ought not to be tolerated. Inasmuch as the Righteous God destroyed the city of Jerusalem and the Land of the Jews and wiped out Jewish sovereignty and gave over the Jews to the rule of the Roman Caesar, it is self-evident that they should not be given new opportunities to adjudicate cases, resolve disputes, to bring fellow Jews to (their) court, to levy taxes, to enter contracts (by their own formulas) or to punish as they wish such wrongdoers as thieves, murderers, or adulterers.[28]

The state increasingly deprived the Jewish communities of the means of control over their own members. In Frankfurt am Main, for example, the privilege of 1617 gave the Jewish community autonomous jurisdiction over everything except "murder, homicide and other important matters" (*ausserhalb Mord, Todtschlag und andere wichtige Sachen*). By the end of the century, the Frankfurt Jews had jurisdiction over only those monetary matters connected with Jewish "ceremonial" law.[29] The state made a distinction, rooted in Christian not Jewish theology, between the "civil" and the "ceremonial" aspects of Judaism. All civil powers were denied to rabbis, *parnasim*, and Jewish courts. The state's preference was that all cases of consequence come before its courts. Only the most trivial matters should be excluded so that the Jews' quarrels not occupy the state courts' precious time.[30] Increasingly, the state supervised the appointment of rabbis and *parnasim*. It required that bookkeeping be in German and that frequent fiscal reports be submitted.

The most significant power taken from the communities was that of the ban (*herem*).[31] Medieval communities could excommunicate wrongdoers, the extent of marginalization being tied to the gravity of the sin or crime. Spinoza had been excommunicated by the Amsterdam community in 1656. Had he lived in Prussia a few decades later, he would most likely have escaped such punishment. In Prussia, the power of *herem* was explicitly retracted in 1730, although evidence suggests that it had been denied as early as 1714. At that time, Jewish courts were reduced to courts of arbitration whose decisions were binding only if the litigants agreed to them. Prussian Jewry law throughout the eighteenth and into the early nineteenth centuries continued to deny rabbis and *parnasim* civil powers. The repeated denial suggests that state policies were not entirely effective in transforming the Jewish communities.[32]

Although many in the communities wanted to hold on to the scrap of ancient sovereignty that autonomy and *herem* represented, a rising educated middle class (*Bildungsbürgertum*) wanted to be free of communal obligations and rabbinic jurisdiction. As Michael Graetz puts it:

> Time and time again, requests for liberation from rabbinical jurisdiction played into the hands of absolutist rulers by making it easier for them to interfere in the internal affairs of the corporate community and encouraging the abolition of certain functions. The autonomy of the court was clearly threatened when community members took disputes about ceremonial and ritual matters, as well as quarrels over money and trade, before the regular courts. They thereby helped to undermine what remained of the old rabbinical authority.[33]

This rising Jewish bourgeoisie consisted of *Hofjuden*, bankers, businessmen, manufacturers, and physicians. Acculturated, German-speaking, and dressing in a Christian rather than a Jewish manner, they were agents of Enlightenment and its vision of human emancipation.

What was that vision? The Enlightenment wanted a rationally designed society, which is to say, a society governed by scientific morality rather than inherited religious taboos and strictures. Except for its most radical spokesmen, however, the Enlightenment did not reject religion per se. It relativized historical religions, qualifying or rejecting the concept of historical revelation. God was known not through miraculous disclosure at Sinai, for example, but naturally, that is, through the light of natural reason. All humans were so endowed as to be able to reason their way to "Nature's God." Neither fallen nor in need of justification, humans were born morally good and mentally fit. They needed to free themselves from the distorting superstitions of their historic societies and from the intellectual vices of their various clergies. The best way to secure this was to curtail the political power of the clergy. The state, which in the German version of the Enlightenment is a benign, paternal, and progressive force, must subdue religion and constrain its role to one of moral suasion. No one should be disadvantaged by his or her historic religious ties, either by the state or by the churches themselves.

Moses Mendelssohn, the principal Jewish Enlightenment figure, was also a proponent of natural religion and of the emancipation of society from the influence of historical religion. Like other *Aufklärer*, he sought a world where civil religion would subordinate sectarian religion. Natural religion, equally available to all, would function as the civil religion of liberal society. Mendelssohn sought to prove against Judaism's cultured despisers that Judaism was fully conformable to Enlightenment civil religion. On Mendelssohn's view, Judaism was (contra Christianity) a religion without dogmas. Its only beliefs were the self-evident truths of reason: the existence of God, his Providence, and his justice. But unlike Locke or Leibniz, Mendelssohn, an observant Jew, wanted to defend historic Judaism. He could not entirely dispense with the historicity or significance of Sinai. He sought the equality of Jew and gentile, not the dissolution of the Jewish people. Therefore, Mendelssohn could not dispense entirely with the concept of election and the Sinaitic revelation on which election was based.

Mendelssohn argued that although Judaism taught no distinctive beliefs, it presented itself as a revealed law (*offenbartes Gesetz*). The commandments were both symbolic and prophylactic. The purpose of the commandments, or at least of those that were still valid, was to induce contemplation of the self-evident truths of reason and to guard against superstition. Mendelssohn distinguished, as did the Prussian law, between ceremonial and civil commandments. The former, as symbolic pointers to eternal truths, were eternally binding and valid for Israel. The latter were purely political. Following Spinoza, Mendelssohn asserted that they derived from the ancient state constitution of biblical Israel. Unlike Spinoza, Mendelssohn retained a core of commandments that had not lost their validity. Jewish national unity, such as it is, is based on voluntary obedience to a ceremonial law, a symbol system designed to ward off idolatrous superstition and instill a contemplative disposition. The nation is in no sense a political unity, nor do its representatives have any right to political power. The Jews are a church of believers and behavers. As Mendelssohn puts it:

> As the rabbis expressly state, with the destruction of the Temple, all corporal and capital punishments and, indeed, even monetary fines, insofar as they are only national, have ceased to be legal. . . . The civil bonds of the nation were dissolved; religious offenses were no longer crimes against the state; and the religion, as religion, knows of no punishment, no other penalty than the one the remorseful sinner voluntarily imposes on himself. It knows of no coercion, uses only the staff [called] gentleness, and affects only mind and heart.[34]

Mendelssohn shifts the basis of Jewish national belonging from obligatory participation in a covenantal political-juridical order to voluntary affirmation of a rational creed, supported by symbolically charged religious actions. To the extent that Mendelssohn has not done away with the obligatory character of the commandments, he did not fully consummate the shift: that was left to Reform Jewry in the next century. But although Mendelssohn is not a nineteenth century Reform Jew for whom Judaism is purely confessional, he lays the groundwork for that position. By denying that there is a valid, continuing civil—that is, political—component to Judaism, Mendelssohn orients Jewish self-representation away from nationhood and toward a kind of Jewish church.[35] He accomplishes this at the cost of historical credibility. He had to deny that the entire development sketched above—the constitution of public authority in post-biblical Judaism—existed. In his view, only under the absolutely unique theocratic conditions of biblical Israel, where God was the immediate ruler of the people, could the religious and civil spheres be identical. After the age of the "Mosaic constitution," this unique unity was destroyed. The civil and the religious can no longer be conjoined.[36] The realm of the religious is strictly one of conscience. There can be no coercion, by either church or state, in matters of faith. Thus whatever residual powers the Jewish communities had to regulate the lives of their members according to halakha and *mishpat ha-melekh* were, in Mendelssohn's sense, anti-Jewish. Civil jurisdiction is not in accord with the deepest nature of Judaism. The scepter is to depart from Judah, at least until a messianic age—which Mendelssohn did not entirely repudiate—restores the original unity.

In the Aftermath of the Jewish Polity

The Mendelssohnian vision of emancipation and integration was realized only slowly and imperfectly in Germany. The last barriers to Jewish legal equality did not fall until late in the nineteenth century. Jewish social acceptance and equality remained elusive. Despite remaining disabilities, or perhaps because of them, German Jews struggled mightily to transform themselves into Germans of the Mosaic persuasion. A uniquely hybridized German Judaism and German Jewry emerged. The medieval concept of sacred Jewish nationhood faded as Jews sought to prove their Germanness. Jewish national consciousness and political institutions, expressed in the now crippled *kehillot*, became mere remnants. Yet nineteenth-century European Jewish thinkers continued to contest the nature and extent of Judaism and the Jews as national and political phenomena. One of the most assertive of these pre-Zionist "nationalists" was the pathbreaking Jewish historian Heinrich Graetz (1817-1891).

A professor at the liberal rabbinical seminary in Breslau, Graetz was a controversial figure. Although a proponent of Emancipation, he was an opponent of Reform Judaism and of an unlimited assimilation. Graetz resisted the confessionalization of Judaism. He clung to the idea of Jewish nationhood and invested that nationhood with a political dimension. He refused to spiritualize Jewish nationhood or ground its lingering justification in an alleged priestly mission to the gentiles. He gave both the endurance of Jewish nationhood and the political dimension of that endurance a key place in his concept of Judaism. For this, Graetz was criticized by both the Jewish liberal integrationists of his time and the German nationalists who found his assertion of Jewish national consciousness unacceptable.[37]

Graetz's offense was "national pride."[38] He resisted the view of Judaism that had become dominant in Reform circles in nineteenth-century Germany, namely, that Judaism had a simple, unchanging essence: monotheistic faith. Reformers used their essentialist credo to historicize and therefore dismiss much of inherited Judaism.[39] If Judaism was essentially unchanging monotheistic faith, then everything other than that faith was temporal, contingent, and of questionable worth. Customs and ceremonies that did not contribute in an intelligible way to the enhancement of faith, which is to say, that did not comport with nineteenth-century moral and aesthetic norms, should be dropped. The essence of Judaism was its prophetic faith, monotheism cum social justice. This was the inner spirit. All else was outer form.[40]

Graetz sought the longed-for "essence of Judaism" elsewhere. He looked to the unfolding of Jewish history and tried to comprise its empirical variety in his own version of essence. No less than the Reform historians and theologians, Graetz was an idealist. He also thought that Judaism had an essence and that this noetic essence expressed itself in the political, social, and religious forms of empirical history. But unlike the Reformers, who believed that these forms could be pared away dualistically from the inner spirit, Graetz held on to the significance of the forms. The Reformers, some of whom were Hegelians, believed that the formal expressions of the spirit succeeded one another in an evolutionary way. Graetz, by contrast, did not believe that Jewish history was a history of progress. The Jews did not outgrow the political form of Judaism represented in the Bible. Nor did the destruction of the Temples represent some progressive refinement of the cultic dimension of Judaism. In Ismar Schorsch's words: "The radical import of Graetz's position is that, unlike the Reform theory, earlier phases of Jewish history are never transcended."[41] Graetz refused to see Jewish history teleologically, to subordinate the past to the present. He had an unshakable belief in the continuity of Jewish history, and therefore in the endurance of the bearer of that history, the Jewish nation.[42]

In his first programmatic essay on Jewish historiography, *The Construction of Jewish History* (1846), Graetz asserted that:

> If an idea has fought its way through into reality, if it has moved through the manifold configurations of history, then we may assume that all the actual

forms brought forth were originally immanent. For history merely ripens the seeds of an idea, and the variety of forms which history yields are only concrete manifestations of the idea.[43]

What is this originary idea that characterizes Judaism throughout all of its historical manifestations? Graetz sees the emergence of Judaism as a protest movement, a "negative force."[44] Judaism emerges in opposition to paganism. Unlike paganism, where the divine was immanent in nature and therefore unfree, Judaism presents a free, sovereign Creator God who is in no way restrained by nature or fate. The Creator's freedom endows human action—the action of the creatures he has freely brought forth—with significance. Human action is not a product of necessity, but is conceived in freedom. Graetz thus pairs the discovery of the Creator God with human moral accountability: "The totality of Jewish life is enveloped by the glory of God. It receives its grace only after the spirit of God has suffused it. Moral freedom, complete self-determination, therefore, is the first consequence of the Jewish principle."[45]

Up until this point, Graetz does not differentiate himself from others who postulate monotheism as the "essence of Judaism" (*Wesen des Judentums*). But Graetz takes the negativity of monotheism, monotheism as the negation of paganism, seriously. As such, he cannot locate the distinctive and enduring idea of Judaism purely in an opposition. He has to give it a positive content. Thus he asserts:

> [T]he monotheistic idea is not even the primary principle of Judaism, as has been widely believed by many until now, but it is a secondary consequence. . . . Therefore, the idea of monotheism in no way exhausts the entire content of Judaism; it is infinitely richer, infinitely deeper. Not even the repudiation of the deification of nature exhausts Judaism; it marks only the beginning of its career, a fact that becomes fully clear in the course of its long history.[46]

The positive concept that complements the negativity of monotheism is that of people and politics:

> Thus the concept of an extramundane God does not hover in the ethereal region of thought, but creates for itself a living people: an adequate political constitution must serve as the living carrier of this idea, which must ultimately become the moral code for society and the way of thinking for the individual . . . .The concept of God must immediately become a concept of the state.[47]

Graetz asserts that the ancient Jewish polity, a theocracy in the true sense of the word, characterizes all subsequent Judaism as well.[48] Although God stood at the head of the ancient Jewish political system, God was not its goal. Its goal was, rather, a national eudaemonism: the nation—not the individual—

should live well in its land. Graetz's formulation radically restores an immanent political aspect to Judaism:

> For Judaism is not a religion for the individual, but for the community, and the promises and rewards attached to the fulfillment of commandments do not refer to the individual—for then the broken promises would serve to contradict Judaism at any given moment—but rather are apparently intended for the entire people. . . . Judaism is not a religion of the individual but of the community. That actually means that Judaism, in the strict sense of the word, is not even a religion—if one understands thereby the relationship of man to his creator and his hopes for his earthly existence—but rather a *constitution for a body politic.*[49]

Had Graetz made this assertion, with all of its implications for Jewish nationhood, law, and politics, only of ancient Israel, he might have avoided controversy. But insofar as it was his conviction that this dimension lay "in the original idea of Judaism, as the tree in the seed," he asserted it of post-biblical Judaism as well. Although subsequent Jewish history enriched and complicated Judaism's essence, it remained true "that the task of Judaism's God-idea is to found a religious state."[50] Graetz's radical view was profoundly subversive of integrationist Jewish efforts to prove Jewish loyalty to the *Vaterland* by disclaiming the more overt reminders of bygone Jewish nationhood. The editor of the journal to which Graetz submitted this youthful piece, the moderate reformer Zecharias Frankel (1801-1875), disagreed with Graetz's bold assertion of Jewish nationhood and appended an editorial critique to the essay when he published it.

Hermann Cohen (1842-1918) reacted to Graetz's early essay in his 1917 article "Graetz's Philosophy of Jewish History."[51] The scene had substantially changed from Graetz's day. Emancipation had been achieved. Antisemitism had been revived, in a modern, politically virulent form. Herzlian Zionism, with its unambiguous reassertion of the national and political character of the Jews, was on the agenda. Hermann Cohen, in criticizing Graetz, addresses these trends as well.

Cohen was the principal intellectual voice of liberal Judaism. He was anxious to defend Jews and Judaism to an often hostile German public and intelligentsia. He did so by arguing for an idealized compatibility between Judaism and Germanness, a complementarity of national ideas. Cohen acknowledges distinctions between Jew and German, and asserts a role for ongoing Jewish peoplehood. That peoplehood is not political, however. Jewish peoplehood finds its fulfillment, in the short term, in the German constitutional state (*Rechtsstaat*) and in the unending task of social justice. Jewish peoplehood finds its ultimate fulfillment in the messianic age, when differences between Jew and gentile are overcome and justice will be the common norm for all. It is crucial to Cohen to justify the distinct continuity of Jewish nationhood (if that is not too strong a term for his understanding of peoplehood) in terms of its messianic intention. Jewish uniqueness intends a universalist overcoming of Jewish separateness. The oneness of the Jews is a sign of the inherent (and messianic) oneness of all humanity. Jews guard their difference because it is in service to the other. The Jews have a right to be, because their being is for all others.

In the following critique of Graetz, Cohen must transvalue Graetz's assertive political nationhood into his own version of messianic-universalist peoplehood. The Jews are the servant people of the nations in the messianic quest for moral unity. Cohen carefully recapitulates the steps of Graetz's argument, trying to restore what he sees as the appropriate balance between foundational monotheism and a chastened political expression. Cohen outlines a concept of politics suitable, as he sees it, for the modern Jew—a metapolitics of national self-abnegation in the name of universal redemption.

"Graetz's Philosophy of Jewish History"

A fundamental methodological question exists for the philosophy of history: does history have its center of gravity in political history or in the collective concept of cultural history?

The history of the Jews may shed some light on this difficulty, since, after the destruction of the Jewish state, the Jews have a history that lacks its own political center. Indeed, the nation came to occupy the place of the state and this might give rise to the appearance of a Jewish history, which, qua history of the Jewish nation, maintains the fiction of a Jewish state. However, there also arises the countertendency of the relationship of the Jewish nation to Jewish messianic religion. The latter cannot be entirely identical with the Jewish state. There is no escaping the fact that a Jewish historiography that takes the Jewish nation seriously, even on account of the Jewish state, must make Jewish religion the irreplaceable and central object of Jewish history. The political center of gravity is thus eliminated in Jewish history. The development of Jewish religion alone has to be presented as the driving cultural force.

For a man of such burning political passion as our Graetz, writing at the time when Moses Hess wrote *Rome and Jerusalem*, it was indeed a difficult trial, put to his scholarly, his religious, and ultimately his Jewish national conscience, to have to decide about this fundamental methodological problem. We do not have a single literary document of Graetz's about these three concepts of state, nation, and religion that posits them as the central problem for his history of the Jews. But it is indicative of the methodological, that is, philosophical, centrality that he ascribed to this issue that he addressed it in advance of undertaking his major work already in 1846, in a journal edited by our teacher, Zecharias Frankel, the *Journal for the Religious Interests of Judaism*. Graetz published a series of articles entitled "The Construction of Jewish History, a Sketch."

Already at the beginning of this project, a very interesting and instructive controversy arose between the writer and the editor over precisely this decisive point in the conceptualization of Jewish history. Graetz, namely, begins with this point: What is Judaism? This question is his first word. He discusses it in a brief exchange with Samuel Hirsch, Steinheim, S. R. Hirsch, whom he refers to as Ben Usiel, the *nom de plume* under which the *Nineteen Letters* appeared, and finally with Mieses. He himself begins with the attempt to "conceptually construct Jewish history." The first concept, by means of which he conceives Judaism as the negation of paganism, arises through the determination: "It (Judaism) appears, as it were, as Protestantism." He constructs the opposition between Judaism and paganism, following Steinheim, as an opposition between nature and spirit. Out of this opposition arises the opposition of natural religion and spiritual religion, as well as the opposition of divine transcendence against immanence.

Now one should think that this religion of the spirit with its transcendent God would undoubtedly be precisely described as monotheism. However, he surprises us with this turn: "not once is the monotheistic idea the primary principle of Judaism." Monotheism is, rather, a negative principle, which requires a positive supplement. And most peculiar: the principle of the unique God is only the negation of paganism and itself requires a positive definition, which, however, must then lie outside of the transcendent concept of God! In what could such a supplement to monotheism exist?

The author continues: "The transmundane idea of God does not float in the ethereal regions of thought, but produces for itself a concrete peoplehood [literally, "ethnic substance"], an adequate state constitution which is supposed to be the living bearer of this idea. The idea of God should be at the same time the idea of the state." This is the supplement that monotheism requires. Monotheism is therefore completed by two concepts: peoplehood and the state constitution. Are these two concepts identical, however? Furthermore, if it seems that the abstract idea of God should first become concrete in peoplehood, it eventually turns out, in Graetz's view, that the state constitution is the first realization of the idea of the divine.

Thus we see Graetz at the crossroads between religion, on the one side, and nation and state, on the other. He formulates his opposition to the usual conception as sharply as possible. "While God alone is the beginning and end of this Civitas Dei, he is not its goal, which remains, rather, a eudaemonistic one: that it may go well for you upon the soil which the Lord has given to you." (Deut. 5:16) This eudaemonism is valid, however, not for the individual, but for the entire group, for the "folk individual."

At this point Graetz introduces the most doubtful of possible expressions: "Judaism is, in the strong sense, not a religion at all . . . but the law of a state." A suspicious reminiscence of Spinoza's defamation of Judaism echoes here. "The law is the soul and the holy land the body of this peculiar political organism." "The Torah, the Israelite nation, and the holy land stand in a, I would like to say, magical rapport. They are indestructibly joined to one another by an invisible band." And now there follows in Graetz's manner, which we recognize from the emotional style of his lectures, a flood tide of sentences against the "sublime, idealized Judaism," which is only a "shadow" and a "dried husk." The core of religion has been torn from the "juicy fruit" of this national-political Judaism. In this way Graetz brings Judaism to its native eudaemonistic condition. But what has happened to the religion of the Spirit as an opposition to the idolization of nature?

Graetz did not fear reaching the following conclusion: "The immortality of the soul has as little a place in Judaism as the dogma of transsubstantiation. Judaism is no religion of the individual." Yet despite all of these deletions, Judaism is supposed to be a monotheism of the Spirit! The question of the essence of Judaism cannot remain hanging in all of these paradoxes. The daring author must be given a helping hand by the editor, who will set the concept aright.

Here we can rejoice in a high point of calm clarity, of solid certainty, of healthy-mindedness, and, not least of all, of philosophical depth, which Frankel had demonstrated with this disastrous assault. He immediately asserted the right of the editor against the contributor and corrected the erring standpoint in a long comment. Monotheism should in no way be thought of as a secondary principle. The uniqueness and the otherworldliness of God are "an indivisible concept." "Judaism, when it came into the world did not need to proclaim that there is a God. But that there is only One God: this was Judaism's original and essential principle." Thus Frankel repudiates the Steinheimian hypothesis that God = Spirit, as this hypothesis is subversive for monotheism.

The politicization and localization of Judaism is also revealed in all of its irreligiosity. "What obligatory quality could the Torah have for these people torn from their own soil? The hope for the resumption of the state and for the messiah could provide at best only weak support for such obligation."

Frankel also makes reference, with ethical clarity, to the false opposition between the state and the individual, which forms the consequence of this error. Next to the factor of justice, which represents the state, Frankel posits virtue as the principle of the individual. He establishes the connection between monotheism and individual morality on the basis of the connection between the commandment to love God with the "Shema Yisrael." "Love can only be asked of the individual who sees himself recognized as an independent person, who feels himself standing near in his immediacy to Him Who asks for love." And so finally, "the divine lawgiver Himself is not only the God of the land, but also that of the whole earth."

These are clear and golden words that, especially in the present day, should gain their instructive significance once again. The religion of monotheism is preserved in all its purity by this liberation from a complex of antinomies that attacks its essence. Monotheism must be protected both from pantheism and from political nationalism. The history of the Jews is removed from the will o' the wisp that must be seen in every other lodestar than that of religion which would become the principle of Judaism.

How did the young historian, who had up until this time primarily worked in religious philosophy, in the history of gnosticism, react to this rebuke? Did he perhaps only change his disposition on account of coercion or did he, rather, grasp the correctness of the editorial critique? Did he even find it easy to submit to it, because he had already basically felt himself to be back on the right way, only temporarily detoured by the contemporary philosophical and political currents that had taken root in the fertile soil of Judaism, although not to the same extent that he himself, with all his knowledge and thought, was rooted?[52]

At the end of his essay, Frankel reports that Graetz had sent him a postscript concerning his "reproof." "We are delighted that the author agrees in essence with our view, " Frankel writes, "and we regret only that we are not able to reprint this postscript on account of space considerations." It would certainly have been instructive if we could have gotten this postscript, but the main thing remains, that understanding had "in essence" been reached. In Graetz's entire further work only slight traces of the original error could be detected.

The real error with regard to this whole distinction between politics and religion has its cause in the failure to recognize that the unification of these supposed opposites is found in social ethics. Social ethics belongs, on the one hand, to politics, and, on the other, to religion. Out of social ethics, the bridge is also thrown down for the individual, who also arises as a problem between politics and religion. This lack of an ethical ground betrays itself quite clearly in the attempt to establish political thought on the basis of eudaemonia. Had the political teaching, in contrast, been based on duty and on the love grounded in duty, then every antinomy would have been equalized in a single stroke. Religion must become politics insofar as it ought to educate the citizens in the duty of love of humanity. Likewise, politics must become religion insofar as every national-political community must revolve around two poles, one of which is the individual, the other, however, the entirety of humanity. The opposition between politics and religion is canceled by messianism, which is both the acme and the root of monotheism.

Graetz divides Jewish history into two halves and three periods, each of which falls into three phases. Already the two halves suffer from this false characteristic: "The agents of the first historical period are political citizens, war heroes, kings with only a slightly religious touch to them, while those of the second are pious men, sages, teachers, students, and sectarians who have only a slight social interest." But the qualification follows immediately. Haven't the prophets already prepared the religiosity of the first period? With this question alone, the characteristic of the first period becomes invalid. And Graetz himself intercedes already for the "indivisible unity" of Judaism.

He also expresses the fundamental conviction that within the essence of Judaism there inheres the power to bring both of these two factors, the religious and the social elements, into view. The connection of the religious and the political, the unity of the supramundane idea of God with the life of the state, becomes the "ideal of Judaism." With these details, the entire dialectical contradiction is eliminated—because the messiah, in the complete fulfillment of the concept, can only be thought of as the idea of all humanity.

Only in the beginning of history are these two factors separated from one another. In truth, however, in the covenant with Abraham, indeed, with Noah, the first glimpse of the messiah already shines. For Graetz, however, the "first page of Jewish history begins" no earlier than in the book of Joshua, in "the camp at Gilgal." The Pentateuch forms only "the interesting introduction." In truth, Frankel demonstrated a very patient editorial conscience.

The first phase of the first period still fought with paganism, nevertheless "the religious element was not entirely null." Fine remarks indicate the religious character of Deborah in particular. The second phase begins with Samuel and his prophetic school, out of which the Psalmist Assaf, who created this genre before David, originated. With David and poetry, however, religion first came alive in the people. This maturity of the nation, which transformed the tribal confederacy into a constitutional state, is also attested in that religious upsurge whose symbol is the Solomonic Temple. At the same time, literature flourished and, in the *mashal*, even produced an analogy to philosophy.

The third phase, initiated by the division of the kingdom, brings with it an escalation in the religious dimension, as the political element declines. Its product is prophecy: "especially the end, which emerges indisputably out of the breakup of the Solomonic empire." The religious character of prophetism is not limited to the postexilic prophets. Isaiah, Hosea, Micah, and Amos are designated as the "quadriumvirat" of messianic prophecy, which embraces "all of humanity." There exists no opposition between patriotism and cosmopolitanism for these monotheists. The people, however, had not yet matured to this ideal stage. And thus there arose, in Isaiah, chapter 42, the servant of God as the ideal image of the people. This idealization of the people comes, through the exile, to the first steps of its realization.

In the second period, which now follows, and in its division into three phases, there are also interesting characteristics throughout. For example, he draws an analogy between the men of the Great Synagogue and the judges, who both bear the cares of the nation "for a moment" and thus also for the duration. In the second phase, the analogy is between kingship and Hellenism, both of which had been received as foreign elements after some initial reluctance. The Maccabees then came, a Davidic reflex, and Greek culture was overcome.

The third phase begins with the struggle of the Pharisees against the Sadducees, which is analogous to the division of the empire into Judah and Israel. Here the author inserts a tribute to the Pharisees. "For them life was solely for the sake of religion." The Pharisees, he suggests at last, because of their religious teaching spurn this worldly happiness for heavenly blessedness. The Sanhedrin is analogous to the prophetic schools. Jesus of

Nazareth is considered as "not the only one" who "strove to make the messianic ideality a reality." It was Johanan ben Zakkai, however, who saved Judaism, and thereby the foundation of the messianic world, through the school, by which he also replaced the Temple. Now there comes the new element of theory, of "intelligence," in the formation of Judaism.

The third period is, accordingly, only the continuation of this now intellectual character. "The historical activity of Judaism in the seventeen centuries of exile was a theoretical activity, directed toward the intellectual upbuilding of its doctrinal concepts and contents." Religiosity "sought a science of its own essence and of its own significance." In the place of the sages of the second period, there now come scholars, religious philosophers, the legal systematizers. "Judaism becomes science." And this science wants to bring forth "a religious-social reality."

Now at once, the two elements, the religious and the political, which were previously separated, appear to be simply united. The theory, the science, has brought this unity about. The diaspora threw the Jews into the life of the world, while Talmudism, superficially considered, seems to have served the purpose of isolation. This isolation, however, first created and allowed for the possibility of endurance vis-à-vis the life of the world: the theory was the fundamental power common to the two forms in which the historical life of the Jews appeared. "Wherever the train of world history went, wherever only a mere grain of world historical life was sown, thereunto followed the migration of the Jews." Talmudism was a defensive weapon against the contempt and the self-loss of this migration. "The same definition which the natural boundaries of Palestine—the high Lebanon in the north, the sandy deserts of the east and south, the half-dividing sea of the West—gave to Judaism to sever the holy land from too intimate a contact with the polytheistic world, was also provided by the fence of Talmudism during the period of exile. Judaism has it alone to thank for its survival." We do not want to quarrel here with the word "alone." Graetz only means that the Talmud in its entirety, insofar as it also contains the aggada and consequently insofar as it allows all of the sides of the Jewish spirit to come forth, thus including prophetism, which endures in poetry and philosophy, by such a Talmudism did Judaism survive. The aggada was only the flower of the halakha, of the real theory.

The martyrs bled for this unified theory during the Hadrianic time. This theory, which unified halakha and aggada, showed itself to be an authentic manifestation of the religious spirit through its distinction between "the religious and the social duties, which appear as "rational and irrational" determinations in Judaism.

Thus the halakha becomes not only an analogy, but itself a type of philosophy. "The production of aggada reaches into the nineth and tenth centuries" that is, until Saadia. Mysticism, which reaches into the seventeenth century, became the other side of this phenomenon. The festival prayers, with their special *piyyutim*, are a further fruit of the aggada.

This prepared the second period of the diaspora. The second period of the diaspora developed the aggadic commentary into a philosophical system.

Now Judaism seeks its justification in a principle. The scientific-scholarly dimension of this principle sustains itself through its connection to a grammatically based exegesis. Graetz tries to "explain the contours of the main systems that make up the epochs of the Jewish life of the spirit." The baselines of these characteristics run very deep. "Philosophical exploration belonged, henceforth, in Judaism." The study of general science, indeed, of both natural science and the humanities, became bound up with the study of philosophy.

After characterizing the age of Saadia, Jehuda Halevi, and Maimonides, Graetz now characterizes the third period, that of Moses Mendelssohn. Mendelssohn's appreciation of the law is not derived from a national point of view alone, but rather, as if no problems were entailed by this view, out of the unity of religion and state. "In Judaism, state and religion are rooted in community, or rather, they are one." Now, all at once, this identity of the ethical principle of monotheism, which he had offended in his treatment of Mosaism and prophetism, is clear to our historian. It seems as if this insight first begins to dawn on him as he makes the fundamental way of thought and disposition of Mendelssohn's *Jerusalem* contemporary. But there are other flashes of insight as well. Already in the second phase, we find the statement that Judaism has "no Middle Ages in the secondary meaning of this concept." Similarly, it reads here: "Judaism is throughout no product of the orient. It constitutes a sharp opposition to the orient." He plays this trump card against Hegel. The essay finally makes explicit reference to Steinheim, Hirsch (Ben Usiel), and Salvador, to the latter for the social-legislative side of Judaism. At the end, however, it reads: "We still lack a single, comprehensive principle of Judaism that can comprise and unite all of these aspects in itself; a principle that must play itself out in the entirety of Jewish life, in the dogmatic, religious, political, historical, even in the stunted dimensions of Judaism." Thus Graetz demands a unified principle of Judaism, which, in its universality, can be nothing other than monotheism.

When will this unified principle of all the phenomena of Judaism become alive for us? When will it bring the world to the recognition that pure, absolute monotheism forms the historical ground for the endurance of Judaism?

The final sentence of the essay is intended as a recapitulation, but also as an adjustment of its basic line of thought. It goes: "It turns out, according to this historical point of view, that it seems to be the task of the Jewish idea of God to organize a religious state-constitution which is conscious of its activity, its goal, and its connectedness with the world as a whole." We would be true to the spirit of our deceased teacher if we rendered this statement in the following way: The monotheistic idea of God has the task of organizing a religious state-constitution as a world organization, that is, as the federation of states of a humanity developing according to the messianic idea.

In the year Cohen's essay appeared, the British government offered the Jewish people the promise of a national home in Palestine. The potential of a restored Jewish nationhood, mooted by Graetz and sublimated by Cohen, began to take on ever more distinct actuality. In Zionism, a political self-representation returned to the Jewish people. Yet integrating an appropriate political image of themselves with a religious one proves no less daunting for twentieth-century Jews than it did for Mendelssohn, Graetz, or Cohen. The balance and interaction of these elements, like participation in the covenant itself, is a task "for all their generations."

Notes

1. Gil Graff, for example, has shown that the Talmudic norm of *dina d'malkhuta dina* (the "law of the kingdom is valid law"), far from being a mere capitulation to the legal and political realities of exile, was a kind of foreign policy strategy. This law enabled Jews to think of the Jewish polity's relations with non-Jewish polities on the model of treaty relations. See Gil Graff, *Separation of Church and State: Dina de-Malkhuta Dina in Jewish Law, 1750-1848* (University: University of Alabama Press, 1985), 10,15. Also, David Biale, *Power and Powerlessness in Jewish History* (New York: Schocken Books, 1987), 56.

2. For a history of the beginnings of the erosion of communal autonomy, see Eric Zimmer, *Harmony & Discord: An Analysis of the Decline of Jewish Self-Government in Fifteenth Century Europe* (New York: Bloch Publishing, 1970).

3. See Michael Graetz, "From Corporate Community to Ethnic-Religious Minority, 1750-1830," *Leo Baeck Institute Yearbook*, Vol. 37, 1992.

4. On the growth of the modern conception of religion as a private, personalistic reality, see Wilfred Cantwell Smith, *The Meaning and End of Religion* (Minneapolis: Augsburg Fortress Press, 1998).

5. Abraham Melamed, "Medieval and Renaissance Jewish Political Philosophy," in Daniel H. Frank and Oliver Leaman, eds. *History of Jewish Philosophy* (London: Routledge, 1997), 417.

6. The debate is introduced in *Sifre* on Deuteronomy (*Piska* 156) with R. Nehorai charging that Israel's request for a king was shameful, entailing the rejection of God as king. R. Judah claimed to the contrary that the Torah commands kingship. The people were punished in the time of Samuel for their request, on Judah's view, not because the request was inherently wrong, but because they acted unilaterally, that is, presumptuously in making it. In B. Sanhedrin 20b, R. Nehorai's position is reiterated, while R. Judah and R. Jose are opposed, declaring the appointment of a king a mitzvah. R. Eliezer claims that the elders, as described in I Samuel 8, were appropriate in asking for a king to judge them. The people, however, were inappropriate in asking for a king to lead them into battle so that they could be like all the nations. Later exegetes align themselves with either of the original positions. Ibn Ezra and, most notably, Abravanel oppose kingship. Maimonides, Nachmanides, and the *Sefer Ha-Hinukh* treat kingship as

a mitzvah. For an able summary of this issue in rabbinic literature, see David Polish, "Rabbinic Views on Kingship—A Study in Jewish Sovereignty," *Jewish Political Studies Review*, vol. 3, nos. 1-2 (Spring 1991).

7. For an analysis of the political and religious repercussions of the transition from judges to kings, see Moshe Weinfeld, "The Transition from Tribal Republic to Monarchy in Ancient Israel and Its Impression on Jewish Political History," in Daniel J. Elazar, ed. *Kinship and Consent: The Jewish Political Tradition and Its Contemporary Uses* (Lanham, Md.: University Press of America, 1983).

8. In B. Sanhedrin 20b, R. Judah (in the name of R. Samuel) and R. Jose assert that the powers enumerated in the Samuel text are permitted to the king (*mutar bo*). Rav and R. Judah see them as a rhetorical invention so that the people may fear the king, but not as actual granted powers.

9. Menachem Elon, *Jewish Law: History, Sources, Principles*, Vol. 1 (Philadelphia: Jewish Publication Society, 1994), 55-58.

10. For an authoritative and nuanced account of the ambiguities of *mishpat ha-melekh* as a mediating principle between the ideals of halakha and the realities of politics, see Gerald J. Blidstein, "'Ideal' and 'Real' in Classical Jewish Political Theory: From the Talmud to Abrabanel," in Zvi Gitelman, ed. *The Quest for Utopia: Jewish Political Ideas and Institutions Through the Ages* (Armonk, N.Y.: M. E. Sharpe, 1992). See also a special issue of *Jewish Political Studies Review* devoted to this topic, *Jewish Political Studies Review*, vol. 10, nos. 3 & 4 (Fall 1998).

11. Blidstein, "'Ideal' and 'Real,'" 47.

12. B. Sanhedrin 5a. Cf. Maimonides, *Mishneh Torah*, Laws of the Sanhedrin 4:13: "The exilarchs in Babylonia stand in the place of the king. They have the right to rule over Israel (*yesh lahen lirdot et yisrael*) in every place and to judge them whether they consent or not (*beyn ratzu veyn lo ratzu*), as it is said, '"The scepter shall not depart from Judah." These are exilarchs in Babylonia.'" For analysis of Maimonides' stand on the Exilarchate vis-à-vis kingship, see Jacob (Gerald) Blidstein, *Political Concepts in Maimonidean Halakha* (Hebrew) (Jerusalem: Bar Ilan University Press, 1983), 46-49.

13. Salo Baron, *The Jewish Community: Its History and Structure to the American Revolution*, Vol. 1 (Philadelphia: Jewish Publication Society of America, 1948), 145-50.

14. Samuel Morell, "The Constitutional Limits of Communal Government in Rabbinic Law," *Jewish Social Studies* 33 (July 1971), 87.

15. Quoted in Morell, "Constitutional Limits," 88. Cf. Elon, *Jewish Law*, Vol. 2, 685-86.

16. See chapter 7.

17. The rabbinic tendency to de-emphasize covenantalism in its strong, social form is explored in chapter 3.

18. For the sources of *hefker bet din hefker*, see Mishna Shekalim 1:1-2; B. Gittin 36b; B. Yevamot 89b, See Gerald Blidstein, "Notes on Hefker Bet-Din in Talmudic and Medieval Law," *Dine Israel* IV (1973), pp. XXXV-XLIX, and Menachem Elon, *Jewish Law*, 507-15.

19. Responsa Rashba, 5, no.126. Cited in Elon, *Jewish Law*, Vol. 2, 515.

20. Responsa Rashba 1, no. 729. Cited in Eliav Shochetman, "Jewish Law in Spain and the Halakhic Activity of Its Scholars Before 1300," in N. S. Hecht, et al.,

eds., *An Introduction to the History and Sources of Jewish Law* (Oxford: Clarendon Press, 1996), 284.

21. Responsa Rashba 4, no. 310. Shochetman, "Jewish Law in Spain," 285.

22. Morell, "Constitutional Limits," 89.

23. Elon, *Jewish Law*, Vol. 2, 682-83.

24. Morell, "Constitutional Limits," 101.

25. Gerald Blidstein, "Individual and Community in the Middle Ages: Halakhic Theory," in Daniel J. Elazar, ed. *Kinship and Consent: The Jewish Political Tradition and Its Contemporary Uses* (Lanham, Md.: University Press of America, 1983), 226. Yitzhak Baer identified the polarity between the decision of the quantitative majority and the decision of the qualitative "majority," that is, of the worthiest members of the community, as deriving from German and Roman law models, respectively. See his classic article, now in English translation, "The Origins of Jewish Communal Organization in the Middle Ages" in Joseph Dan, ed., *Binah*, Vol. 1 (New York: Praeger, 1989), 80.

26. On elections, see Salo Baron, *The Jewish Community*, Vol. 2, ch.10. In general, the procedures of Jewish communities for electing leadership resembled those of the host society. See also Jacob Katz, *Tradition and Crisis: Jewish Society at the End of the Middle Ages*, Bernard Dov Cooperman, trans. (New York: New York University Press, 1993), ch. 11.

27. For the relationship of rabbis and lay leaders in the evolving (and declining) *kehilla*, see Katz, *Tradition and Crisis,* 73-75, 106.

28. Translation by Gil Graff in his *Separation of Church and State,* 31-32. Original in Azriel Shochet, *Beginnings of the Haskalah Among German Jewry* (Hebrew)(Jerusalem: Bialik Institute, 1960), 75.

29. Shochet, *Beginnings of the Haskalah*, 76.

30. This was the view of the well-known Christian chronicler of Frankfurt Jewry, Jakob Schudt. See Shochet, *Beginnings of the Haskalah*, 76. A detailed accounting of the decline of communal powers in Germany on the basis of available documentary evidence is given in Shochet, 75-88.

31. Katz, *Tradition and Crisis*, 84-86.

32. For external pressures on the community, see Michael A. Meyer and Michael Brenner, eds. *German-Jewish History in Modern Times*, Vol. 2 (New York: Columbia University Press, 1997), 100-105.

33. Graetz, "From Corporate Community to Ethnic-Religious Minority," 74.

34. From Mendelssohn's *Jerusalem*, quoted in Allan Arkush, *Moses Mendelssohn and the Enlightenment* (Albany: State University of New York Press, 1994), 226.

35. On Mendelssohn's voluntarism, see Arkush, *Moses Mendelssohn and the Enlightenment*, 228.

36. Ibid., 265.

37. For the famous attack of the Prussian historian Heinrich von Treitschke on German Jewry and Graetz in particular, see Jehuda Reinharz and Paul Mendes-Flohr, *The Jew in the Modern World: A Documentary History* (New York: Oxford University Press, 1995), 343-46.

38. Ibid., 346.

39. For typical examples of the approach Graetz rejected, see Max Wiener, *Abraham Geiger & Liberal Judaism: The Challenge of the Nineteenth Century* (Philadelphia: Jewish Publication Society of America, 1962), 179-83.

40. For a survey of nascent Reform theology, see Michael A. Meyer, *Response to Modernity: A History of the Reform Movement* (Detroit: Wayne State University Press, 1995), 89-99.

41. Heinrich Graetz, *The Structure of Jewish History and Other Essays*, Ismar Schorsch, trans. and ed. (New York: Jewish Theological Seminary of America, 1975), 44.

42. Ibid., 51.

43. Ibid., 65.

44. Ibid., 66.

45. Ibid., 67.

46. Ibid., 69.

47. Ibid.

48. In Nathan Rotenstreich's view, Graetz uses history as a third term, a synthesis, between two antithetical positions: Judaism as revealed law (Mendelssohn) and Judaism as religious creed (Graetz's Reform-minded contemporaries). The synthesis has both elements, that is, a political-legal foundation and a faith in God, inextricably intertwined. Rotenstreich claims that Graetz, while holding on to the duality of this complex, deemphasized the purely political, state character of Judaism, in favor of Jewish society, that is, the historical Jewish people and its community as the appropriate mode for the political-legal element in postbiblical Jewish history. Nathan Rotenstreich, "Graetz and the Philosophy of History," (Hebrew) *Zion*, September 1942: No. 1, 53.

49. Ibid., 70 (italics mine).

50. Ibid., 124.

51. Hermann Cohen, "Graetzens Philosophie der jüdischen Geschichte," in Bruno Strauss, ed., *Hermann Cohens Jüdische Schriften*, Vol. 3 (Berlin: C.A. Schwetschke & Sohn, 1924), 203-212. Translation my own. The original essay appeared in the *Monatsschrift für Geschichte und Wissenschaft des Judentums*, Vol. 61 (1917), 356-66.

52. It is worth noting that, unlike Cohen, Schorsch does not believe that Graetz changed his point of view. See Ismar Schorsch, *The Structure of Jewish History and Other Essays*, 40.

Chapter Two

The Recovery of Covenant: The Politicization of Jewish Origins

As we saw in the last chapter, a political understanding of Jews and Judaism declined at the dawn of the modern era. The autonomous, medieval Jewish community was progressively dismantled from the fifteenth century on by gentile rulers who sought direct control of Jewish assets and of Jews. The Enlightenment (and its Jewish correlate, *Haskalah*) deprived the autonomous community of its symbolic efficacy as a distant echo of ancient Jewish sovereignty. Mendelssohn and his followers envisioned a Judaism shorn of political dimensions and constituted by a rational-ethical creed. In Mendelssohn's case, the creed was surrounded by a supporting architecture of still binding *mitzvot*. But the purpose of the *mitzvot* was personal *Bildung*, not the securing of a good society in the form of a distinctively Jewish, political commonwealth. In a modern classic such as Hermann Cohen, the political has been transformed to the point of effacement.

Yet the Enlightenment, if not yet the Haskalah, also contained the potential to renew a political self-understanding by facilitating a politically sensitive reading of Scripture. For the Enlightenment facilitated the possibility of a purely *secular* reading of Scripture, that is, a reading in which the assumption of a human provenance for Scripture predominated. Against such a background, the social and political conditions that shaped Scripture and that Scripture arguably reflects came to the fore.

47

In this chapter, I argue that the new emphasis on the historical, social, and political dimensions of the Bible provided an opportunity for a new understanding of one of the key political concepts of Scripture: covenant. The political dimension of covenant was retrieved at first by Christian Bible scholars, and later by Jews. Covenant is a central concept for any political reading of the Bible. Before turning to an analysis of the seminal figure in this process, Max Weber, let us briefly consider why the concept of covenant is key.

Covenant as a Political Concept

The idea of covenant was born in the world of the ancient Near Eastern city-state in the second millennium before the common era. The city was the basic unit of political life. In order for stability to prevail beyond the borders of the territory that the city controlled, it needed to enter into alliances with other cities. Early attempts at building empires also required that lesser rulers swear fealty to more powerful rulers, allying their cities with that of the overlord. The device by which these alliances were formalized was the covenant. The partners to a covenant were either equal or unequal to one another in terms of power. What they had in common, in any case, was their pledge of fidelity to one another.

Covenants arose because the power of governments by nature only extends so far. In a police state—the most extreme version of governmental power—the ruling elite seeks to regulate the behavior, the "private life," of every member of the polity. Indeed, there is to be no truly private life in the sense of a life sheltered from the demands of public conformity or compliance with shared codes. The total state, most famously imagined in Plato's *Republic*, aims to control all aspects of life. But Plato also taught (as we know from *Statesman* and *Laws*) that such a system can never be supported by coercion alone. Even the most powerful state cannot post policemen on every corner or in every living room. Loyalty to the state, internalized support of its existence and policies, is a necessary complement to necessarily limited power. The approval of citizens, whatever form such approval is to take, initiates the transformation of power into authority. Authority denotes rule by right, and right is conferred, at least in part, by consent.[1]

In the ancient Near East, rulers sought a way to inculcate and secure loyalty from their allied or conquered subjects. After the conquering army returned to its own city and the immediate threat of force vanished, the vassal city had to remember who was in charge. Covenanting was the solution to that dilemma. Covenanting involved a formal ceremony full of symbolic acts conducted in the presence of the gods of the consenting parties. A history of the acts of the superior party vis-à-vis the inferior one served to ground the relationship that the partners now cemented. Past acts of graciousness established the context for the gratitude and loyalty the vassal must show the lord. The vassal pledged himself to a catalogue of performances, as well as to an attitude of faithful devotion, in exchange for which the lord would faithfully support and protect him.[2] The various gods bore witness to these solemn promises. Curses were invoked on the party that would violate the provisions and the spirit of the agreement.

Covenanting responds, I suggested, to what might be thought of as a defect: the limits of a ruler's power of enforcement. But it also introduces a positive element: it puts consent at the center of authority. Covenant represents the awareness that power alone, in the sense of the ability to compel humans to comply with one's will, is an insufficient basis for government. It represents a movement away from rule based on fear to rule based on right. A covenantal ruler believes, as do his subjects, that he has a right to expect compliance because his subjects have agreed to conduct themselves in a compliant way. Equal parties to a covenant believe that they have a right to expect certain courses of action from each other. They have a right to mutual respect and cooperation based on their having made promises to one another.[3] Covenant lends a moral quality to power. It invites reflection on the nature of authority. It marks authority off conceptually from mere power.

Covenant is thus a way of organizing the relationship between central conceptual features of political life: consent, authority, sovereignty, obligation, freedom, and justice. It is, of course, not the only way to organize these concepts, but it has been a historically powerful one. Covenant entered the political vocabulary of the West in part through ancient Israel's adoption of the covenant formulary from her neighbors and subsequent adaptation of that device to express both her mode of social life, her legal order, and her relationship with God. Covenant has resonated throughout the Western political experience, for wherever Jews and Christians have drawn from biblical ideas for social organization, covenantal themes have entered their politics.

From Transcendence to Immanence

The rise of modern biblical studies permitted a secular appraisal of the sacred literature. For the first time, the Bible could be viewed as an edited collection of historical materials originating in the life of an ancient civilization, rather than as a divine teaching originating in the mind of God. Spinoza first gave systematic expression to this profane approach. Not surprisingly, he called his exegetical treatise the *Theological-Political Treatise* (*Tractatus Theologico-Politicus*, 1670). When the Bible fell from grace, as it were, into history, the context in which it was shown to have originated was the national, i.e., political, life of ancient Israel. Spinoza understood the text not as revelation but as the documentation of the political evolution and aspiration of a historical people.[4]

Spinoza, like other seventeenth-century philosophers such as Hobbes and Locke, both read the Bible as a political document and attacked the Bible as such. That is, they acknowledged that the Bible provided a political teaching and they used that teaching insofar as (in Spinoza's and Locke's case) it could support their republicanism. But they also felt compelled to disparage the Bible's political teaching insofar as the apologists for absolute monarchy and the divine right of kings based their claims on Scripture. An uncomplicated, republican reading of Scripture, such as Althusius's at the beginning of the seventeenth century, was replaced by a much more ambivalent, contested one at the century's end. What was Spinoza about?

The fundamental issue for Spinoza, as Leo Strauss pointed out many years ago, is the question of revelation. Spinoza is radically opposed to the concept of revelation in the sense that the "natural light" of reason requires guidance from beyond its own ken and that, furthermore, Scripture is the record of this gracious, divine guidance. Spinoza's *Theological-Political Tractate* is a frontal assault on the Mosaic authorship, indeed, the divinity of Scripture. Spinoza was concerned to avoid both a "skeptical" and a "dogmatic" hermeneutic. "Skeptical" in this context means skeptical of reason. That is, we ought not, on Spinoza's account, suspend our rational knowledge of the world and take, for example, biblical miracles at their face value. But neither should we follow Maimonides (a "dogmatist") and assume that Scripture always conforms to reason if only we interpret it through philosophical allegory. Spinoza does not want Scripture to be either a scandal to reason or an encoded philosophical text. He proposes, rather, a naturalistic hermeneutic through which the meaning of Scripture in its original setting is allowed to emerge. This becomes, essentially, the stand of modern hermeneutics for which the truth of the text is no longer the issue. The meaning or significance of the text-in-historical-context is what counts. This is, in fact, Spinoza's move. Not truth but meaning is what counts.

Spinoza is convinced that Scripture is not about truth. It is no more and no less than the cultural product of the ancient Hebrews. Its "meaning" (Spinoza, like Kant who follows him on this score, believes that Scripture has an essential, overriding meaning) is moral: love God and love your neighbor as yourself. Almost all the rest is, as it were, commentary: historical-cultural detritus to be jettisoned. Spinoza hopes to preserve the moral kernel for political purposes after the husk of narrative and the fiction of revelation are discarded. It is wellknown that the political thinkers of the seventeenth century read Scripture (and criticized it) *as* a political text. But Spinoza went far beyond, for example, Locke of *The First Treatise* or of *The Reasonableness of Christianity*. Spinoza organized the premises and initiated the project of higher criticism. Spinoza inserted the Bible into the dimension of secular history and forever after its status as divine revelation (as the medievals understood it) has been problematic. Other than the most orthodox of the Orthodox, the Jews have never regained their confidence that the words of Torah are the words of God. But if Spinoza framed the problem, he also mooted the purported solution. He crafted the liberal Jewish compensatory mechanism: the eternal commands of conscience, the moral law, speaking through the text are, as it were, the voice of God.

In its Spinozist incarnation, the immanentization of Scripture has a clear political thrust. Higher criticism is meant to contribute to a solution of the theological-political problem of emerging modern societies. It is meant to reduce the authority of competing sects and clergies by reducing the authority of Scripture. In place of a Scripture, contention over which foments civic unrest, the modern society proposes a rational religion that promotes civic peace. Spinoza, like Rousseau who follows him, is convinced that civil society requires civil religion. He arrives at this conclusion in part for "Judaic" reasons. His critique of Scripture required a critique of prophecy, particularly of that philosophical version of prophecy promoted by Maimonides and other medievals. Spinoza had to argue that revelation (via prophecy) was not a higher form of knowledge but an inferior, because imagination-driven, expression of natural knowledge. Revealed religion makes no defensible cognitive claims. Prophecy has more to do with the prophet's passional psychology than with objective reality. Having severed revelation and thus Scripture from truth (or theoretical reason), what was left was a connection of Scripture with law and ethics (or practical reason). Scripture's main purpose was to stipulate moral and civil law for the ancient Israelite polity. Judaism is a religion of law; its faith is simply a posture of obedience to law.

By claiming that the emerging modern civil society requires a civil faith whose content is primarily a moral law inculcating obedience to the state, Spinoza gives civil religion a "Judaic" turn. (This sorry caricature of Judaism as a religion of law without distinctive knowledge or belief later was also to have a long afterlife, promoted by both Jews such as Moses Mendelssohn and enemies of Judaism such as Kant.) Spinoza in effect turns modern persons into Jews: their "faith," whatever notional significance it may have for them on a personal level, is in fact a matter of obedience to the civil sovereign. This faith, like the faith of biblical Israelites, does not per se bring happiness. It does, however, secure civil peace within which individuals can work out their happiness. For Spinoza, the *optima respublica* is a democratic, commercial republic where citizens have access to education and commercial opportunity against a background of legally secured liberty. The civil faith is a foundation of this civil society. In a metaphysical sense, however, it is only an appendage to ultimate felicity.

Spinoza's construction of Scripture and Judaism, and its role in the economy of the emerging liberal political theory which he taught, both endures in and is transformed by thinkers such as Lessing, Kant, and Hegel. There is no doubt that Spinoza had a very considerable impact on the *Aufklärung* as well as romanticism. Indeed, it was in the nineteenth century when Spinoza's purely secular approach to Scripture established itself against the continuing theological and religious interests within the guild of biblical scholars. Julius

Wellhausen stands within and represents that transition. When he published his great work, *Prolegomena to the History of Ancient Israel* (1878), he no longer believed himself capable of training students for the ministry and resigned from the faculty of Protestant theology at Greifswald. He became an orientalist and professor of Semitic languages at Goettingen and then Marburg. His own biography indicates the shift toward the secularization of interpretation. In regard to covenant, however, Wellhausen does not achieve an adequate appreciation of the political dimension of the covenant idea. Despite situating it within a historical and political context, he continues to emphasize the theological character of the idea. It is not that he treats covenant as only a theological or ethical construct, but that he privileges the theological element over the political one. I treat Wellhausen's theory of covenant below as an important example of how the political dimension can be slighted even by a writer whose predominant interest is secular and historical.

For the emergence of a consequential, political construction of the covenant idea, we must turn to a younger contemporary of Wellhausen, Max Weber. Weber's *Ancient Judaism* represents the first major scholarly treatment of covenant as a political idea. Weber builds on, while departing from, the tradition of modern biblical studies consolidated by Julius Wellhausen. While Weber follows Wellhausen's Documentary Hypothesis in essential respects, he also abandons a central contention of Wellhausen's, namely, that covenant is a late and unhistorical biblical motif. Weber rehabilitates the antiquity and original political character of covenant. Those German and American scholars such as Martin Noth and Walther Eichrodt, George Mendenhall and Delbert Hillers, who in the latter half of the twentieth century promote a more fully political reading of covenantalism stand in Weber's debt. Accordingly, this chapter focuses on Max Weber's particular contribution to understanding this central motif of the Jewish political tradition. I shall first sketch Wellhausen's reading as a foil to Weber's, then explore Weber's reading in some detail. Finally, I will note how a contemporary Jewish critic of Weber's, Julius Guttmann, demurred, in a manner reminiscent of Hermann Cohen vis-à-vis Heinrich Graetz, from attributing a proper political character to the covenant idea. That demurral is important, for it is typical of the way in which Jewish scholars, for theological reasons, continue to underplay the political significance of covenantalism. Together these authors represent enduring possibilities or types of interpretation of the covenant idea.

Stages in Theorizing about Covenant

Modern research into the covenant traditions of ancient Israel falls into three distinct stages.[5] The first scholarly stage is dominated by Wellhausen (1844-1918). The second stage, after World War I, refutes Wellhausen and brings the social and political dimensions of covenant into greater prominence. Max

Weber's work is pivotal for this stage. The third stage, after World War II, sees a strengthening of the sociopolitical perspective initiated by Weber. This strengthening is brought about by an increasing reliance on Hittite and other treaty formularies as the basis for Israelite covenantalism.

In Julius Wellhausen's view, enunciated in *Prolegomena to the History of Ancient Israel*, the covenant idea is a relatively late development in Israel, stemming from the time of the great eighth-century prophets. Prior to this period, Israel conceived of the relationship between itself and God as a natural one, as that of Father and son. Referring to the time of Moses, Wellhausen writes:

> The relation of [God] to Israel was in its nature and origin a natural one; there was no interval between Him and His people to call for thought or question. Only when the existence of Israel had come to be threatened by Syrians or Assyrians, did such prophets as Elijah and Amos raise the Deity high above the people, sever the natural bond between them, and put in its place a relation depending on conditions, conditions of a moral character.[6]

Conceived in terms of a "naturalistic" relationship, God was characterized as a helping, provident parent whose bond with his child was indestructible. God was originally the god of Moses' family or extended clan. Moses' success in uniting Hebrew tribes and imparting a sense of group solidarity to them elevates his god to the god of the nation. But this god belongs to the nation in the same sense that Zeus belongs to the Hellenes: he is a national, tribal, and particular god whose efficacy, furthermore, is limited to the worldly needs of the group.

> But "God" was equivalent to "helper" that was the meaning of the word. "Help," assistance in all occasions of life,—that was what Israel looked for . . . not "salvation" in the theological sense. The forgiveness of sins was a matter of subordinate importance; it was involved in the "help," and was a matter not of faith but of experience. The relation between the people and God was a natural one as that of son to father; it did not rest upon observance of the conditions of a pact.[7]

The religion of this god called for sacrifices and prayers. He was effective in war, but was moody and had to be propitiated. Israel did have, however, more than a cultic form of interaction with its god. God was also understood to be the source of law. In tribal life under Moses, Joshua, and the judges, priestly oracles determined the law, which consisted of specific instances of guidance in response to specific social problems. Wellhausen does not believe that the legal materials of the Bible reached any systematic form until Deuteronomy in the seventh century, and the priestly writings in the postexilic age. Until that time, law had an oracular, episodic status. For this reason, "the priestly Torah was an entirely unpolitical or rather pre-political institution; it had an existence before the state had, and it was one of the invisible foundation pillars on which the state rested." [8]

Wellhausen draws a sharp distinction between the prepolitical communal life of the Israelites up through the era of the judges, and the emergence of the Israelite state.

> Moses certainly organised no formal state, endowed with specific holiness. The old patriarchal system of families and clans continued as before to be the ordinary constitution, if one can apply such a word as constitution at all to an unorganized conglomeration of homogenous elements. What there was of permanent official authority lay in the hands of elders and heads of houses; in time of war they commanded each his own household force, and in peace they dispensed justice each within his own circle. But this obviously imperfect and inefficient form of government showed a growing tendency to break down just in proportion to the magnitude of the tasks which the nation in the course of its history was called upon to undertake. [9]

Under the threat of the Philistines, Samuel realized the advantages of consolidating the families and tribes into a kingdom and discovering Saul as its leader. Saul, and initially David as well, while kings, ruled basically along the lines of the charismatic war chieftains that had come before them. Success in war confirmed David's fitness for the throne. With Solomon, the regime loses its final affinities with the charismatic authority of the judges, and acquires the political lineaments of a centralized, Canaanite monarchy. [10] With these three, the Israelites emerged from the "state of nature" to the "civil state." They "first made out of the Hebrew tribes a real people in the political sense . . . . It was they who drew the life of the people together at a centre, and gave it an aim; to them the nation is indebted for its historical self-consciousness." [11]

Before proceeding with Wellhausen's account of the covenant, a few observations on his premises are in order. Wellhausen has a strongly statist approach to political reality. His distinction between prepolitical and political society turns on the emergence of the state. Politics is a state monopoly. The Israelites under Moses and his successors share a rather fragile national consciousness, but they do not constitute an organized public body fit to act on the stage of history. Only a society organized into a state with an efficient central administration engages in politics.

A debate continues over the extent to which Wellhausen was influenced by Hegel. [12] This debate usually focuses on Wellhausen's theory of religious evolution, but it might just as well focus on whether Wellhausen's assumptions about politics owe anything to Hegel's consummate expression of the teleology of the state. What is at least clear is that in this respect Wellhausen was very much a man of his time: the achievement of a united Reich under the sovereignty of the Prussian king could not but influence the philosophical outlook of a nineteenth-century German civil servant such as Prof. Wellhausen.

One cannot quite avoid the impression that in Wellhausen's history of the beginnings of the Israelite state, one glimpses a reflection of the Franco-Prussian war and its aftermath.

One acquires another impression as well: the return of Spinoza's thesis about the decline and fall of the Israelite state. Spinoza ascribed the demise of both Israelite polities not only to the aggressions of Assyria and Babylonia, but to the inherent flaws of those polities. For Spinoza, the religious constitution of the polity inhibited its rational freedom of action. Wellhausen does not make precisely this claim, but he does implicate the prophets in the decline of the state. The prophets are chiefly responsible for the invention of theocracy, based on covenant, which ends the old form of naturalistic religion even as it saps the state's confidence in itself. Under the impact of the prophets, religion becomes more than civil religion. The state loses its automatic legitimacy, and demands for righteousness are placed on it that are so high that it cannot help but betray them.

The prophets advanced an ethical conception of God. God became righteous and demanding. Israel's relationship to him was no longer one of kinship, but of contingency. Beginning tentatively with Elijah and crystallizing in the great literary prophets of the eighth century, the view took hold that if the state were to be lost, God must not be lost with it. God is not in service to the nation or to its state. Nation and state must serve God in order to continue to exist. This was a stunning and paradoxical reversal of popular consciousness. The Day of the Lord would bring darkness, not light. The fact that the Lord knew Israel alone ensured their punishment, not their victory. Through this transvaluation of all values, ethics is freed from custom. The moral becomes transcendent.

> What [God] demands is righteousness,—nothing more and nothing less; what He hates is injustice. Sin or offence to the Deity is a thing of purely moral character; with such emphasis this doctrine had never before been heard. Morality is that for the sake of which all other things exist; it is alone the essential thing in the world.[13]

The natural bond between father and son was shattered. The prophets devised the motif of the covenant to express this sense of contingent relationship: Israel's bond with God, no longer organic and indestructible, is entirely conditional upon ethical performances.

> Thus the nature of the conditions which [God] required of His people came to the very front in considering His relations with them: the Torah of [God], which originally, like all His dealings, fell under the category of divine aid, especially in the doing of justice, of divine guidance in the solution of difficult questions, was now conceived of as incorporating the demands on the fulfilment of which His attitude towards Israel depended. In this way

arose, from ideas which easily suggested it, but yet as an entirely new thing, the substance of the notion of covenant or treaty . . . . This use of Berith (i.e. treaty) for law, fitted very well with the great idea of the prophets and received from it in turn an interpretation, according to which the relation of [God] to Israel was conditioned by the demands of His righteousness, as set forth in His word and instruction. In this view of the matter [God] and Israel came to be regarded as the contracting parties of the covenant by which the various representatives of the people had originally pledged each other to keep, say, the Deuteronomic law.[14]

For Wellhausen, the covenant at Sinai was not a historical event. The Sinai Covenant represents a retrojection of the ethical-prophetic form of religion onto an age that could not have conceived of religion in such a manner. In no sense did Moses' teaching, his Torah, initiate a civil order, an incipient polity, with the Sinaitic covenant as its constitution. That is a retrojection from the age of Ezra, given its initial impetus by the prophetic revolution.

Prophecy set Israelite religion on a new footing. Its implication for the reconstitution of the people and for their long-term survival was benign, but its implications for the state were malign. Prophets such as Isaiah and Jeremiah, equipped with the new concept of the covenant, set out to reform the institutions of the state. But even under willing rulers such as Hezekiah or Josiah, it was not possible to do so. It was not possible for a political order to sustain the demands of God's righteousness. The prophets were not, in Wellhausen's words, "practical men." Consequently, the prophetic project of reform increasingly restricted itself to the reform of the cult. Centralization of the cult elevated the importance of the priesthood. This new (and ironic) emphasis on priestly religiosity was to have tragic consequences in the postexilic period *pace* Wellhausen.

At any rate, it was only after the destruction of the state that the grandiose reforming program of the prophets, now freed from the burdens of realpolitik and under the aegis of the greatly enhanced priesthood, could be put into play. Under Ezra, a full theocratic system, that is, a holy community understanding itself as a covenant community living under a comprehensive, divine law comes into being. Now we speak of Judaism, a religious polity leading an artificial life divorced from both the early state of nature and the later civil state.

> [This] theocracy, the residuum of a ruined state, is itself not a state at all, but an unpolitical artificial product created in spite of unfavourable circumstances by the impulse of an ever memorable energy: and foreign rule is its necessary counterpart.[15]

Wellhausen adds something distinctively Lutheran to this Spinozist paraphrase: "In its nature it is intimately allied to the old Catholic church, which was, in fact, its child. As a matter of taste it may be objectionable to speak of a Jewish church, but as a matter of history it is not inaccurate, and the name is perhaps preferable to that of theocracy, which shelters such confusion of ideas."

What is also strikingly Lutheran about Wellhausen's view is the implicit two-kingdom theory of governance. Wellhausen takes it for granted that the spiritual realm, the domain of true faith, must remain categorically distinct from the domain of civil administration. The *realpolitische* activity of the latter need not, indeed ought not, give an account of itself before the eyes of faith. God has given it license to do its dirty but necessary business. The prophets become good Lutherans, in a sense, as they recognize the calling of the state to be the highest earthly authority. The state is a natural fact. True, they want the state to live up to an impossible ideal of holiness, but they themselves glimpse the futility, the inner contradiction, of that aspiration. Ultimately, they situate, however tentatively, true faithfulness in the apolitical, interior, private life of the individual. Communities, no less than states, cannot achieve holiness. Only individuals, with the grace of God, can. Judaism, like the Catholic church it spawned, failed to recognize this incipient prophetic insight and settled for the vain and self-defeating hope of building a holy community on a covenantal basis, but the true covenant is a covenant of individuals in their solitariness with their God.

> Their [the literary prophets'] mistake was in supposing that they could make their way of thinking the basis of a national life. Jeremiah saw through the mistake; the true Israel was narrowed to himself . . . . Instead of the nation, the heart and the individual conviction were to him the subject of religion.[16]

It is but a short step from this "correct conception" of covenant to Christianity, in Wellhausen's view.

It cannot, of course, be said that Wellhausen's account neglects the political dimensions of the covenant idea. As a historian, he could not conceptually divorce covenant from its role in the social and political thought of ancient Israel. In his own way, he honors those dimensions of the idea. Nonetheless, his statist assumptions and taken-for-granted Lutheran premises prevent him from recognizing the idea as an early and original political motif, and to constitute it primarily in theological and moral terms. This was not a promising beginning for understanding covenant in its political dimensions. Nonetheless, with his controversial thesis that the Sinai covenant tradition was late and unhistorical, Wellhausen at least awakened critical interest in the issue of the antiquity of this dimension of Israelite thought.

Before turning to Weber, let us briefly consider an intermediate thinker who forms something of a bridge between the two dominant figures. A fertile exploration of the covenant idea was undertaken by Richard Kraetzschmar (1896). Kraetzschmar's point of departure was an awareness of the ambiguity of the term *brit*. Wellhausen had hinted at this, but had failed to explore it in any satisfactory way. Kraetzschmar knew that *brit* did not signify a unitary concept, but rather stood for a variety of relationships. Some of these entailed mutual obligations and performances. Some were more one-sided than reciprocal. Some covenants in the Bible involved God. Others were purely intrahuman devices. Some covenants were conditional on stipulated performances and revocable, while others were unconditional and eternal. Some were divinely initiated. Others stemmed from human initiative. Some were tendered by mediators, while others were not. Kraetzschmar was the first to try to sort out the various categories of covenant. He argued that there were four categories of relationship comprised by the idea of covenant:

> 1. A solemn assurance of a superior to an inferior (*Zusicherung*) or, by contrast, the imposition of obligations upon an inferior party, e.g., Genesis 15:1-12; Numbers 25:10-13; II Samuel 7:11b-16, 23:1-7; Psalms 89:1-4. In these texts, God obligates himself to support Abraham, Pinchas, and David, respectively. Kraetzschmar believed this form of covenanting to be the earliest.
> 2. An agreement between parties stipulating mutual obligations in order to achieve a mutually desired goal (*Bund*), e.g., Exodus 20:1-17, 34:10-28. Kraetzschmar thought that this form was the latest.
> 3. A treaty or contract between two states or individuals (*Vertrag*), e.g., II Samuel 5:1-3.
> 4. A vow taken by a group to perform duties to God (*Gelübde*), e.g., Ezra 10:1-4, Nehemiah 9.[17]

Kraetzschmar follows Wellhausen to the extent that he sees the solemn, unconditional assurance as the earliest form of covenant, and the reciprocal agreement as the latest. The earliest form reflects the organic, paternal conception of God, while the latest form expresses the demands of righteous and ethical contingency. But Kraetzschmar departs from Wellhausen by assigning an important social and political role to covenant. He argues that the Rachel tribes united with each other for mutual protection by an oath, and that this served as Moses' model for the Sinai covenant. Scholars such as Schwally, Eerdmans, and Budde also introduced the idea that Israelite tribes (or Israelites and non-Israelites, Midianites, e.g.) united by oath under God for mutual assistance. It is this idea that Weber picks up and develops in an especially powerful way.[18]

Weber is a link between the pre- and post-World War I stages of scholarship. Later scholars, such as Sigmund Mowinckle, Albrecht Alt, and Martin Noth were much more willing than Wellhausen, and even Kraetzschmar, to situate the covenant idea at the point of Israel's origins. The perspective shifts from covenant as a primarily theological idea to covenant as a functional social institution. One of the most important influences on this shift was the new discipline of the sociology of religion practiced by Weber. Weber ascribed a constitutive social role to religious ideas. It was now possible to conceive of the nexus between theology and politics represented by covenant in a more accurate and fertile way.

Weber's Recovery

Before turning to Weber's contribution to our understanding of covenant, let us first consider some aspects of his background and method.

Max Weber (1864-1920) may seem at first an unlikely contributor to our modern understanding of the political traditions of the Jewish people. A product of the nineteenth-century German university, Weber, no less than Wellhausen, partook of its many prejudices toward and preconceptions about the Jews. While not an anti-Semite, neither was Weber a pluralist. He believed that Jewish identity in the modern world was a traditionalistic anomaly that had no real place in the German nation-state. The problem of the Jewish "pariah people," a term he did much to popularize, was to be solved through radical assimilation. In views such as this, Weber was of a piece with the entirety of the liberal movement in Wilhelmian Germany.[19]

With respect to his textual exegesis, Weber also inherits the subtle and not so subtle anti-Judaism of the biblical scholars on whom he relied. Yet it cannot be said that he followed them blindly. Insofar as Weber was explicitly devoted to putting the sociology of religion on a sound scientific basis, he was alert to the infiltration of theological or metaphysical elements.[20] To a greater extent than Wellhausen, he succeeded in freeing himself from standard theology-driven methodological assumptions.[21] On the other hand, Weber remains solidly committed to what we today denominate as a "hermeneutics of suspicion." He assumes that the actual course of Israelite history differs radically from the narrative presentation of that history in the Bible. He is convinced of the basic soundness of source criticism and is confident that P, for example, is the latest stage in the redactional process. Weber buttresses this assumption by his own formidable theory of rationalization. While this assumption is not necessarily anti-Judaic, it does imply a notion of increasing rigidity and decline. Weber does not free himself from such views.

What then can Weber contribute to an understanding of covenant, and of the Jewish political tradition as a whole? His contribution, in my view, is three-fold: substantive, methodological, and cautionary. His theses, his sociological approach, and his limits are instructive.

Substantively, Weber was the first modern scholar to work out the implications of a concept of covenant rooted in sociopolitical rather than strictly theological categories. Weber's posthumous classic, *Das antike Judentum* (1921), had a profound impact on the development of subsequent German and American Bible scholarship. Our modern understanding of covenant as the form of the Israelite polity is directly indebted to Weber's interpretation.[22]

Weber's substantive appreciation of covenant follows from his methodology. Methodologically, all subsequent sociologists of religion are, more or less, in Weber's debt. Let us now briefly review some of the methodological aspects of his sociology of religion.

Weber was a practitioner of what came to be called the sociology of knowledge. He learned from Marx to implicate the world of ideas in a network of material factors.[23] Unlike Marx, however, Weber did not believe that material factors *caused* constellations of ideas and values in a straightforward manner. The ideational sphere is not, in Weber's thought, simply an expression of the play of material interests. Neither is it ever the case that religious ideas alone determine the historical process, as a typical misunderstanding of Weber's thesis on Puritanism and the rise of capitalism would have it. The interrelation of ideas and material factors is more problematic.

To start, Weber rejects Marx's monocausal emphasis on the determinative force of economic factors. He faults Marx for failing to distinguish between an idea being *caused* by economic forces and economic forces being relevant to the progress of an idea. In Weber's celebrated thesis on the Puritan ethic, capitalism is not caused by Puritanism. Puritanism is, rather, relevant as a factor among factors in the development of the type of mentality that was able to rationalize the organization of production.

Weber is more concerned to study the interrelatedness of all spheres of social life—economic, political, religious, technological, aesthetic, military, legal, and ideational—than he is to privilege any of them. All of these orders are linked in relations of causation, expression, and affinity. Unlike Marx, Weber rejects historical necessity as an illicit philosophical concept that ought to have no role in science. Weber sees a great deal of accident, arbitrariness, and, of course, uniqueness in social reality. Social arrangements do not cause ideas. Rather, arrangements and ideas coexist. Ideas and values are often produced by extraordinary, charismatic individuals for idiosyncratic, unpredictable reasons. Once an idea becomes available, social groups, driven by particular interests, may find an affinity with it and institutionalize it. The chosen idea then becomes an ideology that endures to the extent that it enables its bearers to survive and succeed. As we shall see, covenant is just such an idea for Weber.

"Understanding" (*Verstehende*) sociology has as its purpose to understand the ideas and values of historical groups as *they themselves understand* them. This emphasis on empathy was a legacy of the German historicist tradition. By affirming *Verstehen*, Weber rejects Marxism's claim to objective knowledge of the meaning of historical events. Objective meaning construed against an essentially metaphysical construction of the process of history is an illicit notion for Weber. What *can* be understood objectively, indeed what *must* be understood objectively (for science requires objectivity), is how historical agents themselves understood or defined their situation. What did the values of a group mean to the group? Why did they choose these values and not others? How did these values affect empirical reality? Did the subjects who chose them act rationally, i.e., consistently, according to them? At a higher level of abstraction, Weber asks, what would ideal, rational behavior according to x values be like?

Using an abstract standard of ideal rational congruence with some set of values, Weber derives the heuristic concept of an "ideal type." Ideal types (e.g., capitalism, Christianity, asceticism, salvation, charisma) are generalizing concepts that enable us to talk comparatively and abstractly about the brute, infinite particularity of empirical reality. Unlike the historicists, Weber, while respecting the unique irreplicability of human events, does not believe that empathy alone suffices to grasp their meaning. Sociology is not an imaginative hermeneutics by which we reexperience the *Erlebnis* of others. Sociology, rather, discerns amid the flux of human events an underlying lawful structure. This structure is described by postulating ideal types.

Ideal types may be compared to the grammar of a language. No one ever speaks a language entirely in accordance with the norms of grammar. Yet grammar, in all its abstractness, describes as well as prescribes how a language functions.[24] Similarly, ideal types—when applied to human relations and social structures—clarify the forms of rationality implicit in a culture. Weber believed that human beings in society often acted rationally, i.e., consistently within a given framework of ideas and values. Insofar as the researcher can rationally explore the rational action of his subjects, *verstehende* sociology is a strictly scientific inquiry.

"Rationalization" refers to the growth of an increasingly coherent, lawful body of governing ideas in society. The coherent ordering of a worldview replaces belief in a mysterious, adventitious, spirit-animated universe. Rationalization in worldview is correlated with increasing systematization and rule-oriented social institutions, ultimately culminating in the pervasive bureaucratic control of society.

Weber's studies of world religions were generated in part by the problem of charting the growth of rationalization in the relevant cultures of the East and West.[25] Weber's specific interest in Judaism stems from his conviction that only Judaism intuited the complete rationalization and hence the complete disenchantment of the world:

> The world was conceived [by ancient Judaism] as neither eternal nor unchangeable, but rather as having been created. Its present structures were a product of man's activities, above all those of the Jews and of God's reactions to them. Hence the world was an historical product designed to give way again to the truly God-ordained order . . . . There existed in addition a highly rational religious ethic of social conduct; it was free of magic and all forms of irrational quest for salvation; it was inwardly worlds apart from the paths of salvation offered by Asian religions. To a large extent this ethic still underlies contemporary Mid Eastern and European ethic. World-historical interest in Jewry rests upon this fact.[26]

Unlike the great ancient cultures of south and east Asia, the Jews did not produce asocial and solitary contemplatives. Man is to be conceived as an instrument for purposive action, not as a vessel for salvific, unitive experience. Action in accordance with the divine will was rationalized in terms of conformity to a legally articulated set of rules. Rational action rather than mystical contemplation of the meaning of the universe as a whole marked Jewish religiosity. "The only problems which could arise were those which were concrete and topical and concerned action in the world; any other problem was excluded." [27] By "inner-worldly asceticism," Weber implies a practically oriented type of activist piety centered on the fulfillment in history and society of the divine will. This form of religiosity, fully articulated by the prophets, originates in the covenantal thought of early Israel at the time of the judges.

The importance and insight of Weber's concept of covenant can best be gained by contrasting it with Wellhausen's. In the latter's view, as we have seen, covenant is primarily a theologically charged symbol of Israel's relationship with God. Weber decisively rejects this strictly theological concept of covenant. For him, by contrast, Israel has its origins in covenant (*brit*). Israel both develops and acquires its peculiar character as an "oath-bound confederation" through negotiated agreements between subgroups and through an overall agreement with YHVH. The "inner political history of Israel developed through ever-repeated ritualistic confederate resolutions" (AJ: 77). Weber believed that individual tribes such as Judah formed through agreements between various ethnic and status groups (AJ: 81); that kings were accepted through covenanting; that Deuteronomy was accepted as a Yahwistic constitution by the polity through covenant and that the procedure of covenanting carried Israel through the Exile and established the postexilic community under Nehemiah (AJ: 78).

To understand the central role Weber ascribes to covenanting, we must first grasp his account of Israelite origins. As stated above, Weber does not accept the bald historicity of the biblical narrative. With higher criticism, he tends to view the patriarchs as eponymous ancestors. Nonetheless, the patriarchal materials—particularly through consideration of their redactional layers—can tell us something about the composition of Israel before the time of the judges.[28] Weber also believes that Moses probably was a historical figure and possibly a non-Israelite. YHVH was a non-Israelite god, worshipped by Midianite bedouin surrounding the Kadesh oasis (AJ: 123). Moses learned of this god from his father-in-law, Jethro. Moses and the group he led out of Egypt, possibly *habiru*, attributed their deliverance to YHVH (AJ: 75). The group gathered around the charismatic Moses covenanted to accept the rites of previous YHVH-worship (prohibition of images, circumcision, oracles by lot, army summons) and became "Israel," which Weber takes to mean "the people of the fighting god" (AJ: 81).

YHVH is a war god of a group originally conceived as a war confederation. His awe and incipient transcendence derive from the fact that YHVH was not originally a domestic numen of the early proto-Israelites. He came from afar, from Seir (Judges 5:4). That Israel did not know or control him gave him a majestic and mysterious otherness. Devotion to him gave the oath-bound confederation its sacral quality (AJ: 124). Although YHVH loses his war-like character and function in the course of Israelite history, assuming the character of a benign providence, his forte remains might, not order (AJ: 126-29). Judaism is a response to his will, not his logos. Insofar as YHVH's original purpose was historical deliverance and guidance, Judaism's conception of salvation is political-historical, not ontic. In this is found the germ cell of " inner worldly asceticism."

Weber does not give an account of how the Moses-group confederates with populations already in Canaan. Insofar as he sees Israel as a confederation of numerous strata from a variety of ethnic groups, including free peasants, Levites, smiths, artisans (whom he takes to be metics, *gerim*), small stock holders, cattle breeders, and urban warlords (*gibborim*), he does not feel compelled to give a unilinear account of Israelite origins from the patriarchs on. All of these various groups occupied different regions of the country and were driven by different interests. They covenanted with each other in shifting alliances to secure their interests. Small stock breeders, for example, had to negotiate traverse rights for their herds with free peasants or with the ever-expanding urban patriciate. Dan becomes a settled tribe in this way (Judges 18:1) Cattle breeders and peasants, often at odds over control of pasturage, had a common interest in fighting bedouin raiders.

> The covenant concept was important for Israel because the ancient social structure of Israel in part rested essentially upon a contractually regulated, permanent relationship of landed warrior sibs with guest tribes as legally protected metics: itinerant herdsmen and guest artisans, merchants and priests. An entire maze of such fraternal arrangements . . . dominated the social and economic structure. (AJ: 79)

Yet such contracting for rights lacks stability. Interests are fluid rather than static. While war, for example, brings about the composition of clans and tribes as fighting units, peace causes organizational disintegration. As the prosperity of peasants or livestock holders increases, so does pressure on land. Clans—associations of families held together by charismatic headmen—disintegrate in the face of economic pressures (cf. the parting of Abraham and Lot) and dissolve into constitutive family units. In Weber's view, the sacred covenant is the technique the Israelites hit upon to solve the problem of chronic social instability. Religious unity, i.e., devotion to a common YHVH cult, was discovered to produce a durable confederation.

Weber is making a Durkheimian point. Religion provides a strong cement for group solidarity. The Rechabites, a Kenite tribe of strict Yahwists, appear in biblical narratives from the time of Jehu through Nehemiah. Weber suggests that groups such as the Rechabites had an adaptive survival advantage that Israelites could have observed and emulated. Israelite elements found an affinity between the covenant idea and their own needs relative to their circumstances:

> Now, the point at issue is not that the life conditions of the Bedouins and semi-nomads had "produced" an order whose establishment could be considered as something like the "ideological exponent" of its economic conditions. This form of historical materialistic construction is here, as elsewhere, inadequate. The point is, rather, that once such an order was established the life conditions of these strata gave it by far the greater opportunity to survive in the selective struggle for existence against the other, less stable political organizations. The question, however, why such an order emerged at all, was determined by quite concrete religious-historical and often highly personal circumstances and vicissitudes. Once the religious fraternization had proven its efficiency as a political and economic instrument of power and was recognized as such it contributed, of course, tremendously to the diffusion of the pattern. (AJ: 79-80)

Weber's rejection of Marxist determinism and his attribution of religious ideas to charismatic sources is clear in the above quote. The transformation of socio-economic contracts into sacred covenants was an innovation of charismatic leaders such as Jonadav ben Rechav. Once such a structure becomes available, it will succeed if it enables a group to successfully compete in the struggle for survival.

Insofar as Weber views the Israelite covenantal community (*Eidgenossenschaft*) as a war confederation under YHVH, he understands the image of Israel in the Book of Judges to have a core of historical value. To be sure, Judges retrospectively attributes too much ethnic and political unity to Israel. It does, however, capture the character of whatever degree of unity did actually exist.

The judges (*shoftim*) were charismatic war heroes whose relative ephemerality indicates the unsettled nature of the life of the stock breeders among whom many of them originate.

> An example of the instability and purely charismatic character of warlordism among tribes of pure cattle-breeders is the view of Jephthah's position in the tradition. The elders of the tribe Gilead initially offered to Jephthah, an East Jordan war hero, only the dignity of a "*kazin*" a war leader corresponding to the Germanic duke (*Herzog*). This was offered for the duration of the war of liberation against the Ammonites (Jud. 11:6). He refused, and the army (*ha'am*, the men), at the proposal of the elders, conferred to him life-long, but non-hereditary, dignity of a *rosh* (chieftain, prince, headman, Jud. 11:11).

The numerous ephemeral judges (*shoftim*) of early Israelite times, partly were mere charismatic war leaders, partly, perhaps, also endowed with the charisma of judicial wisdom, were apparently, of the same type. Their power remained purely personal. (AJ: 40)

Eventually, the institution of kingship will emerge from the precedent of warrior nobles who recruit on the basis of their personal charisma. Weber sees that transition occuring in Judges with the story of Abimelech of Shechem (Judges 9). Abimelech's usurpation of the rights of Shechem's traditional patriciate (the local *bne hamor*) is presented by the text as tyranny. Both Abimelech and, in time, the kings will continue to have to reckon with the power of the landed, urban patriciate (*bne chayil*) and the traditional authority of the elders who are considered to be authentic representatives of the people (AJ: 19). In other words, political authority, as portrayed by Judges, is both traditional and charismatic.

By portraying the judges as primarily charismatic war heroes, Weber means to cast doubt on their "judicial" role. From time to time, proven war heroes may have been called upon to settle civil matters in peacetime, but in general Weber finds that role to be the traditional prerogative of the elders (*zekenim*). He takes Samuel's multifaceted activity to be an anachronistic retrojection (AJ: 85). Only Solomon takes legal matters into his own hands. Weber makes this point in order to assert that the Israelite confederacy had no permanent political organs until the time of the kings. Power was broadly diffused (AJ: 18). Whatever unity there was found its expression in a YHVH-certified war hero who was able to claim authority outside of his or her tribe, as for example in the case of Deborah (Judg. 4:5).

As far as can be determined this unstable Israelite confederation till the time of kings had no permanent political organs at all. The tribes engage in occasional feuds with one another. The religious international law, which, for example, prohibited the cutting down of fruit trees, applied—if at all extending back to ancient times—presumably to such feuds as occurred within the organization. The league members in the Song of Deborah partly withheld their support. Occasionally this led to their being cursed and to holy war against the oath-breaking member. There existed no common citizenship. Such was present, apparently, only in the tribe. To be sure, grave violation of metic rights, which every Israelite enjoyed in every other tribe, under certain circumstances was revenged by the confederacy. But there existed, obviously, no unitary court or unified administrative organ of any sort in times of peace. (AJ: 83)

Weber's characterization of Israelite society at the time of the judges appears paradoxical. On the one hand, he gives the concept of covenant a strongly political dimension. On the other, he deprives the polity, ordered in the name of covenant, of any stable political structures. This ambivalence reflects Weber's larger social theory. Weber wanted a political order in which bourgeois individuals would have maximum freedom of action. The somewhat anarchic regime of a traditional or charismatic leader held a certain appeal. On the other hand, Weber not only described (often with foreboding) but endorsed the growth of the modern, centralized, efficient state. He saw the state as the proper object of political obligation, as the most legitimate actor on the historical stage. Weber was both pathologist, prophet, and partisan vis-à-vis modern political life. His profound ambivalence imparts a pathos to his work that forms a source of its perennial appeal.[29]

A Cohenian Demurral

Julius Guttmann, in his extensive 1925 review essay of *Das antike Judentum*, sensed this incoherence in Weber's political reading of early Israelite covenanting. In terms reminiscent of Hermann Cohen's critique of Heinrich Graetz, Guttmann faulted Weber for his stress on the primacy of the political dimension as the framework for Israelite unity. Guttmann's critique clarifies what is at stake in as strong a sociopolitical reading of these texts as Weber provides.

Guttmann rejects Weber's reading of the political character of the covenant. On Weber's account, Israel's sense of unity is due to its covenantal act of mutual commitment in wartime. Yet Guttmann is troubled by the postulation of a polity without political institutions. He therefore follows a more traditional reading of the text and asserts that religious unity precedes and transcends political unity. Israel conceived of itself as a natural unity (*eine naturliche Einheit*) and a religious whole prior to any alleged political need to do so.[30] His proof of this is that after the division of Solomon's kingdom, despite political differentiation, Israel continued to conceive of itself as a religious unity. A primordial consciousness of religious unity suffices to explain, for example, the obligation to mutual assistance in wartime. No postulation of a political confederacy is required. Israel's God is the God of the community of Israelite persons (*Gott der Personengemeinschaft*), not of the State or of the Land, a point Weber himself makes.[31] Why interpolate a statelike entity between YHVH and Israel?

In line with this ascription of primordial religious unity to Israel, Guttmann believes that Weber has over politicized Israel's concept of God. If God is first and foremost a God of covenant (*seinem primären Charakter nach ist Ihvh Bundeskriegsgott und sozialer Verbandsgott*), we are at a loss to explain this god's apparent activities in nature.[32] Guttmann believes that Israel must have had early religious experiences of God, such as those of the patriarchs, in which the nature and universality of God were intuited. Israel understood the God of the covenant to be the same God as that of its primordial experience and that is why Israel consented to covenant with him. Essentially we have a reversion to the Wellhausian position here, albeit with a twist. That position posits that a natural people (or at least a people with a more or less natural self-understanding) exists prior to the covenantal moment. At a subsequent point in its history, covenant enters the scene as little more than a symbol of how this now less-than-natural people begins to think about its God and its own origins. The twist is Guttmann's embrace of a phenomenological method. It is basically at this point that he runs into conflict with Weber.

The argument between Guttmann and Weber is essentially methodological. Guttmann actually advocates a more radical application of *Verstehen* than Weber does. Guttmann is phenomenologically oriented. He wants to grasp those structures of consciousness that are the necessary preconditions for the self-presentation of Israel in its sacred texts. As such, he locates a primordial consciousness of religious unity in the earliest Israelite experience. He views such unity as a precondition, not as an instrumental value or effect. Guttmann believes in phenomenologically pristine religious experience, apparently taking the biblical descriptions of revelation more or less at their word. In this, he carries on the kind of quasi-theological scholarship that Weber rejects in the name of science.

Weber, while not excluding the possibility of religious experience, places much more emphasis on the pragmatic employment of religious ideas, derived from the religious experiences of charismatic individuals, in a social system. His accent is less on ideational structures than on value-laden behavior. Furthermore, Weber's sociological concern for discerning different occupational and status groups and specifying their interests undercuts ascriptions of unity and thematizes conflict. The Israelites, who are, at any rate, an amalgam of numerous ethnic groups, continue to harbor the same intergroup conflicts as the Canaanites before them. It makes little difference, in Weber's view, whether the small livestock breeders squeezed by the urban patriciate are Israelites or Canaanites. Economically informed interests carry their own momentum. Guttmann's critique therefore faults Weber for insufficiently pursuing the method of *Verstehen* and placing too much weight on "objective" factors.

Wellhausen and Guttmann, different though they are from each other, represent one sort of possibility in how we conceive of covenant. Weber represents another. The first pair are not oblivious toward covenanting as an actual social practice. Nonetheless, this is not what they mean to emphasize. Their emphasis is on covenant as a symbol of the divine-human relationship. "Covenant," in their vocabularies, refers to a social practice taken from its originary context and applied to a religious reality. We might call this the "soft" sense of the term *covenant*. Insofar as the reality of the divine-human encounter can only be captured by symbolic language and insofar as the religious reality is what counts, the soft sense of covenant rightly predominates. Their view is certainly legitimated, to an extent, by the phenomenology of religious consciousness. To the extent that the term *covenant* is used to mention the encounter of divine-human relationship, a figurative reading, that is, one that depresses the social-functional role of the term, is in order.

Weber, largely on account of his sociological method, brackets out the divine-human relational referent of the term. That is simply not his province. He practices methodological agnosticism. He anchors the term completely in political-historical reality. He does not slight the integrity of the religious dimension, as a reductionist would, but neither does he provide any theoretical access to it. Weber stipulates a "hard" sense for the term *covenant*.

No less than Wellhausen or Guttmann, Weber also represents an enduring approach to the phenomenology of covenant. For covenant is, once again, a political instrument. It is both a practical device for organizing a political community and an intellectual device for thinking about a community's organization, origins, and goals. Covenant is an idea that organizes the concepts of politics. That dimension is often lost in theologically oriented discussions, but it must not be. It is that function of the idea that we wish to retrieve here, without losing the connection to the more purely religious frame of reference. We must constantly keep in mind the dual referents of the idea even while emphasizing only one of them. That is not easy to do, for it is not easy to demarcate a line where politics ends and religion begins. The line becomes especially broken in rabbinic literature, to which we now turn.

Notes

1. I do not mean to imply that consent is a sufficient condition for legitimate authority, but I do want to argue that consent is a necessary condition for legitimate authority. Jewish sources are unusually insistent on the value of consent. This stems from the prominence of covenanting as a ground of legitimate authority in the Jewish political tradition. However, the construction of the doctrine of consent will be somewhat different from its construction in the modern liberal tradition, given a different philosophical anthropology. Critics of consent, beginning in Aristotle with *Politics*, book 3, chapter 9, operate with a model of consent as a matter of sheer human convention alone. I believe that it is possible to hold on to the centrality of consent for political legitimacy without subscribing to a conventionalist account of justice. That is precisely what covenant provides. Thus, covenant is not only a way of organizing concepts such as consent for an operational political system. It is also a way of conditioning them. Covenant gives to consent a character that it would not otherwise have. The modern liberal tradition, although postcovenantal in important ways, has resources for correcting a purely conventionalist view of consent. Locke's doctrine of consent as consent to what is right will go a long way, without question begging, toward correcting a decontextualized and distorted view of consent. It will also move us into the way the classical Jewish sources consider the matter. For a critique of consent from the point of view of a contemporary Jewish philosopher, see L. E. Goodman, "Toward a Jewish

Theory of Justice," in Daniel Frank, ed., *Commandment and Community* (Albany: State University of New York Press, 1995).

2. From an anthropological perspective, covenanting might be thought of as a highly developed example of gift exchange. For a highly suggestive exploration of the dynamics of exchange, see Marcel Mauss, *The Gift* (London: Cohen & West, 1954)

3. In classical Hittite treaties, however, the lord does not make the kind of explicit, stipulated promises that he expects from his partners. This is not true in the Bible, where God does commit himself to specific promises to his covenant partner, Israel. See Delbert Hillers, *Covenant: The History of a Biblical Idea* (Baltimore: Johns Hopkins University Press, 1969), 34. Furthermore, as Jon Levenson points out, since treaties are made between kings, Israel becomes a sort of priest-king people by implication. Jon Levenson, *Sinai & Zion: An Entry into the Jewish Bible* (New York: Harper & Row, 1985), 31-32.

4. Spinoza was not the first heterodox thinker to challenge the Mosaic authorship and hence divine authority of the text, but he was the most far-reaching and radical in his conclusions. He was the first to glimpse an entirely secular comprehension of Scripture. See Richard Popkin, "Spinoza and Bible Scholarship," in Don Garrett, ed., *The Cambridge Companion to Spinoza* (New York: Cambridge University Press, 1996). For a recent study of Spinoza's political thought, see Steven B. Smith, *Spinoza, Liberalism and the Question of Jewish Identity* (New Haven: Yale University Press, 1997).

5. See Ernest W. Nicholson, *God and His People: Covenant and Theology in the Old Testament* (Oxford: Clarendon Press, 1986).

6. Julius Wellhausen, *Prolegomena to the History of Ancient Israel* (New York: Meridian Books, 1965), 417.

7. Ibid., 469.

8. Ibid., 436.

9. Ibid., 436.

10. Ibid., 413, 466. The administration of justice and the concept of law, however, remain localized and unsystematic as in "prepolitical" times.

11. Ibid., 413.

12. For an appreciative, non-Hegelian reading of Wellhausen, see Steven Grosby, "Men Blow Kisses to Calves," *The American Scholar* 60:4 (Autumn 1991).

13. Wellhausen, *Prolegomena*, 472.

14. Ibid., 418.

15. Ibid., 422.

16. Ibid., 491.

17. Nicholson, *God and His People*, 16.

18. Ibid., 20-22.

19. Gary A. Abraham, *Max Weber and the Jewish Question* (Urbana: University of Illinois Press, 1992), chs. 2, 3. On Jews and liberalism in imperial Germany, see Marjorie Lamberti, *Jewish Activism in Imperial Germany* (New Haven: Yale University Press, 1978) and Ismar Schorsch, *Jewish Reactions to German Anti-Semitism* (New York: Columbia University Press, 1972).

20. Freddy Raphael, "Max Weber and Ancient Judaism," *Leo Baeck Institute Year Book*, Vol. 18, 1973, 47.

21. This was noted with appreciation by Julius Guttmann in his 1925 review essay of *Das antike Judentum*, "Max Webers Soziologie des antiken Judentums," *Monatsschrift für Geschichte und Wissenschaft des Judentums*, Vol. 69 (1925), 198.

22. Nicholson, *God and His People*, 38-44.

23. H. H. Gerth and C. Wright Mills, eds., *From Max Weber* (New York: Oxford University Press, 1978), Intro.

24. Georg G. Iggers, *The German Conception of History* (Middletown, Conn.: Wesleyan University Press, 1968), 164.

25. Weber's studies of particular religions appeared over a sixteen-year period in the *Archiv für Sozialwissenschaft und Sozialforschung*. They are compiled in a posthumous collection, *Gesammelte Aufsätze zur Religionssoziologie*, 6 vols. (Tübingen: Mohr/Siebeck, 1972) and are available in English as: *The Protestant Ethic and the Spirit of Capitalism* (New York: Scribner's, 1958); *The Religion of China: Confucianism and Taoism* (Glencoe: Free Press, 1951); *The Religion of India: The Sociology of Hinduism and Buddhism* (New York: Free Press, 1958), and *Ancient Judaism* (Glencoe: Free Press, 1952). His chief synthetic study, "Religionssoziologie" appeared in his magnum opus, *Wirtschaft und Gesellschaft*, and is available in English as *The Sociology of Religion* (Boston: Beacon Press, 1963).

26. Max Weber, *Ancient Judaism*, Hans. H. Gerth and Don Martindale, trans. (New York: Free Press, 1952), 4. Subsequent references to *Ancient Judaism* will be indicated by AJ and page number in parentheses.

27. Raphael, "Max Weber and Ancient Judaism," 51.

28. The patriarchs are portrayed as metic, small livestock breeders who must contract with urban patricians for pasturage rights. Weber held this situation to be typical in Canaanite and early Israelite times. While the patriarchs appear to be humble yet shrewd small stock breeders, the texts also present them as cattle breeders and warrior heroes. Weber suggests that the redactional process transformed them from *gibborim* to pacifists owing to a general transformation from semi-nomadism to urbanism. The disintegration of cattle-breeding tribes such as Shimon and Reuven, in evidence in Moses's Blessing (Deut. 33), supports this thesis, in Weber's view. See *Ancient Judaism*, 41-42, 52.

29. On Weber's politics and political thought, see Fred Dallmayr, "Max Weber and the Modern State," and David Beetham, "Max Weber and the Liberal Political Tradition," in Asher Horowitz and Terry Maley, eds., *The Barbarism of Reason: Max Weber and the Twilight of Enlightenment* (Toronto: University of Toronto Press, 1994).

30. Guttmann, "Max Webers Soziologie des antiken Judentums," 202.

31. Ibid., 203.

32. Ibid., 210.

Chapter Three

Covenant and Tradition: The Dynamics of Consent

In the last chapter, we tried to differentiate two different approaches to, and two different senses of, the idea of covenant. The "hard" sense stressed the political dimension of the term. The "soft" sense emphasized a more forthright theological concern with the divine-human relationship.[1] In this chapter, I want to consider this distinction against a different background, namely, the transformation of covenantal thought in rabbinic Judaism. In the emerging Judaism of the post-70 C.E. sages, covenant loses some of its relationality, whether that relationality is construed in political or purely religious terms. Covenant seems to stand less for an active relationship or matrix for relationship than for an inherited condition, a standing rather than a founding. There seems to be a movement from choice to encumbrance, from election to tradition. As such, the constellation of political values attending and underlying covenant shifts. The focus moves from the primacy of consent to the habit of participation. Participating in a social world of inherited, traditional customs looms larger in this political framework than deliberate consent to a constitutional model.

In studying this historical shift, we must also attend to the political-theoretical implications of traditionalism (versus active consent) as a ground for political obligation. Among the modern thinkers who have sought to problematize consent and promote traditionalism as the principal basis for political loyalty, David Hume is arguably the most useful. It is then to his political thought that we shall turn after surveying some of the historical background for rabbinic covenantalism. Yet it is an odd pairing, the sages and Hume. The sages could not possibly agree with much of Hume's thought. His ethical naturalism, for example, is alien to their own ethic of *imitatio dei*. Nonetheless, there is a point of contact between the two in Hume's repudiation of the theory of social contract with its exclusive emphasis on consent as the sufficient basis for the legitimacy of the polity. Hume argued that political association, and hence political obligation, were not based on some putative ancient promise that our ancestors made to a sovereign, thereby voluntarily relinquishing their natural rights and entering a civil state. Hume unmasked contract theory as a myth or noble lie. Be honest, he urged, and admit that the polity is a product of force, often violent, and accident. Our loyalty to it is based on brute habit and calculations of individual or mutual interest. The polity, and the allegiance of its citizens to it, endure not because of promises kept, but because of habits sustained. It endures only as long as the habit of deference is to everyone's advantage.

The rabbinic parallel with this view is subtle. It is found in how the rabbis use consent as a doctrine of political obligation, and how they, at the same time, contextualize and transform consent. The framework for this treatment of consent is the transformation of the idea of covenant in rabbinic literature. With this transformation, the society-founding and sustaining role of covenant becomes more obscure. Covenant continues to loom large as a theological concept and as a historical datum, but it shrinks as an operational principle. Arguably, the dimension of active consent or of repeated communal renewal has been reduced to an epiphenomenon.[2] Might we say that if the biblical authors were Lockeans, the rabbis were Humeans?

To answer this question, we need to get a better grasp of the rabbinic construction of covenant and how it compares with biblical usage. The term *covenant (brit)*, I have suggested, has both a hard and a soft sense. The hard sense is that sense which continues to embody the origin of the term as a *socio-political practice*, rooted in the diplomatic and treaty relations of ancient Near Eastern societies. If the biblical scholars are correct and Israelite covenantalism was an adaptation of Hittite and other suzerainty formularies, then this hard sense is the root idea, and other biblical uses constitute metaphorical adaptations of the concept. The soft sense, therefore, represents the increasingly symbolic extension of the original politically anchored idea into a generalized concept of intense, mutual, and binding relationship. Both hard ("political") and soft ("religious") senses have in common that covenant refers to relationship. Relationship is the constant. Type or range of relationship is the variable. Insofar as it is not possible to demarcate a purely political form of relationship from a purely religious form of relationship (for even secular treaties have a religious dimension), the hard and soft senses are not mutually exclusive. They represent the range of legitimate uses for the term.

When we come to rabbinic literature, however, something has changed. The rabbis seem to promote a very soft usage indeed. Their usage is so soft that it may be extra-categorical in terms of my distinction. The point is that for the rabbis, the term does not necessarily signify a relationship at all. It often signifies a substantive such as circumcision, Torah, or Shabbat. A process of reification and reversal has occurred. That which was once a sign of the relationship (*'ot brit*) has been substituted for the relationship. Circumcision, for example, was a sign of the covenant. In the earliest rabbinic usage, it *becomes* the covenant. Of course, the older senses, both hard and soft, are also preserved and used, especially in the halakhic midrash collections and Talmuds. But one senses a decline, particularly in the need for the practice of covenant renewal, which is common in the Bible.[3] With this decline, I will argue, comes a decentering of the importance of consent. It is not that consent vanishes altogether from the theoretical stage, but that it does not have the lead. And here we come to the resemblance with Hume. For both the rabbis and Hume, consent remains an important prop of political obligation. But for both, it is not the most or the sole important prop. Other Humean motifs such as tradition, custom, and habit are given a role to play.

Covenantalism and Rabbinic Judaism

We do not doubt today that the concept of covenant is key to understanding much of the biblical literature. As biblical scholar Jon Levenson has written, "the format of covenant served as the controlling metaphor for Israel's relationship to God through most of biblical history . . . . The literary legacy of ancient Israel is incomprehensible apart from covenant theology."[4] Biblical scholars still argue about whether this "controlling metaphor" was introduced earlier or later into Israel's thought or about whether (or to what extent) it derived from the suzerainty treaties of various ancient Near Eastern peoples. They do not, however, doubt its importance for the Bible as a whole.

Is the same true for rabbinic Judaism? Is covenant a "controlling metaphor" describing Israel's relationship to God as conceived by the rabbis of the first centuries of the common era and their intellectual heirs down to our own day? Here the record is much less clear. One could marshal much evidence on behalf of an affirmative claim. The rabbis do continue to use the term *brit* (*kayam* in Aramaic) to refer to the relationship God initiated with the patriarchs, as well as to those mutually obligating relationships undertaken with all Israel at Sinai, with David and his heirs, and with Aaron and his descendants. The rabbis seem to understand the system of law that they themselves did so much to advance and elaborate as a witness to this covenantal relationship, in the sense of being both a product of the relationship and a framework for it. They elevate certain legal observances within the system, such as the observance of circumcision, the sabbath, or the daily recitation of the *Shema* to defining moments of covenantal fidelity. To undergo circumcision (*brit milah*) is to enter and participate in the *brit*. To recite the *Shema* is to accept the yoke of the kingdom of Heaven. These are ways of enacting fidelity to the covenant in the midst of the covenant community.

For all this, however, it is far from obvious that covenant served, in the rabbis' form of Judaism, as a *controlling* metaphor to describe social life and political organization to the same extent that it did in the Bible. In the Bible, covenant is both a theological motif and a political idea. The book of Exodus, for example, conflates the hard and soft senses: the tribes of Israel enter into a binding relationship with God and *with each other*. Their form of association is covenantal in the sense that they retain their individuality as social groups, even as they federate for common purposes under the supreme authority of God. The idea of covenant describes both the sacred reality of the divine-human bond and the "secular" reality of human political association. Scholars such as Richard Kraetzschmar, as noted in the preceding chapter, sought a typology of covenant adequate to the many uses of the term. Max Weber was particularly attuned to the secular, political function of the idea in the life of ancient Israel.

The hard sense of covenant is not difficult to find in Scripture. It is prominent in incidents such as those described by Joshua, chapters 9 and 24. In the former text, Joshua and the elders enter into a covenant with the people of Gibeon, who have succeeded in tricking the Israelites into thinking that they are not local Canaanites but a distant nation. Despite the Gibeonites' deceit, the Israelites feel themselves duty bound to respect the new treaty relationship with the Gibeonites and to protect them against other Canaanites. In the latter text, the tribes of Israel renew their loyalty to God and to one another in a covenant renewal ceremony at Shechem. They reaffirm their political association as a confederacy under the God of Israel in advance of their leader's impending death. In each of these cases, covenant is more than a metaphor. It is a political institution, an instrument for organizing a political association.

The political character of covenanting is visible in the Dead Sea Scrolls in a far more explicit way than in the rabbinic literature. The Qumran literature documents annual covenant renewal ceremonies as well as elaborate confessional and oath-taking procedures for entering into the community. These procedures are explicitly modeled after biblical covenant-making episodes such as Deuteronomy, chapter 27. In the "Community Rule," for example, this modeling is fairly explicit:

> All those who join the order of the community shall enter into a covenant before God to do all that he has commanded and not to turn back from following him through any fear or terror or trial which takes place during the reign of Belial. When they enter the covenant the priests and the Levites shall bless the God of salvation and all deeds of his faithfulness, and all

those who are entering into the covenant say after them, "Amen, Amen!" The priests recount the righteous acts of God manifested in his mighty deeds and proclaim all his gracious acts of love towards Israel. And the Levites recount the inquities of the children of Israel, and all their guilty transgressions, and their sins during the reign of Belial. [And all] those entering into the covenant confess after them and say: "We have committed inquity [and transgressed,] we have [sin]ned and acted wickedly, we [and] our [fath]ers before us, in that we have walked [contrary to the covenant of truth] and righteous[ness . . .] his judgment upon us and upon our fathers, but he has bestowed his loving grace upon us from everlasting to everlasting."[5]

In passages such as these, it is easy to see that covenanting functioned at Qumran as a means of establishing entrance into and maintaining the community. Covenant seems to have a far more political role for the Dead Sea sectarians than it had for the rabbis. Taking an oath, explicitly consenting to a sacred law as a condition of entrance into a holy society, is far more evocative of Joshua, chapter 24, for example, than being circumcised as an eight-day-old infant.

Gordon Freeman has suggested that the rabbis did, in fact, abandon the polity-forming, polity-sustaining use of covenant. Freeman refers to this aspect of covenant as its "operational character."[6] In Freeman's view, the rabbis were aware that sectarian groups, such as the Qumran covenanters and the early Christians, were keen to use covenantal language and adopt covenantal practices in order to demonstrate that they were the true heirs of the biblical ancestors. By renewing the covenantal practices of biblical times, they could style themselves as biblical Israel. The rabbis, accordingly, limited the use of *brit* and substantially transformed the idea. First, the rabbis made the term *brit* synonymous with crucial observances: *brit* becomes coextensive with *brit milah*. Where once covenant signified a relationship with the divine and a means of structuring a polity, it now signifies a ritual practice that marks membership in a community. Second, the rabbis back away from use of the term *brit* entirely. They elevate the term *Torah* as the favored designation for the focus of Jewish life. "In substituting Torah for the covenant, the rabbis were demonstrating that by their study, interpretation and application of the Torah to the life of the Jewish people [their group] was the only group continuing and living according to the original covenant. The use of *brit* specifically as covenant was no longer necessary, since the covenant had once and for all bound God and Israel . . . Renewal of the original covenant was not necessary."[7]

Freeman believes that although the rabbis virtually abandoned the full semantic range of the term *brit*, they continued to think of the Jewish people as a covenantal community. That is, the Jews were not simply a natural *Volk*, bound together by ancestry, custom, and tradition, but a consensual political association. Rabbinic Jews were no less covenantal in this sense than the Qumran sectarians or Jewish Christians who actually employed covenantal practices for generating their associations and sustaining loyalty to them.

A similar conclusion is reached by Jon Levenson. Levenson traces the evolution of the covenant idea from its hard to its soft sense, that is, from a purely political instrument to a cosmizing metaphor to describe God's relationship with Israel. Already in the time of Hosea, covenant becomes a symbol to describe God's passionate (and stormy) love affair with Israel. The political (or in Levenson's language "juridical") sense of covenant is already undergoing a process of transvaluation. Levenson, like the majority of biblical scholars, sees a full and complex range of meanings associated with *brit* emerging early on. The later Jewish transformations of meaning have been well-prepared within the biblical process itself.[8] Nevertheless, Levenson does admit that the full-orbed biblical idea of covenant has suffered a certain loss of centrality in rabbinic religion. "There is no rabbinic ceremony in which Jews are said explicitly to be renewing their partnership in the Sinaitic covenant . . . ."[9]

Like Freeman, however, Levenson wants to preserve the essential content of covenantal thought and practice for rabbinic religion despite a loss of form. Levenson argues that the central liturgy of rabbinic Judaism, the daily recitation of the *Shema* (Deut. 6:4-9, 11:13-21; Num. 15:37-41) is "expressive of the classical covenant theology."[10] In an ingenious exegesis, Levenson interprets the three paragraphs as a condensed exposition of the ancient covenant formulary. The first declaration: "Listen Israel: YHWH is our God, YHWH alone" is "manifestly an echo of the requirement of the old suzerainty treaties to recognize one lord alone."[11]

> The second paragraph, which stresses performance of the stipulations, derives mostly from the blessings and curses of the covenant formulary. . . . What is interesting in light of the putative disappearance of the covenant renewal ceremony is that the rabbis selected these three texts to make up one prayer, for the three are not contiguous in the Torah. . . What links the three paragraphs is that they constitute the basic affirmation of covenant.[12]

In Levenson's view, "the recitation of the *Shema* is the rabbinic covenant renewal ceremony."[13]

Although both of these scholars recognize that something has changed for the rabbis, they are still anxious to preserve an essential continuity with the political, that is, the society-forming and sustaining function of biblical covenanting. Each wants to foreground a doctrine of consent and at this point both of them, it seems to me, are open to Hume's critique.

Hume on Consent

In "Of the Original Contract," Hume argues that it is absurd to think that men actively form their governments, generation after generation, by deliberation and choice. Societies are formed by force and accident and maintained through habit and the inertia of tradition:

> Did one generation of men go off the stage at once and another succeed, as is the case with silkworms and butterflies, the new race, if they had sense enough to choose their government, which surely is never the case with men, might voluntarily and by general consent establish their own form of civil polity without any regard to the laws or precedents which prevailed among their ancestors. But as human society is in perpetual flux, one man every hour going out of the world, another coming into it, it is necessary in order to preserve stability in government that the new brood should conform themselves to the established constitution and nearly follow the path which their fathers, treading in the footsteps of theirs, had marked out to them.[14]

Hume's position is subtle. He does not deny that there once was an original contract between early humans. Indeed, he cannot imagine how association would have otherwise occurred. Hume denies to this early contractual association, however, any political or moral status. The primordial horde could not be described as a true political society, for it lacked regular and stable institutions. Hume imagines a time similar to the period of the biblical judges, when humans followed charismatic chieftains, especially for purposes of war. Their submission to these leaders was based on the latter's efficacy in warfare and persuasiveness, not on their *right* to rule. The difference then between a horde and a "state of civil government" is that the ruler of the latter has a right to compel obedience and a right to expect obedience. The leader of a horde will prevail as long as his charisma holds out. Hume depicts the transition from the as yet unmastered *status naturalis* to the civil state in this way:

> The chieftain, who had probably acquired his influence during the continuance of war, ruled more by persuasion than command; and till he could employ force to reduce the refractory and disobedient, the society could scarcely be said to have attained a state of civil government. No compact or agreement, it is evident, was expressly formed for general submission, an idea far beyond the comprehension of savages. Each exertion of authority in the chieftain must have been particular and called forth by the present exigencies of the case. The sensible utility resulting from his interposition made these exertions become daily more frequent; and their frequency gradually produced a habitual and, if you please to call it so, a voluntary and therefore precarious acquiescence in the people.[15]

The transition to organized political society is brought about empirically by the regularization and effectiveness of the chieftain's rule. Its moral foundation, however, is the people's habit of acceptance. The habit of obedience is not based on an act of consent or the making of a promise to a ruler. It is based on the simple recognition that unless there is obedience to a sovereign and to a system of law, "society could not otherwise subsist."[16]

Hume has three basic arguments against exclusive reliance on consent. The first is historical and empirical. Although he grants that historically an original contract must have led to the first quasi- or proto-political society, he believes that this was lost in the mists of time and no conclusions can be drawn from it. There is no memory of it. Furthermore, not only is there no memory of the contract, there is no knowledge of it as a legitimacy-conferring mechanism. As a matter of empirical fact, most men in most of the world do not believe that the legitimacy of their sovereign rests on their consent.

Consent theorists are generally required to defend a doctrine of passive or tacit consent because they must concede to Hume that, for the most part, explicit moments of active consent hardly ever occur. (The exception is naturalized citizenship.) Hume's second line of argument finds tacit consent, however, incoherent. For tacit consent to be meaningful, people must believe that they are, in fact, consenting to their government and that the government's legitimacy depends upon their mental attitudes or physical acts. But Hume has already asserted that, in fact, outside of a few republican philosophers, most men do not believe that their sovereign's legitimacy depends on their consent.

> Should it be said that, by living under the dominion of a prince which one might leave, every individual has given a *tacit* consent to his authority and promised him obedience, it may be answered that such an implied consent can only have place where a man imagines that the matter depends on his choice. But where he thinks—as all mankind do who are born under established governments—that by his birth he owes allegiance to a certain prince or certain form of government, it would be absurd to infer a consent or choice which he expressly in this case renounces and disclaims.[17]

The intention of the subject is the existence condition for tacit consent. Where the subject has no such intention, tacit consent cannot be said to exist.

Hume's third argument is directed against what he takes to be a false moral anthropology. Moral duties are of two kinds, he tells us. Primary duties are impelled by a natural instinct. The love of our children, gratitude to our benefactors, pity to the unfortunate arise in us spontaneously. The second class stems from a sense of obligation, nourished by rational reflection on our social condition. We observe that our felicity in society depends upon our curbing our appetites and accommodating ourselves to respect our neighbor's property and the various conventions that make social life possible. The second class of duties, comprising such values as justice, fidelity, and allegiance, is less immediate and instinctive for us, but no less fundamental to our nature. Hume faults consent theorists for basing allegiance (to a polity) on fidelity (that is, keeping one's promise), for in his typology of moral duties, allegiance is no more and no less primary than fidelity. Both belong to the same class and stand on the same foundation. As second-order duties, both require an appraisal of our welfare and an appreciation of our circumstances with an eye toward maximizing utility. It is a mistake to found one on the other. They are both founded on the same calculation.[18]

At the end of the day, Hume does not want to debunk consent altogether. He wants to rein in its philosophical enthusiasts and substitute what seems to him a more realistic, empirically founded account of legitimate political authority. Speaking of a chastened doctrine of consent, he writes:

> My intention here is not to exclude the consent of the people from being one just foundation of government. Where it has place, it is surely the best and most sacred of any. I only contend that it has very seldom had place in any degree, and never almost in its full extent, and that, therefore, some other foundation of government must also be admitted.[19]

Hume's position has distinct strengths and distinct weaknesses. Some of its strengths are also among its weaknesses. It is creditable that he attacks contractarianism on empirical and historical grounds. There is an air of unreality that hangs about social contract theory when it seems to rely on a historical claim.[20] Hume shows clearly that even on the assumption that such contracting actually occurred it would not have been sufficient to found a government in any recognizable sense. He also argues persuasively that even during times when government is dissolved, such as during a revolution, and new governments are instituted, the process is still marred by violence, demagoguery, and accident. Consent has seldom actually functioned in the way its proponents have imagined. The weakness of this empirically-oriented argument is that it is open to empirical falsification. Political values and culture have changed since Hume's day. Far more people today do, in fact, believe that the legitimacy of government rests on their consent. The bonds of tradition and order-sustaining habit so praised by Hume and Edmund Burke are far more frayed and far less authoritative than they were in Hume's time. The venerable antiquity of an institution no longer constitutes an implicit claim for its authority. Hume would have to confront the inadequacy of his empirical account of loyalty. It is also possible that had Hume lived another decade to read *The Federalist Papers* or to witness the constitutional deliberations in Philadelphia, he might have had to revise his view that governments are never really empirically founded on consent.

But Hume's real target was never the adequacy of social contract theory as a historical thesis about political origins. His criticism was focused on the normative use to which the historical thesis was put. The more serious weakness in Hume's position is that his counterproposal for the justification of political obligation is far less adequate than the one he attempts to demolish. His proposal has no critical edge. Since the legitimacy of government is founded only on its ability to secure an advantageous order, Hume provides no standard for judging when order becomes oppressive and unjust. Injustice can also be advantageous. It often is, at least to someone. Because he has no expectation for government higher than order, there is no value to which order is subordinate. Unjust order might not be unjust for a polity governed by Humean conventions. The classic problem of justice for utilitarians ("if the sacrifice of one innocent man could secure a greater advantage for the group . . .") raises its head.

Despite this not inconsiderable defect, Hume's account has its virtues. It focuses attention on the intellectual gymnastics defenders of a pure consent-based theory of obligation have to perform to bring coherence to their view. It directs us to the actual forces that motivate political allegiance and inform political obligation. At this juncture, let us return to the Jewish sources and see whether Hume's disenchanted account of communal allegiance does not better capture the phenomenology of Jewish belonging than consent-oriented theories do.

Jewish Obligation and Consent

Following Hume, we might say that the consent-oriented theories of Levenson and Freeman ascribe a political character to what are arguably apolitical acts. Under the influence of the Bible's covenantal emphases, they want to extend the political dimensions of covenanting and covenant-renewal into a sphere where their place is more metaphorical than operational. This is very similar to Hume's objection to the Lockean view that when a subject remains in a kingdom rather than fleeing abroad he thereby expresses his tacit consent and affirms the legitimacy of the king. Locke ascribes a political function to a state of affairs that Hume sees as largely nonpolitical, namely, daily life. Hume finds it absurd to count as "tacit consent" what is, after all, people just doing their daily business without the real possibility of an alternative. He objects to the politicization, as it were, of everyday life. He wants to give the habits and practices of everyday life their due. Habits of participation, traditions, and customs rather than deliberate acts of assent keep a society afloat.[21] Levenson and Freeman may be open to the same sort of objection. Are Torah study, performance of commandments, and daily recitation of the *Shema* polity-maintaining, consent-expressing actions or are they simply the traditions and habits of the observant Jew? These traditions and habits, to be sure, keep the polity going. They transmit and reproduce a culture. Religiously, these actions are expressive of accepting the divine sovereignty or are expressive of allegiance to Jewish law or the Jewish people. But that still places them on the soft side of the political sense of covenanting.

To sharpen the contrast between the hard sense of covenant and the soft religious-metaphorical one within the rabbinic idiom, let us consider some typical ways in which the rabbis use the term *brit*. We begin with a so-called hard usage, wherein the term actually does signify a consensual relationship between two parties.

> *"A God merciful and gracious:"* Rav Judah said: A covenant has been made with the thirteen attributes that they will not be turned away empty-handed, as it says, *Behold I make a covenant.*[22]

This text is taken from a famous aggada in which God instructs Israel how to plead before Him to secure mercy. God Himself acts like the emissary of the congregation, draws His shawl over His head, as it were, and institutes a ritual of petition. The core of the ritual is the recitation of Exodus 34:6-7, which the rabbis designate the "thirteen attributes." Our text then goes on to explain why the recitation of one segment of these verses is especially efficacious. God has made a covenant (*brit k'rutah*) with the thirteen attributes. He has obligated Himself to respond in an appropriate manner when Israel recites the attributes. The "proof" that God has entered into the covenantal relationship with the attributes is Exodus 34:10, where it is announced that God will make a covenant. But with whom? Grammatically, the biblical text does not supply an object. The rabbis imaginatively answer the implied question (a covenant with whom?): God makes a covenant with the thirteen attributes discussed in the preceding verses.

Now this is certainly a highly "religious," metaphorical text, filled with reification and fancy. It may seem surprising that I have selected it as an example of the "hard" political use of *brit*. And yet, metaphorical as it is, it does use *brit* in a certain biblical way. *Brit* refers to a solemnized, binding relationship between two "parties." The issue of consent is a bit sticky, however. Could God's own qualities have chosen not to link themselves to Him? The question indicates the limit of the citation's usefulness. Although this is a genuinely "political" usage, the applicability of the text to our ideal type of political significance is limited because of its metaphorical character.

A similar usage can be found at B. Yoma 38a. The covenantal relationship depicted in this text also involves symbolic entities.

> Nicanor experienced miracles with his doors: Our Rabbis taught: What miracles happened to his doors? It was reported that when Nicanor had gone to fetch doors from Alexandria of Egypt on his return a gale arose in the sea

to drown him. Thereupon they took one of his doors and cast it into the sea, and yet the sea would not stop its rage. When, thereupon, they prepared to cast the other into the sea, he rose and clung to it, saying: "Cast me in with it!" [They did so, and] the sea stopped immediately its raging. He was deeply grieved about the other [door]. As he arrived at the harbour of Acco, it broke through and came up from under the sides of the boat. Others say: A monster of the sea swallowed it and spat it out on the dry land. Touching this, Solomon said: *The beams of our houses are cedars and our panels are* berothim [*cypresses*] (Song of Songs 1:17). Do not read *berothim* [cypresses] but *brit yam*, i.e., covenant of the sea.

The discussion here concerns the miraculous eastern doors of the Temple, which, Jonah-like, survive abandonment at sea. They survive because they have made a covenant with each other to stay together, despite formidable forces that would tear them apart. Although the story is completely fanciful, the use of *brit* is political, albeit in a highly derivative sense. *Brit* refers to a binding, mutually obligating agreement between parties.[23]

Perhaps the best example of *brit* in this sense is the early rabbinic midrash on the giving of the Torah at Mount Sinai, the covenantal episode par excellence. In the *Mekilta de-Rabbi Ishmael*, we read:

I am the LORD Thy God. (Exod. 20:2) Why were the Ten Commandments not said at the beginning of the Torah? They give a parable. To what may this be compared? To the following: A king who entered a province said to the people: May I be your king? But the people said to him: Have you done anything good for us that you should rule over us? What did he do then? He built the city wall for them, he brought in the water supply for them, and he fought their battles. Then when he said to them: May I be your king? they said to him: Yes, yes. Likewise, God. He brought the Israelites out of Egypt, divided the sea for them, sent down the manna for them, brought up the well for them, brought the quails for them. He fought for them the battle with Amalek. Then He said to them: I am to be your king. And they said to Him: Yes, yes.[24]

This text understands God's offer of covenantal relationship in classic covenantal terms. The people are entitled to choose whether they want the relationship. They have the right of consent. As in ancient Near Eastern covenant formularies, the treaty has a historical prologue indicating what the suzerain has done for his would-be covenant partner. The text interprets the entirety of Genesis and Exodus, chapters 1-19, as a historical prologue to the covenantal stipulations. In this sense, the text aligns itself with authentic, politically salient, covenantal thought and praxis. The midrash continues:

Rabbi says: This proclaims the excellence of Israel. For when they all stood before mount Sinai to receive the Torah they all made up their mind alike to accept the reign of God joyfully. Furthermore, they pledged themselves to one another. And it was not only concerning overt acts that God, revealing Himself to them, wished to make His covenant with them but also concerning secret acts, as it is said: *The secret things belong to the Lord our God and the things that are revealed [it is for us and our children ever to apply all the provisions of this Teaching* (Deut. 29:28)]. But they said to Him: Concerning overt acts we are ready to make a covenant with Thee, but we will not make a covenant with Thee in regard to secret acts lest one of us commit a sin secretly and the entire community be held responsible for it.[25]

Here, the Israelites are concerned that they will consent to conditions that will later be injurious to them. Using God's own Torah (that is, the verse in Deuteronomy) as their leverage, they engage in negotiation with their divine covenant partner, insisting on favorable terms before they consent to the relationship. Covenantal societies foster a culture of bargaining. Bargaining insists on ordering the relationship between discrete parties on the basis on equity. The Israelites are willing to assume the rights and responsibilities of the *brit*, but only if the punishment they might incur for noncompliance is just. If they could be punished for the secret sins of one of their number, they would never have any public, rationally available standards by which to judge their performance. The text further shows an acute awareness of the mutuality and solidarity a covenantal society requires: They covenant with one another to be corporately responsible to God. They assume that it is just for them to be punished as a group, but only for those things over which they, as a public, have control. This is covenantalism, and incipient rabbinic republicanism, at its best.

But it is also rather rare. In many, if not most, rabbinic uses of *brit*, the term no longer refers to the explicit relationship between parties, as above, but to a substantive term such as circumcision or the Torah per se. The following text records a controversy as to whether *brit* actually *means* circumcision or Torah. In any case, its original signification of a relationship founded on and maintained by consent is virtually obliterated.

It was taught: Rabbi said, Great is circumcision, for none so ardently busied himself with [God's] precepts as our Father Abraham, yet he was called perfect only in virtue of circumcision as it is written, *Walk before me and be thou perfect* (Gen. 17:1), and it is written, *And I will make my covenant between me and thee* (Gen. 17:2) . . . Another version [of Rabbi's teaching] is this: Great is circumcision, since but for it heaven and earth would not endure, as it is written, *[Thus saith the Lord,] but for my covenant by day and night, I would not have appointed the ordinances of Heaven and earth* (Jer 33:25). Now this [statement] conflicts with R. Eleazar's: for R. Eleazar said, Great is the Torah, since but for it heaven and earth could not endure, as it is written, *But for my covenant by day and night, I would not have appointed the ordinances of heaven and earth.*[26]

More than one version of Rabbi's teaching is recorded. Both take circumcision to be the meaning of *brit*. (A third version, which I have left out, supports a process of reasoning, according to Rashi, that led Rabbi to conclude that *brit* = circumcision.) Rabbi Eleazar's teaching conflicts with Rabbi's. For him, *brit* = Torah. For neither exegete does *brit* refer to the relationship, per se, to a consensual covenant between parties.

The Jeremiah citation, on which this rabbinic teaching turns, has God in covenant with the natural world. In a more adequate translation than the one excerpted above, the text reads:

> Thus said the LORD: As surely as I have established My covenant with day and night—the laws of heaven and earth—so will I never reject the offspring of Jacob and My servant David; I will never fail to take from his offspring rulers for the descendants of Abraham, Isaac, and Jacob. Indeed, I will restore their fortunes and take them back in love. (Jer. 33:25-26)

In the Bible, the natural, or better, the created order is understood in covenantal terms. The heavens operate lawfully not because of immanent natural law, but because of God's covenantal guarantee. Just as little as God will violate His covenant with the natural world, so would He not deprive Israel of His covenantal fidelity. God's loyalty to Israel, on account of the covenant, is parallel to His fidelity to nature. The point is not that, just as nature is permanent, so too will Israel be permanent, but rather that God exercises *hesed* in both cases. Both relationships are governed by the same rule.

In the rabbinic use of Jeremiah, however, nature is thought to endure because of either circumcision or Torah. Nature/Creation was brought into being for the sake of circumcision or Torah. The created order is an inert object rather than a subject of relationship. It is not a party to a covenant. Covenant, rather, has been equated with either a holy practice or the divine teaching, for the sake of which the world endures. These objects have, of course, entered into a relationship between God and humanity, but the relationship per se is not what the Talmudic text has made thematic.

In a sense, the rabbis have violated the use/mention distinction. Despite some reification, the word *covenant* was still used in biblical Israel to mention relationships between human subjects, or human communities, or humans and the divine suzerain. For the rabbis, the word *covenant* seems to be used self-referentially, that is, it is used to mention itself. "Covenant" has become a hypostasis. The reality toward which "covenant" points is the covenant per se. It no longer signifies a relationship. Rather, it has become its own signifier.

A typical, if slightly paradoxical, case of this is the oft-cited apothegm, "as for circumcision . . . thirteen covenants were made in connection therewith." (B Shabbat 132a) In Genesis 17, where God commands Abraham to circumcise himself and his household, the term *brit* is mentioned 13 times. God repeatedly declares that He will make a covenant with Abraham and his descendants. The stipulation of the covenant is that Abraham will circumcise himself and his household. In the rabbinic reading, however, *brit* has moved from its biblical significance of being a stipulation and sign of the covenant to being the goal or point of the covenant. Thirteen covenants were concluded, it is alleged, for the sake of circumcision. After circumcision replaces more primary meanings of covenant, it subordinates the primary meaning altogether. Covenants are contracted for the sake of circumcision. This reading is somewhat paradoxical because it preserves the political sense of the biblical original to a degree, while inverting its significance. Instead of the mitzvah being the *sign* of the relationship, the point of the relationship is the mitzvah. This example shows that the political sense of *brit* cannot really be eliminated, even when it is being substantially transformed. Readings such as Levenson's and Freeman's respond to this faint political echo in the rabbinic texts.

Although *brit* no longer conveys as much of a political sense as it once did, the rabbis do continue to think in a politically salient, covenantal way. They believe that Israel consented to its covenant with God, and that Israel maintains its covenant through a sort of transgenerational consent. Perhaps the clearest instance of this is in the famous, if idiosyncratic, aggada about how Israel was coerced to accept the Torah. A rabbi moots the idea that Israel did not freely consent at Sinai but was pressured by God to enter the covenantal relationship with Him. The rabbis then quickly reject this reading and try to restore a moment of true, free consent albeit post facto.

> *And they stood under the mount* (Exod. 19:17): R. Abdimi b. Hama b. Hasa said: This teaches that the Holy One, blessed be He, overturned the mountain upon them like an [inverted] cask, and said to them, "If ye accept the Torah, 'tis well; if not, there shall be your burial." R. Aha b. Jacob observed: This furnishes a strong protest against the Torah. Said Raba, Yet even so, they re-accepted it in the days of Ahasuerus, for it is written, *[the Jews] confirmed, and took upon them* [etc.] (Esther 9:27): [i.e.,] they confirmed what they had accepted long before.[27]

Raba's reading is based on a verse from Esther. In context, the Jews confirm (*kiyyamu*) and accept (*kibblu*) the days of Purim as holidays for themselves and their descendants. Raba, however, reads the verse as a reference to Sinai, interpreted in terms of the overturned mountain. The Jews there accepted, without confirming, that is, without true consent. Now, in the days of Ahasuerus, the Jews at last freely confirm (or consent to) what they once accepted. The appeal of this aggada, as Gerald Blidstein points out, is that

> it reflects the complex and ambivalent feelings of the Jew who has accepted upon himself the yoke of the Torah and its commandments. It offers graphic

expression of the heteronomy and coercion which an observant person experiences side by side with his sensibility of "Happy are we! How goodly is our portion, how pleasant our lot, how beautiful our heritage!"[28]

Jon Levenson describes this same ambivalence as a dialectic of autonomy and heteronomy: "Chosen for service, they must choose to serve."[28] One cannot but agree with Blidstein, Levenson, and Freeman that despite their extensive transformation of the concept of covenant, consent remains important to the rabbis as a part of their theory of obligation. What must be stressed, I believe, is that consent is only a part: it does not function for the rabbis as extensively as a social-contract-oriented thinker would like. The rabbis acknowledge other elements in their theory. And here we come back to the position of David Hume. He did not reject consent altogether. Rather, he tried to coordinate it with other, in his view, more predominant reasons for the legitimacy of our obligations.

Hume maintained that something more diffuse than a deliberate act of consent, of promising, or of oathtaking instills in us a sense of loyalty to our government and, normatively speaking, grounds its legitimacy. That diffuse something is the sheer efficacy of tradition. Hume suggests that people both do and ought to approach their traditions, ancestral practices, and institutions with a sense of awe. The rabbis share this belief that the category of tradition per se makes normative claims upon us, as is clear from the following exegesis.

R. Yohanan said: The prophet refers to one [transgression] that is equal to two. What is it? Idolatry. As it is written, "For My people have done a twofold wrong: They have forsaken Me, the Fount of living waters, and hewed them out cisterns, broken cisterns." (Jer. 2:13) It is written [concerning the people]: "Just cross over to the isles of the Kittim and look, send to Kedar and observe carefully, [See if aught like this has ever happened:] Has any nation changed its gods, even though they are no-gods? But My people has exchanged its glory for what can do no good." (Jer. 2:10-11) A Tanna taught: Cuthites worship fire and Kedarites worship water. Even though they know that water extinguishes fire, they have not exchanged their gods. "But my people has exchanged its glory for what can do no good."[29]

The text argues that if gentile peoples such as the Cuthites and the Kedarites show loyalty to their ancestral gods (which are, after all, false gods), how much more should the Israelites show loyalty to their God (who is the true God). While the idolatry of the gentiles is implicitly criticized, their habit of devotion to their traditions is not. It is esteemed. Furthermore, it is esteemed in the face of its patent irrationality.[30] They believe, as it were, because it is absurd. Awe and gratitude, it is implied, are powerful psychological forces for the maintenance of tradition. Tradition is a powerful social force for the maintenance of order.

Tradition is constituted by taken-for-granted thought and action, a skein of practices that give the social world significance and order. Whereas consent calls for decision and requires individuation, tradition calls for emulation and stresses sociality. An interesting echo of the emphasis on traditionality is found in Nachmanides' comment to Exodus 15:25: "There He made for them a fixed rule (*hoq u'mishpat*), and there He put them to the test." The context for this verse is the incident at Marah. The recently liberated people are already beginning to grumble for lack of water in the wilderness. Moses is instructed by God to throw a stick into bitter water and it became sweet. Then this verse follows. The question is, of what does the "fixed rule" consist? Rashi, following the Talmud (B. Sanhedrin 56b), believes that God has taught Israel several distinct mitzvot. Nachmanides, on the other hand, construes *hoq u'mishpat* not as commandments per se, but as civilizing behaviors (*hanhagot*), habits that will be useful for them until they reach civilization (*yishuv ha-medinot*).[31] Nachmanides takes the subject of the sentence ("he") to be not God but Moses. Moses, acting as it were according to *mishpat ha-melekh*, gives the people *nomoi* so that they can sustain their fragile polity.[32] Significantly, Nachmanides learns this analysis of *hoq u'mishpat* from Joshua 24:25, the stirring conclusion of the covenant renewal ceremony that Joshua undertakes with the people settled in their new land. "On that day at Shechem, Joshua made a covenant (*brit*) for the people and he made a fixed rule (*hoq u'mishpat*) for them." Nachmanides interprets *brit* not as the laws of the Torah (*eynam huqei ha-torah*), but as behaviors tending toward the maintenance of a civilized society. Here is a striking example of the transformation of the covenantal into the traditional.

The affirmation of the traditional man over the rational, autonomous, consenting man of classical liberalism defines the split between conservatism of the Burkean and Humean type, and liberalism. I have tried to call attention here to elements such as traditionalism in order to counter our occasional tendency to transform rabbis into republicans. The elements of tradition and habit, whether of the rabbinic or the Humean type, present us with a more difficult material to manufacture into a theory of obligation than does consent. Nonetheless, they are elements of Jewish political thought and deserve a theoretical articulation. They ought to give us pause whenever we hear, for example, that the Jews should be reconceived as a "choosing people," rather than as a chosen one. Because they were reared on a democratic ethos, it is easy to overstate the extent of the domain of consent, of voluntarism, of the choice of affiliations and loyalties. It is easy to see Jewish belonging as one of Hume's second-order moral duties, a product of rational reflection and choice based on some calculation of utility or on some personal persuasion of meaningfulness. To conceive of Jewish belonging in this way assumes an anthropology of primordially undefined and unattached persons, of existence preceding essence, of an originary freedom as freedom from all attachments. Preserving or maximizing freedom means only committing ourselves to those attachments we believe we ourselves have chosen. Judaism teaches, of course, that the freedom to covenant, to consent to attachments of the most consequential and defining sort, is real. Nonetheless, Judaism also teaches that pure consent is a moral and political fiction. Part of the story of our lives has been written before we are born. We are placed into an order of traditions beyond our choosing, many of which, both good and bad, we continue to enact as a matter of course. The extent to which we can form ourselves through deliberately chosen attachments is always balanced by the formative power of the attachments into which we have been born. This unclear mix of choosing and being chosen is basic to the Jewish condition, indeed, to the human condition as such. We cherish consent as a mark of human freedom and dignity, but there is also dignity to be found in embracing the self that we have been given. The Jewish self, at least the self of the born Jew, descends from the choice of parents and earlier ancestors. The proper response to this is gratitude.

Notes

1. I employ these senses of covenant as ideal types. In reality, actual usages of the term *covenant*, as well as actual instances of covenanting, will most likely have mixed political and religious elements. For a discussion of ideal types, see chapter 2, 61.

2. The debate over the extent to which rabbinic Judaism may be characterized as covenantal was initiated by the response to E. P. Sanders's *Paul and Palestinian Judaism* (Philadelphia: Fortress Press, 1977). Sanders described rabbinic Judaism as a "covenantal nomism." Earlier studies of rabbinic thought, such as George Foot Moore's *Judaism in the First Centuries of the Christian Era* or Ephraim Urbach's *The Sages*, did not use the concept of covenant as a way of describing the structure of rabbinic religion. The studies considered in this chapter generally support Sanders's application of covenantalism to rabbinic Judaism. I argue that although there is much sense in this approach, a change in the basic emphases of covenantalism occurs in rabbinic Judaism.

3. Two important technical studies of covenant in rabbinic literature, by Lawrence Schiffman and Friedrich Avemarie, deal with the continuities and discontinuities of rabbinic usage vis-à-vis biblical usage of *brit*. In general, early rabbinic usage (*mishna, tosephta*) tends to identify the content of *brit* with circumcision, or to use the term to mention historical examples of biblical covenanting. The halakhic midrashim (*Mekhilta, Sifra, Sifre*) expand on these uses and use *brit* to mention Torah, the Noachide covenant, the commandments as a whole, and secular agreements. According to Lawrence Schiffman, terms such as Torah function as indicators of the Sinai covenant, rather than as ends in themselves. Thus *brit* preserves what I have termed a relational rather than a substantive content. Nonetheless, the term still mentions something derivative of a relationship, rather than the relationship per se. There is thus still some distance between this sense and the hard senses preserved in the Bible and at Qumran.

Furthermore, there is no evident covenant renewal ceremony. In conversation with Prof. Schiffman, he seemed to accept my point. See Lawrence Schiffman, "The Rabbinic Understanding of Covenant," *Review and Expositor* 84:2, (Spring 1987), 289-98. For a thorough study of *brit* across the rabbinic corpus, as well as a critical review of the scholarly literature, see Friedrich Avemarie, "Bund als Gabe und Recht," in Friedrich Avemarie and Hermann Lichtenberger, eds., *Bund und Tora* (Tübingen: J. C. B. Mohr/Paul Siebeck, 1996), 163-216.

4. Jon D. Levenson, *Sinai and Zion: An Entry into the Jewish Bible* (New York: Harper & Row, 1987), 36.

5. IQS I:16-II:1. Michael A. Knibb, *The Qumran Community, Cambridge Commentaries on Writings of the Jewish & Christian World 200 BC to AD 200*, Vol. 2 (Cambridge: Cambridge University Press, 1987), 82. For an analysis of covenanting in Qumran in relation to the covenantal traditions of biblical Israel, see Klaus Baltzer, *The Covenant Formulary in Old Testament, Jewish and Early Christian Writings*, David E. Green, trans. (Philadelphia: Fortress Press, 1971), pt. II, sect. B.

6. Gordon M. Freeman, *The Heavenly Kingdom: Aspects of Political Thought in the Talmud and Midrash* (Lanham, Md. University Press of America, 1986), 61.

7. Ibid., 64.

8. See, for example, Walther Eichrodt's history and typology of the development of the covenant idea. Walther Eichrodt, *Theology of the Old Testament*, Vol 1, J. A. Baker, trans. (Philadelphia: Westminster Press, 1961), 45-69. Unfortunately, like most Christian scholarly treatments until quite recently, this one is marred by pervasive bias against Judaism. His typology is worked out against the dichotomy of love versus law, so foreign to the very texts he investigates.

9. Levenson, *Sinai and Zion*, 82.

10. Ibid., 82.

11. Ibid., 83.

12. Ibid., 83-84.

13. Ibid., 86.

14. Charles W. Hendel, ed., *David Hume's Political Essays* (New York: Liberal Arts Press, 1953), 52.

15. Ibid., 45.

16. Ibid., 56.

17. Ibid., 51.

18. In chapter 6, I argue that Jewish philosophers, such as Saadia Gaon, founded our political obedience on what Hume terms "gratitude to benefactors." Political allegiance, a second-order duty, would rest on a first-order "natural instinct" on this account. This would invalidate one prong of Hume's three-pronged argument. In general, the distinction between first-order and second-order duties is probably misleading.

19. Hendel, *David Hume's Political Essays*, 50.

20. For Locke's explicit (and not very convincing) defense of the historicity of the social contract, see *Second Treatise of Government*, ch. 8, paras. 99-113.

21. For a contemporary critique of consent theory that replaces consent with the concept of *participation*, see Benjamin Barber, *A Passion for Democracy* (Princeton: Princeton University Press, 1998), 3-18.

22. *B. Rosh Hashanah* 17b, Soncino ed.

23. For another instance of a covenant with an inanimate object, see commentaries on Numbers 18:19, "covenant of salt." Rabbinic commentators such as Rashi understand the biblical phrase *brit melah* (covenant of salt) in the sense of a covenant with salt. Just as salt will not lose its ability to prevent foods from perishing, so too will Aaron not lose his priesthood.

24. *Ba-Hodesh*, ch. 5, in *Mekilta de-Rabbi Ishmael*, Vol. 2, Jakob Z. Lauterbach, ed. and trans. (Philadelphia: Jewish Publication Society, 1961), 229-30.

25. Ibid, 231.

26. *B. Nedarim* 32a.

27. *B. Shabbat* 88a. Gerald Blidstein convincingly demonstrates that the motif of the overturned mountain and the coercion it implies is a minority voice in the Tannaitic, midrashic tradition. The vast majority of rabbinic interpretations of acceptance of the Sinai covenant stress the Jews' willing consent. Cf. Gerald Blidstein, "In the Shadow of the Mountain: Consent and Coercion at Sinai," *Jewish Political Studies Review*, 4:1 (Spring 1992.)

29. Jon Levenson, *Creation and the Persistence of Evil* (New York: Harper & Row, 1988), 148.

30. *B. Taanit* 5b.

31. The rabbis are implicitly raising here the issue of the rationality (or irrationality) of the commandments. Idolatry is patently irrational, yet devotion to ancestral gods is praiseworthy. The case for devotion to God and His covenantal stipulations, the text implies, can be rationally made out. The Israelites are doubly sinful: they are disloyal and they are irrational. The issue of the rationality of the commandments is pivotal for the rabbis. They are divided on the question of whether it is even permissible to inquire into the rationality of the commandments. According to some sages, they should simply be practiced as divine decrees without question. According to others, they should be investigated to uncover the reason why they were commanded. The entire question bears on the issue of consent, which necessarily has a rational orientation versus habitual, customary behavior. The classic treatment of this theme is found in Isaac Heinemann, *Ta'amei Ha-Mitzvot b'Sifrut Yisrael* (Jerusalem: Jewish Agency, 1966).

32. See Nachmanides on Exodus 15:25, s.v. *sham sam lo hoq u'mishpat.*

33. See R. Bahya ben Asher's commentary where he takes Moses, not God, as the subject of the sentence and adds that "In line with plain meaning of scripture, statute and ordinance, (*hoq u'mishpat*) are the customs how to regulate their lives in the desert, for Moses king in Jeshurun, a leader chastised his people and commanded them how to regulate their lives in the desert." Quoted in Charles B. Chavel, trans., *Ramban: Commentary on the Torah, Exodus* (New York: Shilo Publishing, 1971), 209.

Chapter Four

The Emergence of the Polity

When Alexander Hamilton, in *The Federalist*, no. 1, asked Americans to consider whether "societies of men are really capable or not of establishing good government from reflection and choice, or whether they are forever destined to depend for their political constitutions on accident and force," he made use of the threefold model by which polities have been held, since Greek antiquity, to develop.[1] Polities have been formed either through acts of conquest ("force"), gradual processes of organic development ("accident"), or, what David Hume thought least likely, the deliberate, considered choices of free, consenting persons.

For many political thinkers, an account of how a polity has been formed is less a historical narrative than a normative framework by means of which one can make judgments about aspects of the political system. How the polity is thought to begin legitimates those constitutional or political-cultural features that a given political thinker most esteems. Aristotle's use of an organic model of polity formation in the *Politics* (Bk. I, chap. 2), for example, ascribes to politics the teleological orientation and tendency toward stasis and self-sufficiency characteristic of the natural world. This orientation in turn validates rule by the natural, stable center of society, which, in Aristotle's view, is the middle class (Bk. IV, chap. 11). Locke's employment of a covenantal-contractual model, in which he stresses autonomous decision and choice, supports his emphasis on rationality, individuality, and rights. Where polities are held to be founded by a single, virtuous legislator who can be brutal ("force") if circumstances so require, as in Machiavelli, a pyramidal hierarchy of power is legitimated (*Discourses*, Bk. I, 9: Bk. III, 1). Thus, a political philosopher's narrative of polity formation plays a supporting conceptual role in an overall system of thought.

This methodological insight may be applied to the political thought generated by religious traditions. Attention to religious narratives about the foundations of some relevant political order can disclose *in nuce* a whole system of political ideas and values. In this chapter, I attempt to show that rabbinic speculations about the first human polity reveal key elements of a Jewish understanding of politics. My purpose is to trace the outlines of a rabbinic account of polity formation and to show how that account displays three interlocking themes of rabbinic political concern: the legitimation of authority, constitutional design, and consent.

Origins of the Polity: Biblical Considerations

Genesis, chapter 10, is the focal point of Jewish reflection on primordial political society. We shall consider this text first in its own context and then in terms of its appropriation by classical and medieval/early modern rabbinic commentators.

Before turning to the text, however, it is necessary to point out that in the Bible, unlike many other sacred scriptures, polity formation does not occur in a cosmological context. This is emphatically not the case in the Babylonian creation epic *Enuma Elish*, which depicts the founding of the holy polity of Babylon. Genesis 1 eschews such particularism and envisages a purely universal horizon.[2] Neither a polity nor a people has an exclusive or straightforward relationship with the sacred. The eventual connection of politics and the sacred will not be ontological, that is, embedded in the nature of things, but moral and historical, that is, the product of choice and contingency. A biblical understanding of the origins of political order, therefore, departs immediately from an Aristotelian one. Political society is not simply a matter of organic, evolutionary development ("accident"), but the result of moral choices made in response to historical contingencies, challenges, and conditions. The absence of an explicitly political narrative in the biblical creation stories points toward the large role that covenant—an idea that assumes historical contingency and volition—plays in Jewish political thought.

Genesis 1, however, is not wholly devoid of political elements. An echo of cosmological political origins can be heard in the terms used in Genesis 1:16,18 to describe the relationship of the sun and moon to the day, night, and seasons. The relevant terms, *memshelet, limshol* (rulership, to rule), have a political resonance. The sun and moon are to "dominate the day and the night and to separate light from darkness" (Gen. 1:18). The text depicts the cosmos itself as a kind of polity, with God as its ruler. The text implies that while God rules the entirety of creation, he delegates his authority to his subordinates (sun and moon) so that they may rule as he rules within their own sphere. Nature is presented not, of course, as an autonomous system of laws, but as a political system ordered by a divine will. Political relations are not implicit in an autonomous natural order, which at any rate is a concept foreign to the biblical worldview, but are derivative of choices God has made.

If this is correct, then a "thesis" about political authority is built into the ground floor of biblical literature. The thesis is that all legitimate authority is founded on divine grant. God delegates and shares his authority—authority is meant to be shared—but those who receive it are answerable to the grantor. The same set of assumptions that govern the authority of the sun and the moon will be transferred to human political authority. The only difference is that since human beings, unlike the celestials, are capable, like God, of decision and choice, they must choose to participate in—that is, they must consent to the gift of—divine powersharing. The vehicle whereby this mutual choosing is expressed is the covenant. By consenting to enter into covenant with God and with each other, human beings can make their political arrangements legitimate examples of divinely delegated authority.

Before we proceed further, some preliminary fleshing out of the concept of consent—in our context, the sometimes explicit, sometimes tacit acceptance of the divine covenant—is in order. Consent functions, in Western political thought, as a theory of political obligation. While consent has been an element of theoretical strategies to justify obligation since the time of Socrates, it has often had to coexist with other approaches such as divine right or the prescriptive force of traditional authority.[3] Since Locke, consent has tended, at least in democratic thought, to exclude other theoretical approaches. As we saw in the last chapter, however, rabbinic sources although they do not underemphasize consent, do not grant it a theoretic monopoly either. The rabbis are, we remarked, more like Hume than Locke.

Whether employed by ancient and medieval or modern thinkers, consent has always entailed numerous logical problems, some of which are reflected in the Jewish sources. To note a few: Why should our ancestors' consent to a presumed social contract obligate us now? Whose consent actually does obligate, the individual's in the present (or past) or the group's? If the group's, then how much of the group needs to consent for the whole group to be obligated, that is, must the consent be maximal (as in Plato or Rousseau) or minimal (as in Aristotle or Locke)? At any rate, why should my fellows' consent obligate me? Furthermore, must consent be formal or explicit in order for an individual to be bound to a political-legal system or can consent be implied by practices such as participation in the system through voting or (according to Locke) merely enjoying the use of a polity's highways? How tacit can "tacit consent" be before it ought not to be called consent at all? What actually is it that is consented to? Does one consent to a system as a whole or only its fundamental principles, values, or rules? Finally, can one knowingly consent to an illegitimate, evil system?

In Locke's thought, as Hanna Pitkin has shown, what one consents to when one assumes political obligation is a society that respects natural law.[4] Locke wants to invalidate the possibility of consent to evil institutions. He also seeks a basis for determining when valid obligations may be said to be suspended given a significant change in the nature of the system to which one consented. Locke locates his criterion in natural law. We cannot consent, under natural law, to make ourselves slaves, for that is against nature. We can only consent to arrangements that protect our freedom. In Pitkin's view, Locke's doctrine of consent has the ironic effect of shifting the criterion for consent from the individual's private judgment to the objective nature of the government. In order of logical priority: you do not consent to be obligated, given a just government, you are obligated to consent.[5]

With this ironic reading of a modern doctrine of consent, we come close to the mood of the Jewish sources. It is not toward the ideal of the solitary, rational individual explicitly choosing his obligations that our sources point, but toward the ideal Torah to which both the rational individual and the nation ought to consent. The divine wish to enter into covenant takes the place of Locke's natural law. Given the ineluctability of divine will, what is significant about Jewish consent doctrine is that it is there at all. A strong version of a divine command theory (a favorite although completely unbiblical caricature held by many philosophers of religion) might well have obliterated any need for human consent. Yet our sources present consent as a necessary element of political obligation.

This mix of command and consent is evident in rabbinic midrashim on Genesis 1. Ever keen to the shading and resonance of biblical terminology, the Jewish sages sensed the political nuance implied by the term *limshol* in Genesis 1:18 and expanded its range. In addition to reiterating the biblical theme of legitimate authority as divinely granted authority, the midrash also introduces rabbinic notions about consent and constitutional design. The Talmud (B. Hullin 60b) preserves a midrash that explores reasons for the fact that although the sun and the moon were originally created equal in size the moon became smaller:

> R. Simeon b. Pazzi pointed out a contradiction [between verses]. One verse says, *And God made the two great lights.* and immediately the verse continues, The greater light . . .and the lesser light. The moon said unto the Holy One, blessed be He, "Sovereign of the Universe! Is it possible for two kings to wear one crown?" He answered, "Go then and make thyself smaller." "Sovereign of the Universe," cried the moon, "Because I have suggested that which is proper must I then make myself smaller?"[6]

One might argue that God is annoyed by the moon's charge simply because it constitutes insubordination and reflects, possibly, undue ambition. But God's response may also counter the substantive political view represented by the moon, namely, that it is improper for two kings to use the crown of kingship. On this reading, the midrash is not antimonarchic, but rather anti-absolutist. It implies that kings have no inherent or natural privileges. Their authority is derived from and conditional on divine approval and can be reduced or retracted when they overstep their bounds. God did not want one determinate power center. He intended a power-sharing arrangement that the moon found "unnatural." The moon is obligated to consent to the constitutional framework that God has in mind.[7] A king must consent to a limited grant of power. Furthermore, the midrash favors a constitutional design in which power is shared and dispersed over multiple authorities, a feature that is typical of rabbinic political thought.[8]

The basic idea of Jewish constitutional design is this: Because God alone is sovereign, human political arrangements must give expression to that sovereignty. It might have been the case that God's sovereignty should be mirrored by an absolute human monarch, but Jewish political thought took a different tack. Rather than mirror divine sovereignty by absolute or sacred kingship, human rule must be a foil for it. That is, the human polity should be characterized by multiple, diffused centers of limited power in order to indicate, as though by counterexample, what divine sovereignty really means. Because God alone is the true ruler, human agents do not rule as much as they discharge necessary administrative functions. The irreducible plurality of functions necessary for the administration of any polity thus requires plural competencies.

The midrash illustrates this with high irony. While the moon is reduced in size, thus seeming to favor a single power center, its authority is not eliminated. The sun cannot become the sole celestial power any more than the moon could have. The moon continues to rule the night. (In addition, the midrash ascribes to the moon a certain power over the day insofar as God allows the moon a role in determining Israel's calendar.) Both sun and moon perform unique administrative tasks. Rashi (1040-1105), the premier Jewish biblical commentator of the Middle Ages, adds that after the moon was reduced in size, God multiplied its retinue, the stars, in order to conciliate it. The moon, now enhanced through its heavenly host, preserves a parity in power and authority with the sun. The kingdom of nature has more than one throne.[9]

Although far from the full-orbed, cosmogonic legitimations of mundane political regimes that one finds in other scriptures, the Bible and the rabbis nonetheless use the language of cosmogony to lay down their basic political principles. Against this conceptual background, we can explore the political implications of Genesis, chapter 10, the so-called table of nations.

Genesis 10 is directly relevant to our inquiry because it suggests, albeit subtly, the differentiation and emergence of political society from pre-political, family-based social life. The chapter details the lines of Noah's sons, Shem, Ham, and Yaphet who, after the flood, father seventy "nations." The entities characterized as nations (*goyim*) share a common descent, a common language, and the possession of a common territory (cf. Gen. 10:5, 20, 31). A formula is used in these three verses which juxtaposes *mishpaha* (clan) with *goy* (nation). A nation is thus made up of clans characterized by linguistic and territorial commonality. The text does not, at least in these formulae, indicate a political factor by virtue of which the clan has become a nation. All that we can say so far is that the biblical text, like Aristotle, distinguishes different levels of social scale and organization: a kinship group is not identical to a nation and a nation is not identical to a polity.[10] The concepts of nationhood and polity intersect in verses 8-10, with the figure of Nimrod. For the first time the root signifying kingship, *m-l-kh*, makes its appearance in the Bible. Nimrod represents the first human ruler. With Nimrod, political institutions (in this case, kingship) emerge and may be differentiated from family and clan-based social structures.

> 8. Cush also begot Nimrod who was the first man of might on earth.
> 9. He was a mighty hunter by the grace of the LORD; hence the saying, "Like Nimrod a mighty hunter by the grace of the LORD."
> 10. The mainstays [*reshit*: other translations: beginnings] of his kingdom [*mamlakhto*] were Babylon, Erech, Accad, and Calneh in the land of Shinar.[11]

Nimrod is not counted among the seventy nations of the table. He is introduced, almost casually, to indicate the historical agent by whose means political institutions arose. Nationhood is the necessary but not the sufficient condition for kingly rule. Political order in the sense of kingship is not—to invoke the threefold model—wholly a natural, accidental occurrence. It is not merely a matter of scale of social complexity or evolutionary necessity. It also requires the action of a particularly powerful individual, a charismatic figure. The text does not present this charismatic figure as a conqueror. Nor does it present him as a leader chosen by consent. This latter omission will be filled by the rabbinic literature, which is sufficiently influenced by the model of covenant as to be convinced that political institutions must arise through some consensual procedure.

Who is Nimrod? It is plausible that the biblical Nimrod reflects an Accadian king of the third millennium such as Naram-Sin, although this cannot be definitively established.[12] Whatever the historical background for this figure, the text as it stands seems to preserve a fragment of an ancient popular song about the exploits of a legendary king. The popular saying reflected in verse 9 ("like Nimrod, a mighty hunter by the grace of the LORD") provides support for this view.[13] Ancient Israel shared in the praise of this charismatic figure. If this is the case, it indicates that the biblical author supports—or at least does not negate—the memory of Nimrod as a man of might, a ruler and the founder of cities. Nimrod is not presented as a sinner, but in a manner that reflects his legendary stature in the common ancient Near Eastern culture outside of biblical Israel. Ancient Israel praised Nimrod's courage. His exploits as a hunter—a common feature of ancient Near Eastern epics of the deeds of great men—exemplify his charisma. Courage is a principal political virtue. Charisma, in classic Weberian fashion, legitimates political authority.[14]

On the other hand, the root *m-r-d*, out of which his name is formed, means rebellion and might indicate, however subtly, a negative evaluation of his exploits. The text may also employ a double pun, for the root *r-d-h* sometimes signifies oppressive rule.[15] Furthermore, the association of Nimrod with Babylon and the anti-Babylonian critique of the next chapter implicitly bind Nimrod to a negative context. It is this implication upon which rabbinic commentary builds.

Origins of the Polity: Rabbinic Considerations

While the Bible is thus suggestively mixed in its view of Nimrod, rabbinic midrash and medieval commentary are overwhelmingly negative. The hint of critical judgment in the Bible becomes categorical for the rabbis. Nimrod is transformed into a villain: the archetypal rebel against God and the evil nemesis of the patriarch, Abraham. What is crucial, however, is that Nimrod is more than just an evil gentile, a wicked king, or even a king per se. The rabbis' problem with him is in part a political problem. The rabbis retain and expand the political implications of the text. Significantly, they move away from the more or less natural or "accidental" framework of the biblical account, and discover and stress human "reflection and choice," that is, consent and deliberate constitutional design in the formation of Nimrod's polity.

The rabbis continue the biblical motif of the charisma and power of Nimrod. *Genesis Rabba* (37:2) portrays him as a persuasive, charismatic figure who is, however, also deceitful. His legendary hunting skills are transformed metaphorically into a talent for the manipulation and entrapment of gullible people.

Like Nimrod a mighty hunter before the Lord (Gen. 10:9): it is not written, Nimrod [was a mighty hunter], but *like Nimrod*: just as one snared people by their words, so did the other [Esau, i.e., Rome] snare people by their words, saying, "[True,] you have not stolen, [but tell us] who was your partner in the theft; you have not killed, but who was your accomplice in the murder."

The midrash's linkage of Nimrod with contemporary Rome constitutes a double-edged critique of illegitimate political authority, yet the focus is more on Rome than on Nimrod.[16] We do not yet know the political, as opposed to the simply moral, significance of Nimrodian deception.

An eighth-century midrash, *Pirke de Rabbi Eliezer*, provides further insight into the deception motif. The coat that God had made for Adam and Eve when he expelled them from the Garden had been inherited by Noah and rested in the ark. Noah's son Ham took it and gave it to Nimrod. When Nimrod wore it, all the animals prostrated themselves before him. Men were astonished by this and, concluding that he must be a mighty man, decided to appoint him king over themselves.[17] The origins of the polity, the midrash implies, have to do with deceit, confusion, and coercion, not genuine consent.

The Nimrodian polity arose when men were tricked and obligated themselves to a system that did not deserve their loyalty or moral approbation. That human beings chose Nimrod, albeit out of fear and ignorance, indicates the persistent character of this political value for the rabbis. The rabbis are unwilling to claim that spurious consent—consent to evil institutions achieved by manipulative means—is no consent at all. Insofar as human beings continued to follow Nimrod, participating in his construction of the tower of Babel, they sustain a tacit consent to, and guilt for, his regime. The limits of obligation to this system are limned by the figure of Abraham, who rejects his political obligation to Nimrod as a consequence of his obligation to God.

This theme is found in *Tanna Debe Eliyyahu*, a large midrash collection composed between the third and ninth centuries. In these midrashim, Nimrod is presented as the king of Abraham's native Mesopotamia. Abraham discovers that there is but one God and that the idols that his father, Terah, makes are worthless pseudo-divinities. Abraham, in an act of political treason, proselytizes his would-be customers in his father's idol shop, showing them the futility and absurdity of idolatry. As word spreads that Abraham has shaken the credibility structure of the local civil religion, the stage is set for a confrontation with King Nimrod.

> When Nimrod came and found him there, he asked: Are you Abraham the son of Terah? Abraham replied: Yes. Nimrod asked: Do you not know that I am lord of all things? Sun and moon, stars and planets, and human beings go forth only at my command. And now you have destroyed my divinity [i.e., my idol], the only thing I revere.[18]

Nimrod considers himself an absolute monarch who is not per se a god, but whose reign is legitimated by the gods. This self-serving delusion is the immediate target of Abraham's attack. Not only Nimrod's followers but Nimrod himself are profoundly mistaken about the nature of legitimate authority and the sources of political obligation.

Like Socrates, Abraham threatens the civil order in a fundamental way. Abraham challenges Nimrod to prove that he is indeed "lord of all" by commanding the sun to rise in the west and set in the east. Nimrod is shaken from his illusions and discomfited, whereupon Abraham reminds him of his lowly paternity and of his mortality. At this, Nimrod sentences Abraham to death by burning in a specially constructed furnace from which he is saved by God Himself.

The complaint of these classical sources is that Nimrod caused human beings to rebel against and reject God as their king and to consent to follow him instead. Yet this is no blanket protest against kingship as such. The emphasis upon deception and manipulation suggests that it is not only (or primarily) primordial human kingship that is bad. The manner in which it was achieved, sustained, and practiced gives cause for offense. Nimrod did not advance to kingship through divine approval and legitimate human consent, but through deceit and, hence, counterfeit consent.

Genuine consent, the rabbis imply, requires not only sound knowledge but sound judgment. We ought only consent to that which truly obligates us. This is, substantively, the biblical tradition. Although the Bible preserves radically conflicting evaluations of kingship, popular consent in tandem with divine right (cf. I Sam. 10:24, I Kings 12) played a fundamental role in the appointment of a king.[19] Precisely at its moments of negative judgment of kingship, the Bible stresses that Israel was informed about the nature of kingship (e.g., I Sam. 8:11-18, 10:25; I Kings 12:14) and was therefore fully responsible for its choice. Nimrod is depicted by the rabbis as offending against the value of consent and therefore undermining the responsibility or accountability of the members of the political community. Furthermore, Nimrod (like the king of Babylon, see Jer. 25:12-14) does not acknowledge God as the source of his authority and the ground for obligation. He is not in a covenantal relationship with God and so becomes a symbol for political illegitimacy.

The medieval exegetes continue this line of political critique. Rashi synthesizes the elements of the classical sources, consolidating the basic negative image of Nimrod for the tradition. Alone among the medievals, Abraham ibn Ezra (1023-1097), however, draws a rather different picture. He departs from the by-now authoritative metaphorical transformation of Nimrod as a hunter of innocent men's minds and a usurper of loyalties and reasserts the plain sense: Nimrod was the first to display the power of man to the beasts. Being a mighty hunter "before the LORD" indicates, according to ibn Ezra, that he built altars and sacrificed the animals he hunted to God. Ibn Ezra distances himself from the midrashic explanation. He affirms Nimrod's kingship over Babylon without a hint of negative judgment and cites a tannaitic text, *Seder Olam Rabbah*, as support for the view that Nimrod was ruler of all seventy nations after the fall of Babel.[20] Ibn Ezra has a very different evaluation of Nimrod from Rashi. His silence on Nimrod's traditional venality may be an effect of his exegetical preference for the plain sense of the text, or it may reflect a substantively different view of Nimrod. Given the silence of the rabbinic tradition on alternative constructions of Nimrod, however, ibn Ezra's approach is probably a function of his exegetical tendency.

Owing to ibn Ezra's rare suspension of criticism, Nachmanides (1124-1200) criticizes ibn Ezra for "making a wicked man just." According to Nachmanides, ibn Ezra was misled by the plain sense of the text while Rashi, following rabbinic tradition, understood Nimrod correctly. After citing Rashi's reiteration of the midrash that Nimrod trapped men with his words and enticed them to sin, Nachmanides characterizes his original, political role:

> The correct meaning (of Gen. 10:8) in my view is "he began to be" a ruler (*moshel*) by means of his might over men. He was the first sovereign (*molekh*), for up until his time there were no wars, nor did a king rule. First he subdued (*gavar*) the men of Babylon until he ruled over them. Then he went to Assur and did as he wished. He grew great and built fortified cities there by means of his power and might.[21]

For Nachmanides, the rise of political order involves domination by a sovereign, rule over a territory, public displays of authority, and the permanent possibility of war. Relying on Rashi, Nachmanides, like the rabbinic midrashim, implies perverted consent as the avenue by which Nimrod achieved power. He then indicts Nimrod for what amounts to a seizure of power: He overwhelms men with force and then rules over them.

The most thorough exploration of the political implications of the Nimrod passage was undertaken by Isaac Abravanel (1367-1459), the last great medieval Jewish commentator. While Abravanel reiterates the usual elements of rabbinic critique, he adds his own dimension of utopianism. Abravanel asserts that until Nimrod:

> Human beings were all equal in rank, for they were all sons of one father. But Nimrod began to dominate and rule over the men of his generation, as it is said: *He was the first man of might on the earth.* (Gen. 10:8) That is to say, he was an officer and a ruler on the earth.[22]

Abravanel's assertion that the state of prepolitical society is a state of perfect equality immediately places political institutions as a whole into tension with the prepolitical, idealized social backdrop from which they emerged. The reasons for this strong antipolitical tendency in, ironically, medieval Jewry's last outstanding political factotum are a matter of scholarly debate.[23]

How was Nimrod able to lift himself out of a primeval society of equality and create kingship? Abravanel echoes *Pirke de Rabbi Eliezer.* Nimrod's skill as a hunter intimidated his fellow humans. "When human beings saw that bears and lions, with all their strength, were conquered by him, they became afraid of him and were subdued before him."[24] Thus, as in Rousseau, humans have themselves to blame for the loss of their own equality. They allowed themselves to become afraid and hence to be manipulated by a now superior force. Drawing on (while distorting) ibn Ezra, he maintains that Nimrod may have built an altar and sacrificed animals in order to impress people with his piety "before God." He was the first practitioner of civil religion; his religious charisma supported his political charisma. Nimrod went on to build fortified cities in order to display the extent of his power. Dread of him fell upon humanity. For Abravanel—and he is the most extreme example of this among Jewish thinkers—all polities (even the ancient Jewish ones) are grounded in fear, coercion, and false religion. The prepolitical condition of humanity is utopian by comparison with political society. Political life is unnatural and craven. It is the primary perversion of the pristine human condition.

Largely following Abravanel but tempering his extreme negativism, the nineteenth-century commentator Meir Loeb Malbim (1809-1879) also understands political life per se to arise out of coercion. Malbim adds, however, the Hobbesian theme of primordial crisis, the war of all against all. He relates the rise of urban society and legal order to Cain: men banded together and subordinated themselves to mutually beneficial laws after Cain murdered his brother and upset the primeval harmony. Urban life then becomes fully political with Nimrod:

> He was the first who gathered military encampments together and made war. He prevailed over the rest of humanity and became king over them, for until that time, every clan (*mishpaha*) lived under its primary patriarch (*avihem ha-rishon*), who was the head of the clan.[25]

Malbim accepts historical, post-Edenic existence as political existence. Political institutions are a lesser evil than the chaos of unbridled personal liberty unleashed by Cain. Nimrod is not righteous, but his imposition of order keeps the ubiquitous threat of chaos at bay.

Given the foundational biblical account and its rabbinic interpretations, what conclusions can we draw about rabbinic political concepts and values? That the rabbis believe political authority derives from divine grant is clear. But the fact that rabbinic texts, and implicitly the biblical text as well, see Nimrod, the first "political leader," as a usurper of and rebel against divine authority raises a large question. What exactly do these texts oppose? Do they oppose any rule other than God's, or do they only oppose a form of human rule that is, for some reason, against God? Is the political vision behind these texts, in other words, utopian and theocratic or merely critical? If we were to read only Abravanel and Malbim, we would probably emphasize the utopian dimension and have to conclude that Judaism is fundamentally antipolitical. We would read the Nimrod texts as Abravanel does and conclude that the rabbis understand political society as a rejection of divine governance. Kingship in general, and certainly gentile kingship in particular, are irremediably wicked. The evidence here points in a different direction, however.

In my view, what the rabbis reject when they reject Nimrod is not the possibility of legitimate human public authority per se, but only a conception of public authority profoundly at odds with their own. What they reject attests to what they affirm. In order for there to be legitimate authority there must first be an acknowledgment of God as the ultimate authority and ground of political obligation. Such an acknowledgment, established through consent, creates a covenant community. Within this communal context, further acts of consent are necessary for any claims to human political authority to be valid. Finally, at the level of constitutional design, human political authority is best exercised when power is diffused between different centers. Once such an order is in place, its authority is maintained by occasional acts of consent, but also by habits of participation and deference. The Nimrod texts present a hypothetical polity in which none of these principles is in force. It is not the fact that Nimrod became the first ruler that offended the rabbis, but rather that he disregarded the principles of their politics.

Where then does that leave our politics? Although our American Declaration of Independence, in good eighteenth-century fashion, invokes "nature" or "nature's God," our Constitution does not. It is famously controversial whether our form of polity requires an appeal to transcendence, to either the God of Scripture or to his eighteenth-century deist incarnation, for its justification. Clearly, many of the American Founders thought that, on some level, American institutions relied on God for their support. But that is a large topic for an ongoing public conversation, not a matter of settled doctrine.

If the democratic conversation should someday settle on a purely secular reading of the authority of our institutions, would we then have a Nimrodian polity, on a rabbinic account? How much room can Judaism make for a wholly secular governance? We will confront a theoretical attempt to answer this question when we examine the work of Rabbi Shimon Federbush in chapter 8. At this point, let us turn to another way of posing the question of secularity as we consider modern theories of rights and traditional Jewish responses to them.

Notes

1. This discussion follows that of Daniel J. Elazar in Daniel J. Elazar, ed., *Constitutionalism: The Israeli and American Experiences* (Lanham, Md.: University Press of America, 1990), 13-16.

2. Jon Levenson, *The Universal Horizon of Biblical Particularism* (New York: American Jewish Committee, 1985), 4, Alexander Heidel, *The Babylonian Genesis* (Chicago: University of Chicago Press, 1967), 48-49.

3. For a review of treatments of consent in premodern political thought, see Stephan Eisel, *Minimalkonsens und Freiheitliche Demokratie* (Paderborn: F. Schoeningh, 1986), 34. Eisel provides both a historical survey and a philosophical analysis of the concept of consent.

4. Hanna Pitkin, "Obligation and Consent," *American Political Science Review* LIX (December 1965), 990-99.

5. Ibid., 996.

6. *B. Hullin*, Eli Cashdan, trans. (London: Soncino Press, 1978), 331.

7. The idea that created things enjoy the form that they have through a mutual relationship with the divine Creator that entails consent is expressed at *B Hullin* 60a. "Rabbi Joshua b. Levi said: All the animals of the creation were created in their full grown stature, with their consent, and according to the shape of their own choice, for it is written, *And the heaven and the earth were finished, and all the host of them*; read not *zeba'am* [their host] but *zibyonam* [their desire]." The word *host* is hermeneutically construed to derive from a root (*tzbh*) implying will, desire, or consent. *B. Hullin*, Eli Cashdan, trans., 330.

8. See Stuart A. Cohen, "The Concept of the Three Ketarim: Its Place in Jewish Political Thought and Its Implications for a Study of Jewish Constitutional History," *Association for Jewish Studies Review* 9:1 (Spring 1984), 29ff. For a thorough working-out of the theme of division of power as a fundamental rabbinic concept, see Cohen's work *The Three Crowns* (Cambridge: Cambridge University Press, 1990). Cohen argues that rabbinic Judaism endorsed a system of multiple authorities: monarchy, priesthood, and prophecy. These three "crowns" constantly negotiated with each other and entered into shifting allegiances. While the actual classes themselves disappear in the course of Jewish history, the principle of dispersal of power through multiple centers of authority remains a constant of Jewish political organization. This principle is expressed *mutatis mutandis* in our midrash.

9. Rashi bases himself on *Genesis Rabba* 6:4, which expresses with perhaps even greater force the rabbinic elaboration of the political nuance of the biblical text: *And the stars* (Gen. 1:16). R. Aha said: Imagine a king who had two governors, one ruling in the city and the other in a province. Said the king: "Since the former has humbled [lit. diminished] himself to rule in the city only, I decree that whenever he goes out, the city council and the people shall go out with him, and whenever he enters, the city council and the people shall enter with him. Thus did the Holy One, blessed be He, say: "Since the moon humbled itself to rule by night, I decree that when she comes forth the stars shall come forth with her and when she goes in, the stars shall go in with her." *Midrash Rabba: Genesis*, Vol. 1, H. Freedman, trans. (London: Soncino Press, 1983), 43. Both the political vocabulary of the midrashim and God's solicitude for the feelings and the authority of the moon after its diminution argue in favor of the present interpretation. See also *Genesis Rabba* 6:3, where the political implications of the lunar/solar inequality are given a messianic thrust.

10. For the concept of nationhood as a socially constructed reality of variable moral and political significance, see Hans Kohn, *The Idea of Nationalism* (New York: Macmillan, 1961), 7-20.

11. This and other biblical quotations, unless otherwise specified, are taken from the New Jewish Publication Society version. *Tanakh: The Holy Scriptures* (Philadelphia: Jewish Publication Society, 1985).

12. Nahum Sarna, *Genesis: The JPS Torah Commentary* (Philadelphia: Jewish Publication Society, 1989), 73.

13. Umberto Cassuto, *From Noah to Abraham* (Hebrew) (Jerusalem: Magnes Press of Hebrew University, 1953), 136-37.

14. On the attribution of hunting skills to political figures, see Cassuto, *From Noah to Abraham*, 136-37. Weber's views on charisma as a legitimating factor for political authority are found in H. H. Gerth and C. Wright Mills, eds., *From Max Weber: Essays in Sociology* (New York: Oxford University Press, 1978), 79. For an example of the role of charisma in a political founding that resembles the Nimrod pericope, see Machiavelli, *Discourses*, Bk. I, 2:5.

15. I am indebted to Prof. Daniel Elazar, who shared this insight with me in conversation.

16. H. Freedman and M. Simon, trans. and eds. *Midrash Rabbah: Genesis* (New York: Soncino Press, 1983), 296-97. For similar references in rabbinic literature to Nimrod as the archrebel who turns men against God, see *B. Pesachim* 94b and Rashi ad loc. and *Targum Pseudo-Jonathan* on Genesis 10:8.

17. *Pirke de'Rabbi Eliezer*, ch. 24, cited in H. N. Bialik and Y. Rivnitsky, *Sefer Aggadah* (Hebrew) (Tel Aviv: Dvir Publishing House, 1973), 22. Nimrod's divine coat was eventually stolen by Esau, who murdered him to get it. (*Targum Pseudo-Jonathan* Gen. 25:27) The Targum implies that Esau, a cipher in rabbinic literature for Rome, is as illegitimate at bottom as is Nimrod and his kingdom.

18. William G. Braude and Israel J. Kapstein, trans., *Tanna Debe Eliyyahu* (Philadelphia: Jewish Publication Society, 1981), 524-25 see another version at the section "Eliyyahu Rabba" ch. 6, Braude and Kapstein, 102-3. A slightly different version of the Abraham-Nimrod encounter is found in a medieval midrash collection *Yalkut Shimoni*. Zvi Hersch Sperling and Dov Berish Luria, eds. *Yalkut Shimoni* (Zolkiew: Lorje and Matses, 1858), vol. 1, 26:11. Many of the midrashim on Nimrod may be found in Louis Ginzberg, *The Legends of the Jews*, vol. 1 (Philadelphia: Jewish Publication Society, 1942), 177-81; 185-203.

19. Jon Levenson argues that popular consent both in the acceptance of Torah and in the appointment of kings was balanced by a factor of ineluctability. Israel could do no other than choose God or kings Saul and David. Human autonomy and heteronomy are both real elements of the Bible's covenant theology and must be dialectically related in Levenson's view. Thus Levenson's observation is in accord with that of Pitkin, Eisel and others who point to the co-existence of consent with other theories of obligation in ancient and medieval sources. This accords with the general weakening of ideal-typical covenantal tendencies that we observed in the last chapter. Nonetheless, even when consent is qualified, it is still presented as an essential element. Jon Levenson, "Covenant and Consent: Biblical Reflections on the Occasion of the 200th Anniversary of the U.S. Constitution," *The Judeo-Christian Tradition and the U.S. Constitution*

(Philadelphia: Annenberg Research Institute, 1989). The famous story of God threatening to drop Sinai on the Israelites in *B. Shabbat* 88a illustrates precisely this: they are obligated to consent to the Torah due to God's will, yet their consent—at least subsequently in the days of Mordechai and Esther—is crucial.

20. Abraham Ibn Ezra, *Commentary to Genesis* (Hebrew), *Mikraot Gedolot*, Warsaw ed. 1766 (Tel Aviv: Pardes, 1957)

21. Nachmanides' commentary to Genesis 10 may be found in *Mikraot Gedolot*, ad loc.

22. R. Isaac Abravanel, *Commentary on the Torah* (Hebrew), Warsaw ed. (Jerusalem: Torah v'Daat, n.d.), ad loc.

23. Herbert Finkelscherer, "Quellen und Motive der Staats- und Gesellschaftsauffassung des Don Isaak Abravanel," *Monatsschrift für Geschichte und Wissenschaft des Judentums*, Vol. 81: (1937), 498. Finkelscherer's view is that Abravanel was influenced by the Church Fathers and classical sources, particularly Seneca, in his highly negative judgment on the inherent sinfulness of the polity. Finkelscherer, unlike Leo Strauss who largely shares this view, finds some Jewish influences as well. See Leo Strauss, "On Abravanel's Philosophical Tendency and Political Teaching," in J. B. Trend and A. Loewe, eds., *Isaac Abravanel* (Cambridge: Cambridge University Press, 1937). I think that it is at least arguable that Abravanel, a Maimonidean, construed political institutions after the fashion of Maimonides' construal of sacrifices (*Guide* III:32), namely, as a historically contingent concession to the cultural level of the nation.

24. Abravanel, *Commentary on the Torah*.

25. Meir Loeb Malbim, *Ha-Torah ve Ha-Mitzvah* (Hebrew) (n.p., n.d.) on Genesis 10:8. See Martin Sicker, *The Judaic State* (New York: Praeger, 1988), 17-26.

Chapter Five

Persons and Rights

Rights have taken center stage in the moral and political drama of modernity. Rights are formalized articulations of the legitimate claims, compelling needs, and inviolable liberties of persons. Rights are held to pertain to persons as such and to be valid in the various social contexts of the human life-world. The most fundamental rights ("human rights") are thought to be valid regardless of the social status or situation of the persons who bear them. Economic, political, and other social factors are irrelevant to a person's possession of basic rights. With this achievement, the modern human-rights-respecting state is thought to have made a great advance over premodern regimes wherein rights were often construed as privileges that persons were granted depending upon their utility to the regime or their standing in society.

What is the ground of such rights? One senses in the claim of universal human rights the Bible's insistence on the universal dignity of the human. The Bible's claim that all human life, regardless of economic, political, and other social factors, has dignity is based on its theological affirmation that all humans are created in God's image (Gen. 1:27). Although this might be the pedigree of the modern claim, it no longer serves as its warrant for modern secular moral or political theory. Indeed, for some, it is more an embarrassment than a warrant. How did modern theory get to this point? What sense do Jews who continue to make biblical affirmations about the nature of personhood make of rights?

107

To speak of rights as being grounded in nothing more (or less) than personhood per se is to invoke a certain notion of personhood—the person as an "unsituated self."[1] Such a self stands before the associations and attachments of which it becomes a part. It is not encumbered, allegedly, by constituting associations other than those it has, at least ideally, freely chosen. This is the self of social contract theory. It is autonomous, a law unto itself. Or rather, this self discovers lawfulness on its own, through interrogation of itself. One place to start an exploration of the rights-bearing person of modernity is with the concept of autonomy.

The Context of Rights: Autonomous Persons

Autonomy means to live under one's own law, to discover the norms of a lawful life, a *nomos*, by or within oneself. Autonomy is not, in principle, anarchic or anomic. Autonomy and authority are, as etymology suggests, paired concepts. Autonomy means that the self becomes its own authority, that authority per se is conditional upon the consent of the self. Autonomy takes self-directedness as its governing principle.

How does self-directedness come to have credibility as a moral concept? In a sense, its origins may be said to lie in the logic of responsibility, in the conditions under which we can attribute blame or praise to an agent. To be fully responsible, an agent must have freely chosen his or her course of action. The idea that we are responsible only if we can be said to have chosen or consented willingly to a course of action is certainly an old one. The German-Jewish philosopher Hermann Cohen attributes its discovery to the prophet Ezekiel. Against the exiles' belief that "the fathers have eaten sour grapes and the children's teeth are set on edge," Ezekiel asserted that every man suffers for his own sin.[2] Ezekiel appears to have displaced the older biblical notion that God will punish the children for the sins of their fathers for several subsequent generations (Exod. 20:5). Blame and punishment are neither collective nor hereditary. They are merited by individuals on a basis of personal desert. If Cohen is correct, the concept of autonomy, in the sense of having to take reponsibility for one's own situation—of having, on one's own, to recognize what is right and to act accordingly—is not new.

What is new is the idea that the discovery of what is right is an idiosyncratic self-discovery. The self, as the field and the agent of moral discovery, acquires a whole new weight. The process of the self ratifying what it has discovered, that is, of consent, takes on a new prominence. In the Bible, every man doing "right in his own eyes" was a sign of grave political and moral disorder. Now it becomes an ideal. The sovereign self, through rational introspection, discovers what is right for itself. Autonomy as an ideal renders the relation of the autonomous self to other selves, to community, to nature, and to divinity enormously problematic. The ethics and the anthropology of the autonomous self represent a departure from prior traditions of Western thought and religion.

The theme of autonomy has been of defining significance for modernity. Indeed, the major intellectual architects of the modern project have put the individual at the crux of their thought. Modern philosophy begins with the individual. For Descartes, often held to be the first modern philosopher, reality per se is discovered in self-reflection. Being depends upon the solitary, thinking ego for its self-disclosure. The self, which was at best a microcosm of a vast, created (or, for Aristotle, eternal) macrocosm, now becomes the only open window onto the world of being. We cannot know, hence we cannot trust in, anything that is beyond what we can think. The self has now become the arbiter of all that is.

If premodern men and women feared such radical independence, such excision from the context of an environing universe, moderns exult in it. Despite all of the modern talk of loneliness and alienation, the modern soul shrinks from attachments that are not of its own choosing. The modern soul, as Edward Shils put it, has a dread of metaphysical encumbrances. This dread is systematically expressed in the modern traditions of ethical and social thought. The newly definitive individual, stripped of constitutive attachments to primal groups and faiths, is an arbiter not only of what is but of what ought to be.

Although autonomy is not antithetical to authority per se, it is antithetical to traditional, heteronomous authority. Autonomy regards claims to authority that cannot be validated by or, in principle, discovered within the self to be suspect claims. Traditional authority is based on claims to a superior wisdom, to divine revelation, or to the accumulated and refined legacy of the ancestors. The modern ideal rejects this as so much paternalism. No prophet, philosopher-king, or historical collectivity knows better than the individual what the individual's good is. No human arrangement that affects our lives and destinies ought to exist that does not arise from or merit the consent of the individual so affected. Furthermore, this consent is a private matter. No one can tell us to what we ought to consent. No society should prescribe our good for us. Only we, who know ourselves best, as John Stuart Mill argued, can decide what is our special good. There are as many goods as there are persons. Autonomy implies that we are epistemic and ethical worlds unto ourselves.

Traditional authority is enfeebled by modernity because it became increasingly difficult to speak persuasively about the good as such: the good of man qua man, the common good in which all humans share. Tradition spoke about human being in broad, species-wide categories. "It is not good," for example, "for man to be alone" (Gen. 2:18). But what if some humans prefer solitude to sociality? Who is to say? The good became atomized into a near infinity of particularities as the postulate of a common human nature lost ground. More precisely: the postulate of a higher human nature lost ground. The old version of a common human nature, which both Jews and Christians developed from Greek thought during the Middle Ages, became incredible with the rise of modern science. In that version, man is a thinking being whose telos is found in the perfection of intellect. Both the process and the achievement of perfecting the intellect constitute a *communio* and an *imitatio dei*. The teleological universe of Aristotle, in which this conception was at home, was replaced by the mechanical universe of Newton. Nature was a gigantic machine, not a purposive process leading toward divinity. The heavens no longer speak the glory of God. They speak the language of mechanics. Without a divinely directed, providentially purposive nature, human nature lost its human purpose. Man came to be defined increasingly by what had earlier been held to be his lower nature. As modernity progressed, it was the only nature that science could know.

The "scientization" of nature, that is, the triumph of the quantitative methods of the new physics and of the technological goal of mastery, as well as the loss of a biblical anthropology, of man as a being with a higher nature, not only atomized the concept of the good into an infinity of particularities, it also shifted the concept of the right, of *justice*, into a different framework. Justice could no longer be a matter of the conformity of human institutions and practices with an inherent natural standard; of *nomos* with *physis* where *physis* was understood to strive toward the divine. Nature, in the earlier thought, implied an immanent natural lawfulness or natural right, which linked the human things with the natural and the divine. Justice, as Plato taught in the *Republic* (369-371e; 456c), was a life lived according to nature. The city must be designed according to nature. In a more theistic key, nature was the field in which divine providence engaged in shaping human destiny. While Greek and Jewish concepts of nature are not equivalent, they share a common horizon vis-a-vis the modern one. In modernity, by contrast, talk about justice need not appeal to a transcendent norm. Justice is conventional. What is just can be a matter of that to which the individual is willing to consent.

Raising consent to the chief or, at least, to a chief criterion of justice shifts the framework within which we understand justice from ontology to history. Justice does not seek ontological legitimation. Appeals to the way of things or the will of God do not matter. Even worse, they signal antimodern reaction. What matters is the history of the society, the ensemble of conventions, in which institutions of justice are found. Suttee would be intolerable to Jews and Christians, but it is more than just, one might argue, for Hindus. Against this relativism and conventionalism, the premodern theorists of natural right insisted that political things be linked to natural things. The modern theorists loosened then severed this linkage. The Jewish thinkers whom we shall consider in one way or other seek to restore the linkage. They insist on setting the rights of persons into a universal and theistic context.[3]

In order to avoid the unhappy implications of culture-dependent relativism, the Enlightenment founders of the modern project posited a universal and primitive attribute of man qua man that could replace enfeebled natural right: human rights. Human rights are held to be culturally invariant human possessions that guarantee basic claims to life, freedom, and dignity for all. It seems clear that, historically, this discourse derives from the prior traditions of biblical anthropology. It is an open question whether, if this historical link between rights and biblical monotheism is lost, rights discourse will collapse as well. There is reason, in this postmodern age, to suspect this. In much of what was the communist world, rights discourse was or is thought to be a parochial, Western, Judeo-Christian language game. Unless a truly universal case for rights could be made, they might appear to be just another guise of cultural imperialism. It is as if there were a law of the conservation of skepticism: that which was designed to replace biblical faith becomes as vulnerable to rational assault as biblical faith. Human rights are no less jeopardized by the intellectual climate of the world that first gave them systematic articulation than they are by governments that abuse and destroy their citizens. The modern writers want universality without foundation. The traditional Jewish writers, to the extent that they retain sympathy for rights at all, want to overcome this foundationless universality and insist on rooting rights once again in the context of God's creation.

A Modern Concept of Rights

To further explore the status of rights in modern or perhaps postmodern times, let us consider the work of one prominent rights theorist, Abraham I. Melden. It is Melden's view that human persons, *solely* by virtue of their status as persons, possess some fundamental attributes that order moral, legal, and political conduct with respect to them. Melden traces the modern turn in the philosophical constitution of the concept of rights to Locke. In his view, Locke takes the revolutionary step of rejecting the attribution of rights to persons on the basis of either natural law or

> divine ordinances comparable to the statutes of civil society . . . . We need no such principles; we need nothing more than the concept of persons, whose features as the moral agents they are suffice for the possession by them of fundamental moral rights, features which enable them to join their lives with one another as they go about their affairs.[4]

While I am doubtful that Locke sustains this reading (see, e.g., *Second Treatise*, chap. 2, para. 6), the fact that a contemporary interpreter such as Melden reads Locke in this way expresses what is typically modern in Melden's conception of rights.[5]

Human beings have rights because they are persons, not because they have duties or are subject to a law or have a role in some cosmic drama. Melden shakes the concept of personhood loose from any scheme of natural or divine law, transcendent principle, citizenship in a terrestrial or celestial state, or biological or cosmic teleology in which it could be (and once was) located. Persons per se, stripped of culture, community, history, and destiny, are held, by virtue of the "mere" fact that they are persons, to be bearers of rights. These atomistic, unsituated selves make moral claims that are justified not by pointing to any schemata beyond the sheer facticity of their personhood, but by their personhood alone. We might arrive at the same assertion by affirming that man is made in the image of God. That too would ground a universal claim of rights and personhood. Yet Melden would disallow such an appeal on principle. That is precisely the sort of nonempirical move he claims Locke freed us from. Personhood is a primitive and need not be grounded on some foundation, such as "the image of God" of the biblical account.

What is it then to be a person, a rights-bearing being, on Melden's account? A person is one who has the status of a moral agent, who can

> choose, decide and act for himself as he pursues his interests—in food, clothing, shelter, in work and in play, or in any of the indefinitely many other activities in which he engages—interests that give point and purpose to his very many different sorts of endeavors.[6]

Personhood is constituted by performances. One looks at the relevant sorts of things human beings in society do. "Person," as Locke said, is a forensic term or, more broadly, an empirical, social term. Persons, on Melden's account, are not Skinnerian entities. They have dignity. Dignity, however, does not refer to

> some esoteric goodness that is intrinsic to human beings and that has its roots in some transcendent realm of which they are members. Nor is it the ability that we have, by deciding how to live our own lives, to achieve that good which as the scholastics put it, is the fullness of our own being . . . . *Dignity*, as Locke once remarked about *person*, is a forensic term, one that applies to persons in the forum in which they conduct their affairs with each other. The moral dignity of persons is the dignity they have insofar as they show themselves capable of being full and unabridged participants in the life of a moral community, comporting themselves with others in the expectation that they will be dealt with on terms of moral equality, and prepared in a way that anyone can see to hold others to account for the infringement of their rights.[7]

The most noticeable feature of Melden's account is its thorough empiricism. He grounds possession of rights on the status of being a person and constitutes that status out of the observable data of moral interaction. He rejects on principle any transcendental turn. He also rejects a scientistic turn in that his discourse derives from the *Lebenswelt*, the life-world of human experience.

It is in the lived world of moral interaction that the categories of personhood and rights are validly constituted. Metaphysically, however, Melden's account is postfoundational. Exactly how he would sustain the irrefragability of the status of personhood against the vagaries of empirical societies is unclear. For while he is precise about how rights exist over and against their empirical violation, he refuses to anchor the construction of personhood (on which rights depend) in any culturally-invariant, let alone transempirical ground. How can he truly overcome a culture in which whole classes of persons are made non-persons, life unworthy of life (*lebenunwertes Leben*)? Locke, with his appeal to God's sovereignty over his creatures and to the natural law of reason, shows greater continuity with premodern approaches than Melden gives him credit for. Yet Melden rejects this approach. Melden, and modern rights-talk generally, insists on the primitive, precontextual character of rights. As soon as we can speak of persons, we can speak of rights. These primitive terms are held to be logically prior to any social context in which they may empirically be located.[8]

Yet that is not really true. Melden's conception of rights and persons uncritically presupposes modern liberal political culture. Like other rights theorists, he can describe how rights language functions, and prescribes how it should function, in a culture where it already functions rather well. The values of autonomy and rationality, the explicit exclusion of transcendent or divine warrants, underlie his entire account. But his theory is not rich enough to ground its wished-for universalism. It is culture-bound. The discourse of human rights, for all of its purported universality, really descends from the idea of civil rights, of the rights acquired when man leaves the state of nature and enters civil society. This idea began to supplant the earlier natural right teaching in the seventeenth century. The Jewish thinkers speak, in a sense, for a pre-Hobbesian understanding. They direct their criticisms at the unsituated, autonomous individual, the empirical constitution of the moral sphere, the isolation of rights from duties, and the bracketing out of a transcendent frame of reference.

Three Traditional Jewish Critiques

Sol Roth's *Halakhah and Politics: The Jewish Idea of a State* attempts a critical conversation between classical Jewish political values and concepts and those regnant, on his view, in contemporary America. The formulations on both sides of the dichotomy are ideal-typical and somewhat caricatured. Nonetheless, the work displays some of the genuine conflicts between these political traditions.

Roth is highly critical of the concept of rights and of the weight it has acquired in modern social and political life. In Judaism, there is a "denigration of rights in the characterization of its conception of freedom [as] a direct consequence of its supreme concern with *duties* or *obligations*."[9] Roth insists (implicitly, contra Melden) that the sine qua non of personhood is the possession of duties. Obligation, not rights, is the primary constituent of personhood.

Roth wants to argue that Judaism is a rigorously deontological system that subordinates the freedom, independence, indeed the individuality of persons to a collective, normative ideal. Thus rights talk, which effectuates individual freedom through autonomy, indicates an inattention to the axiological primacy of duty. Why should duty have primacy? For, in an unproblematic sense, rights and duties are correlative or coeval. They logically imply one another, so neither one should, strictly speaking, have priority. Roth analyzes this phenomenon and tries to show why rights, nonetheless, are subsidiary to duties.

Rights and duties are coeval in the negative sense that one has a duty to do x, if and only if one has no right to refrain from doing x. So too one has a right to do x, if and only if one does not have a duty to refrain from doing x.[10] Rights and duties are positively correlated in the sense that if someone has obligated himself to someone else, the latter person has rights vis-à-vis the former. If Reuven has promised Shimon that he will do something, Shimon has a right to expect this of Reuven. In these two senses, rights and duty are "naturally" correlated. (Rights, we might also add, appear as "natural" features of any moral landscape where persons have obligations.)

Roth argues that although these terms are logically correlated, there is, in fact, a substantive difference in moral life depending on which term is stressed by a culture.

> Notwithstanding the correlative character of rights and obligations, there is a considerable difference between deducing obligations from rights and inferring rights from obligations. One major difference is the way in which the notion of freedom is defined in these contrasting perspectives. Those to whom human rights are paramount, and who recognize obligations as legitimate only if they flow from rights, will insist that human freedom is to be construed in terms of the right to do whatever one wishes so long as one does not interfere with others in the pursuit of their inclinations. Indeed, this is the American point of view. If, however, obligations are assigned priority, as is the case in Judaism, acting on inclination receives limited sanction. Freedom, in the Jewish perspective, though it is valued and celebrated, is defined, not in terms of the right to do what we want, but in terms of the power to do what we should, that is, in terms of the capacity to fulfill our obligations.[11]

Roth is arguing that when rights are given priority, the individual is presented as radically independent of his or her potential deontological entanglements and predisposed to be critical toward them. From a rights-oriented perspective, freedom is negative. It is freedom from those interferences and associations that delimit autonomy. From a duty-oriented perspective, freedom is positive. It is freedom to fulfill those obligations that constitute the core of personhood. For the Jew, of course, those obligations—the *mitzvot*— constitute both personhood and community. Performing the *mitzvot* is a communal project. Thus, for the Jew, being tightly bound to others in the "community of commitment" takes precedence over atomistic versions of personhood.

> A perspective in which rights are assigned priority is one which fosters self-directedness, a paramount concern with oneself. In such an emphasis, importance is assigned, not to *relations* that attach person to person, but to the person himself, that is, the individual. It is true that, even in such an ambience, people respond to obligations; but they do so because they recognize that the assumption of obligations will serve to secure their rights, and this is their essential thrust. Those, however, for whom obligations are prior are other-directed. They perceive themselves primarily as the bearers of obligations, and even their rights are understood to be functions of the obligations of others to them.[12]

Thus far, Roth's critique is based on the charge that an emphasis on rights engenders self-orientation rather than a social orientation. (Why one is better than the other, Roth does not say.) A further and devastating consequence, in his view, of an emphasis on rights is that the theorist is not able to argue why an individual should not have unlimited rights over his or her own body.

> [I]n a rights-oriented, self-centered society, a human being has no obligations with respect to himself that are not subservient to his interests as he understands them, and that when he perceives an action, on balance, as in his interests, there is no reason for him to refrain from undertaking it: that is, his rights with respect to his own person are unlimited.[13]

From the point of view of rights, Roth sees no counter-argument to suicide, for example. He believes that justice, where rights prevail, is strictly conventional. What is just is whatever an individual is willing to consent to. If obligations are primary, however, then rights are construed within a normative framework that has already ruled out certain choices.

The force of this critique is to deny normative status to the idea of a right altogether. Rights are, as Roth says, "interests on which legitimacy has been conferred," yet the very concept of an interest indicates something empirical or psychological, while the notion of conferral suggests something arbitrary. Ultimately for Roth, it is impossible for modern philosophy to establish primary, valid rights, say, in the sense of human rights. Attempts to derive such rights from nature or human nature run aground on the fact/value distinction. Attempts to derive them from the empirical observation of moral practices as

Melden or H. L. A. Hart have done turn putative human rights into "sociological fact rather than . . . ethical norm."[14] Roth's reply to the perceived failure of rights-oriented philosophy to accomplish its own objectives is to speak about universal, divinely ordained obligations (the so-called Noachide laws or *sheva mitzvot b'nei Noach*) from which universal human rights might be derived. It is because God requires of us, for example, that we do not steal (universal obligation) that we may be said to have a right to private property.[15] Without divinely revealed duties, rights lack all foundation.

Roth's critique has emphasized the dangers of egoism and the threat of relativism implicit in modern rights discourse. As for egoism, things are not so simple. It is worth pointing out that Mill, whom Roth presumably has in mind, argued that individuals ought to be maximally free to pursue their own interests in part *because* of the probable benefit of that freedom, in the aggregate, to society. The very notion of the "greatest good for the greatest number" is social to its core. Indeed, the classic anti-utilitarian argument (How would the utilitarian disallow the sacrifice of an innocent man if it were to promote the greatest good?) is an argument over social good. So too, Melden's work locates rights at the place where persons join their lives together in mutual endeavor, not merely in the egoistic pursuit of private objectives.

Thus, Roth's depiction of American society as a libertarian free-for-all of rights-claiming egoists is a bit of a caricature. Nonetheless, it captures a fundamental problem. In his own idiom, he points toward what Michael Sandel has called the "procedural republic."[16] A society in which the concept of a right trumps all other moral concepts is one in which politics tries to stay neutral with respect to competing concepts of the good. Politics and law come to be about enforcing the rules of the game, the procedures, rather than promoting substantive ideas of a good and common way of life. In part, the procedural republic rises from the same root as autonomy and the scientization of nature described earlier in the chapter. Given an indefinite pluralism in conceptions of the good, that is, of the good life, politics can no longer be about the good. The good has become unwieldy. The focus of politics shifts to matters of right. An indefinitely plural good cannot be prescribed; it cannot be generic to the human species as such. The older philosophical politics erred in seeking to bring citizens to virtue. Politics ought to be about protecting spheres of private life where the indefinitely many visions of the good can be enacted. These spheres are demarcated by the concept of rights and safeguarded by the "procedural republic."

Although he does not use this language, this is the point of Roth's critique. Even though he speaks of "duty" rather than the "good," he is really talking about a society constituted by a very thick, shared concept of moral excellence grounded in *imitatio dei*. Roth is speaking out of a Jewish tradition that has strong republican elements at its core. The Torah, no less than the republican tradition, aims to bring about a good society based on the active participation of a citizenry committed to training in moral virtues that promote civility. The republican tradition is leery of rights insofar as they demarcate individual space and individual claims. In the congressional debate over the Bill of Rights, for example, those who thought the Bill unnecessary thought that it was unworthy of free persons in a republic. Rights define one's sphere of action against a state, where the state is assumed to be prone to violate one's life and liberty. In a republic, however, the people in principle own the state. Their freedom is not freedom from the state, but freedom to rule themselves. Their guarantee of dignity and equality is not a set of parchment barricades, but rather their active participation in the life of the political community.[17] It would be a mistake to identify Jewish political thought with the republican tradition in all of its particulars. Nonetheless, the emphasis on realizing the fullest extent of one's humanity through participation in a (in the Jewish case, covenant) community, on liberty as freedom to rather than freedom from, and on citizens having a thick web of obligations toward one another is unmistakable. Roth's critique of rights adumbrates these concerns, but has not quite found a compelling language in which to articulate them.

Another argument against according primacy to rights is found in the thought of the German-Jewish thinker Isaac Breuer (1883-1946). An Orthodox scholar and political leader trained in neo-Kantian philosophy and law, Breuer developed a comprehensive philosophy of Judaism and a critique of modern epistemological, legal, moral, and political values.[18] While Breuer, like Roth, deprecates the concept of rights due to its presuppositions of individuality and autonomy, he does not dismiss human interests as brusquely as Roth does. Breuer believes that humans qua humans have at least one legitimate interest protected by right: the right to freedom.

Breuer does not restrict the normative dimension of social life to that sphere of obligations derivative of the Noachide commandments and the Sinaitic revelation. Outside of the Torah, there is a sort of social salvation. Building on the work of the neo-Kantian legal philosopher Rudolph Stammler, Breuer argues that sociality is intrinsically normative. That is, the very decision to found a society, be it a family or a polity, is a value-laden decision. To live together is to make a moral commitment. Any social judgment—from the judgment to establish community to judgments about how to live in community—is answerable to the categorical imperative. Unlike animal societies where social life flows from causal necessity, human societies are grounded on the intention to realize human freedom. That is, human societies are not products of causes but of goals: they express an inherent moral teleology and may be judged over/against their performance with respect to the realization of their inherent ideal (i.e., they may be judged according to the categorical imperative).[19]

Stammler believed that law—the rules which order social life—aims by nature toward a telos, which he termed "right law" (*richtige Recht*). Breuer adopts this perspective and believes that all human societies, when viewed from the vantage point of their legal systems, aim at realizing core values such as freedom. To be fully human is to realize freedom. One has a fundamental right to fulfill one's humanity in this sense. Given such a value-laden perspective, Breuer would not assert, as Roth does, that "natural" human interests are merely empirical unless coordinated with supervening, divinely revealed obligations.

On the other hand, Breuer does not believe that persons—on the basis of their "mere" personhood—possess a catalogue of basic human rights that they might assert against the claims made upon them by God in the form of the Noachide laws and the Torah. Following Stammler (who follows Kant), Breuer is convinced that the basic problem of human life, both in its individuated and in its social dimensions, is freedom. How are persons and societies to be truly free? Breuer believes that a rights-oriented perspective, although aiming at freedom, necessarily fails to provide its adherents with freedom. Only submission to Torah, which subordinates rights to the acceptance of divinely imposed duties, secures that freedom for which our created nature longs. Why?

Throughout his corpus, Breuer develops epistemological, metaphysical, and jurisprudential approaches to this basic question. Here I will discuss only his jurisprudential approach. In 1911, Breuer published a weighty legal essay, "The Legal Philosophical Grounds of Jewish and Modern Law (*Die Rechtsphilosophischen Grundlagen des jüdischen und des modernen Rechts*)" in response to a contemporary controversy.[20] A Russian Jewish woman, living in Germany, sought a divorce from her husband. The husband refused to give the wife a Jewish divorce, and the wife brought her case to a civil court. The German judge ruled that the husband's defense—that under halakha he did not have to grant his wife a divorce—was worthless. German law supersedes Jewish law because Jewish law, since it denies the wife a right to petition for divorce, enshrines immoral inequalities and is therefore inferior to German law. German law (Breuer takes this to be typical of all modern law) does not recognize sex-based inequality in matters of basic rights. Jewish law offends the good morals of German law. It is a kind of tribal law, which must give way before the superior morality of modern, rights-based jurisprudence. While the implications of this judgment greatly distressed the liberal German-Jewish bourgeoisie, it provided Breuer with an opportunity to attack modern law and its fundamental values head-on.

Breuer argues that modern law seeks to achieve the social ideal of maximal freedom for each, compatible with maximal freedom for all. On the surface, it appears that attributing equal rights to all serves this ideal. Indeed, the Jewish system of enshrining prima facie inequalities seems to fly in the face of this ideal. Yet Breuer argues that the discovery of such fundamental equality had already occurred within the experience of ancient Israel. Israel's truth that man and woman are made in the image of God first made known the radical equality the German judge claims to protect. Why then does Israel's law seem to ignore its own egalitarian presupposition?

Breuer argues, in an apologetic manner, that while modern law *aims* at protecting equal rights for the sake of freedom, Jewish law *presupposes* equal rights and then moves on to dispense unequal duties for the sake not of freedom but of holiness. The "social ideal" of Jewish law is holiness (gained through obedience to *mitzvot*). The modern faith that rights secure freedom is presupposed by Judaism, but not determinative for it.

Of course, this answer simply begs the question. If Breuer is genuinely concerned about freedom and believes that humans have a fundamental right to it, then how can that right not be protected by laws that bear on one's freedom of action? Breuer's general approach is first to offer a rather apologetic answer and then, sensing the inadequacy of his answer, to offer a more subtle (although no less dogmatic) line of argumentation. He proceeds as follows: In fact, modern law is condemned to fail in its attempt to secure freedom through its postulation of equal rights. What is freedom? Freedom refers to the will's determination of itself according to the categorical imperative. The free will is the will that achieves the status of a universal legislator (of general validity or *Allgemeingültigkeit* in Kantian terms) when it composes its maxim, that is, the principle on which it will act.

Breuer argues that this is actually impossible in modern law. In modern law, law and ethics are fundamentally alienated from one another. Ethics, and consequently the possibility of freedom, has to do with the internal state of the will and the private, albeit universalizable, action. Law has to do with general classes of actions, with balancing interests to maintain the highest degree of social freedom. There is a phenomenological gulf between ethics and law. Ethics applies to law at the boundaries. That is, ethics becomes a kind of criterion, inter alia, for legality, but ethics and law are not identical. Ethics functions as a check on law at the level of the judge's or legislator's conscience. Ethics is the conscience but not the essence of modern law. Additionally, the mere fact that modern law relies on the state's coercive power undercuts the law's claim to "good morals." How can a moral agent freely will law-abiding and law-affirming behavior when the quite heteronomous motive of avoiding sanctions constitutes a ubiquitous element of his will?

Breuer thus claims to have deflated the pretensions of modern law to possess a higher morality than does Jewish law. It remains to be seen, however, why Jewish law better integrates law and ethics such that freedom is a real possibility under Jewish law (and only under Jewish law). In the essay here under consideration, Breuer reverts to an apologetic argument for the unity of ethics and law in Judaism, based on the nature of the law as God's will. The argument moves into a metaphysical vein, as Breuer relates Jewish law to "creation law" (*Schöpfungsgesetz*). Jewish law mirrors the implicit logos/telos of creation. Thus action according to Jewish law expresses the innermost dynamic of creation, i.e., freedom.

Breuer does not invalidate the concept of rights. He seems to agree with Kant that freedom "is the only one and original right which belongs to each man by reason of his humanity."[21] Breuer's argument centers on the fatal inability of legal systems outside of Judaism, as he sees it, to secure the freedom to which that original right entitles human persons. One might argue that Breuer's critique of non-Jewish legal systems is a critique from the point of view of an ethics of pure conscience (*Gesinnungsethik*). That is, Breuer assumes that freedom is primarily an inner state of the will. The purity and goodness of the free will is a necessary though not a sufficient condition for genuine ethics. To construe ethics in this manner necessarily divorces the ethical from the legal. The difference between the two is simply categorical, though not necessarily invidious. Thus, Breuer's invidious distinction between Jewish and non-Jewish legal systems rests on a category mistake. He is judging the non-Jewish systems by an irrelevant criterion. Beyond this, he is treating Judaism's weakness, somewhat disingenuously, as its strength. Non-Jewish legal systems are embedded in functioning, sovereign polities. Because of their political embodiment, the legal systems suffer a divorce of ethics from law. Judaism, by contrast, enjoys the luxury of its apolitical condition. Its law need not be divorced from ethics insofar as no mundane sanctions enforce the law's provisions. This is hardly an honorable argument.

In another work, *The World as Creation and as Nature* (*Die Welt als Schöpfung und Natur*), Breuer tries another approach, which avoids this problem.[22] In this study, Breuer is concerned to contrast the historical career of the "Torah State" with that of its ideal-typical contender in history, the Power State (*Machtstaat*). Essentially following Hegel, Breuer sees secular history (as opposed to Jewish counter- or metahistory) as the history of states conceived as virtually divine entities. The state does not arise out of covenant or contract: it is not an expression of its individuals. Rather, the state is the highest integral expression of reality. It is its own Idea. On this view, individual rights are merely privileges given by the state.

In Breuer's view, Roman law created individual rights by drawing a legal distinction between the home and the state. The law allowed for a private space in order to allow the state uncontested domination of the public space. The personal, private freedom of the Roman citizen expresses a fundamentally false consciousness: what one does in one's private life provides an illusion of freedom. Individuality then is a product of the Roman *Machtstaat*. Far from serving as a check on state power, it is a willing accomplice in it. Breuer writes a history of individuality as a political concept. He traces Christian otherworldliness ("render unto Caesar what is Caesar's") and its contemporary secularized successor, bourgeois philistinism, from Roman antecedents. In this account, the political and legal language of rights expresses the fallenness of history. Secular history is a "slaughter bench," a history of exile *(Golusgeschichte)*. It is the history of states in estrangement from God and the divine law. Individuality and rights are pseudoethical inventions that indicate the unrestrained pretensions of the power state. Jewish history, on the other hand, indicates a different concept, indeed a different reality of statehood. The Torah constitution empowers neither state nor individual. It creates both ideal community and ideal personality through a harmonious dispensation of duties. Breuer does not believe that the Torah State exists in its fullness at the present time. (As a political leader, he worked against the Zionist movement to create a religious countermovement, the goal of which was to create a state governed by Jewish law.) Nonetheless, wherever Jews live in appropriately traditional communities the political authority of the ancient Torah constitution continues to govern them. The scepter of Judean political legitimacy has never departed from the Jews.

Breuer's position is somewhat paradoxical. On the one hand, he rejects autonomy in the Kantian sense of willing law for oneself. (Only obedience to Torah ultimately secures what the categorical imperative is meant to secure, namely, freedom.) On the other hand, he accepts the Kantian premise that freedom, understood as autonomy, is in fact the highest value. Breuer does not dispute that freedom is a matter of self-realization, of bringing the judgments one makes into accord with the categorical imperative. What he disputes in Kantianism is the claim that this can be done without the Torah. Submission to the "creation law," to the Torah, rather than pure, unalloyed autonomy, is the way to achieve the freedom that Kant intends autonomy to secure for the self. Breuer, like Kant, draws on a German tradition that situates freedom beyond politics. His concern is less for the republican value of self-rule as a way of realizing freedom, than for a metapolitics of self-control. Self-rule in this sense is a largely private and interpersonal matter. It is a matter of spiritual transcendence. Transcendence entails lifting oneself up out of the exilic isolation of individuality (Breuer frequently uses the medieval philosophical term *principium individuationis*) and bringing oneself into harmony with the creation law, the Torah-logos. He criticizes rights because they seem to strengthen the metaphysical dead end of individuation, of falsely understood autonomy. Furthermore, he continues to see rights as privileges granted by a state that, by definition, fails to achieve its presumptive moral ends. The truly moral state would be the *Torastaat*, the Torah State, where divinely assigned duties form the content of moral and political life and eclipse the distance between the two. These divinely assigned duties do not seem to confer rights on the duty-bound. The only significant right for Breuer is the right to freedom, but freedom has been construed along metapolitical lines.

For both Roth and Breuer, the concept of rights has been either partially or completely invalidated for metaphysical and moral reasons. Roth sees rights as part of a package of unbridled autonomy, leading to relativism and a loss of foundations. He believes that when rights are in the foreground, community suffers in favor of individuality. Breuer sees rights as partly legitimate, insofar as the right to freedom is a component of our humanness, but the moral-political mechanism for realizing this fundamental claim to freedom cannot be effectuated by modern law and politics, that is, by the modern conception of rights.

A third thinker, David Novak, embraces rights to a much fuller extent than either Roth or Breuer. Novak places rights in the center of Jewish political and moral thought, accepting the modern elevation of the concept of rights as justified. Like Roth and Breuer, however, he rejects features of the modern account of rights. Rights should not be thought of as primitives, as stand-alone features of autonomous, unsituated selves. Novak embeds the concept of rights into an order of creation and revelation: rights become meaningful as signs of a relationship between God and humanity, as well as the relationship of humans, created in the image of God, with each other. Rights take on their fullest meaning in the covenant community created at Sinai.

In *Covenantal Rights: A Study in Jewish Political Theory*, Novak seeks to ground or (as he often puts it in the language of phenomenology) to "constitute" rights on an unabashedly theological basis. Unlike Roth or Breuer, who see rights as a modern intrusion into Jewish moral and political discourse, Novak wants to show that the framework of rights (and correlative duties) is the best way of understanding Jewish political thought. Furthermore, Novak wants to enter the contemporary debate between liberal and communitarian political theorists over the respective spheres of individuality and society and to show how it can best be resolved through articulating the theological basis on which a valid doctrine of rights must stand. Analytically, he uses the concept of rights, and the duties always correlated with them, as a tool to describe an idealized Jewish polity. That is, he wants to show that the concept of rights is fully at home in the biblical/Jewish tradition.[23] To do this he has to deconstruct the modern concept of rights, with its emphasis on autonomous individuals, and reconstruct a biblical and Jewish one. Indeed, he argues that this biblical/Jewish understanding is the proper framework for a meaningful concept of rights. Secular rights talk must be overcome.

Novak argues that talk of individuals and societies must be translated into the less abstract, more experiential concepts of "persons" and "communities." Unlike individuals, who can be thought of in opposition to society, persons are inevitably members of communities, indeed, of several communities at once. Personhood is inconceivable without community. Since persons, for example, are partly constituted by their being language users, their knowledge of language was instilled through their membership in discursive communities such as the family. Person and community are mutually dependent. This better mirrors reality than the more abstract and contested relationship between individual and society. Translating "individual" into "person" allows the opposition between individual and society to be partially overcome. Society, for its part, should be understood as an abstraction constructed out of numerous primary, overlapping communities.

Use of "person" and "community" can help overcome the limitations of social contract theory. The social contract, which relies on the ideas of individual and society, fails to explain fully why alleged autonomous individuals should enter into mutual relationship with each other to form a society. It overlooks the human fact that relationship is based on trust and on communal practices that presuppose trust. Yet trust is not a feature of social contract theory's account of individuals. On that account, they give up a measure of their power (their natural right) for a measure of protection (out of which flow duties toward their new society). The discourse is about power and its correlate, fear, not about trust. But in reality, human persons grow into fuller and more extensive communal relations on the basis of trust learned in the most primal of communities, the family. Social contract theory overestimates the degree of autonomy that individuals have, while underestimating the necessity of the primal discursive communities in which persons are formed.

Rights and duties must similarly be led back to more experiential, primal, and natural terms. Rights should be thought of as the justified *claims* of persons on one another in community (or of God on persons, or of persons on God). Duties should be thought of as mandated responses to these claims.[24] Both rights and duties presuppose a third party, an authoritative community that can guarantee that the rights will be honored and the duties performed. But that third party, normally society, is never fully able to guarantee rights and insist on duties. In the larger context, the claims of persons and the responses of persons to those claims can only be guaranteed by God. Indeed, as Creator, God is the holder of rights: He makes a primordial claim on us to which we must respond. All rights are ultimately God's; all duties are ultimately owed to him. "The universe itself is the ultimate social context for the operation of rights and duties."[25] Novak stipulates that

> rights talk by Jews must not be confined to the rights of individual persons, who are only one component of the covenant. Rather rights must now be seen as being exercised by God and the community as well as individual persons . . . constituting all three of these claimants enables us to constitute a truly coherent way of ordering their conflicting claims.[26]

The ontological priority of God's existence over human existence, as well as the moral priority of God's claims on us over our claims on him, ensures that the transactions of claim and response, or right and duty, take priority over moral categories such as the Good, or Virtue. Novak sees the concept of the good as secondary.

In this way of looking at the normative world, "good" functions primarily as an adverb modifying verbs that describe transactions. It is a qualification, not a ground. Thus when a right has been properly made or responded to, one can say "you have done right," where "right" is a synonym for "good" or "well," which modifies action. Secondarily, "good" functions as an adjective modifying various things or institutions that function within these transactions for their sake. For example, one can say about a social institution like marriage, "it is a good thing." That is, it functions well by facilitating the natural claims of persons for family and the community for its own continuity.[27]

Using both ontological and phenomenological arguments, Novak develops his concept of rights in terms of their operation in both a natural law and a covenantal context. Under both natural law and the covenant (which are on a continuum with one another), the moral and political relations among God, individuals, and the community are ordered by claims and responses. There are seven normative frameworks in which these relations occur: between God and persons and between persons and God; between God and community; and between community and God; between persons; between community and persons; and between persons and community. The first term in the relation signifies the rights holder. The second term indicates the agent duty-bound to honor the right. Novak surveys the vast edifice of biblical and rabbinic law on moral issues relevant to each of these categories. As the chief contemporary proponent for a Jewish natural law theory, he argues for the "naturalness" of Jewish rights and duties, for the naturalness, that is, of the Jewish political vision. His aim is to provide an ontology for rights, to overcome the foundationlessness of the modern account.

As we have seen, Novak's basic argument against the inadequacy of the modern concept of rights as the attribute of autonomous individuals is that rights, so considered, cannot account for why persons enter into binding, sustained relationships. In social contract theory, individuals are conceived as independent centers of authority. They fear the state of nature in which they live and therefore give up some of their power, that is, a portion of their natural rights, in order to gain civil rights. They then have a duty to the communal authority that they have created. Their right precedes their duty. Novak argues that a relationship between persons culminating in a political community could neither be entered into nor sustained on this basis. Right does not precede duty. Claim and response arise together with personhood.

Persons enter into relationship with each other not merely because they hope to avoid mutual harm. Even if that were true, they would have to have enough trust in one another and in their political community to believe that promises will be kept and duties maintained. Trust, not fear, is the basis of relationship. Trust, however, is learned in community. It does not precede community. Trust is both learned and enacted among persons. Furthermore, we learn to trust because others respond to us as persons with valid claims. Our parents care for us because they respond to our valid claims for life, nurture, and love. In Novak's view, the moral logic of relationship is given with personhood as such. There can be no amoral *status naturalis*, as Hobbes claimed (*Leviathan*, Pt. 1, ch. 13). There is no distinction between a state of nature and a civil state with respect to justice. Justice is the total system of valid claims being met by proper responses.

From what Novak has argued thus far, we might have concluded that rights, in the sense of valid claims, are primitive attributes of autonomous individuals. But here Novak's theism intervenes. Human persons come with valid claims because God has so created them. God, as creator, makes claims on his creatures to which they must respond. The human creature's ability to respond endows him or her with dignity, with a fundamental claim requiring response from both God and all other humans. Humans have both duties *and rights* toward God (contra Breuer), as well as toward one another. Novak sees the logic of claim and response as defining all of the relationships, both divine and human, in which human beings are enmeshed. The divine-human, as well as human-human, context in which these claims and responses are enacted is the covenant. Hence, the idea of covenantal rights. Rights talk, so understood, becomes the key to unlock Judaism's theological, moral, and political wisdom.

Novak points to the various inadequacies of the liberal bias toward individual rights and the communitarian penchant for duties to community. Rights on the liberal account do stress the need to protect the dignity and inviolability of persons from majoritarian injustice. However, the stress on the individual does imperil the maintenance of strong civic communities. The communitarian emphasis on the duty to work for a common good does overcome the problem of a weak, atomized society, but it does not offer sufficient protection against the majoritarian tyranny rightly decried by liberals. Novak's own holistic vision of claims and responses working through the contexts of overlapping communities ultimately nested in a universe ruled by God has great conceptual sweep. But would it actually persuade a nonbeliever or a theorist committed to a strictly secular account of rights?

Essentially Novak wants to return to a pre-Hobbesian understanding of rights and nature. He rejects Hobbes's view that humans have a right, as it were, to do wrong in the state of nature. God also rules over the state of nature, hence no one there can escape the claims and responses that are instinct to human life. The flaw in Hobbes, which led him to the presupposition of natural amorality, was impiety. As Alexander Hamilton wrote of the "justly decried" Hobbes:

[He] disbelieved in the existence of an intelligent super-intending principle, who is the governor, and will be the final judge of the universe . . . . Good and wise men, in all ages, have embraced a very dissimilar theory. They have supposed that the deity, from the relation we stand in, to himself and to each other, has constituted an eternal and immutable law, which is, indispensably, obligatory upon all mankind, prior to any human institution whatsoever.[28]

Novak puts the same sort of argument to the modern theorists of rights, who, in their secular point of departure, resemble Hobbes. Of course, the modern theorists, such as Melden, reject many of Hobbes's premises and conclusions. They also posit that individual rights precede entrance into society. And yet, by rejecting a universal, divinely given moral order, they cannot resist relativism and conventionalism. They claim that rights are prior to government, but they presuppose the ruling conventions of a certain form of government, the liberal political order, in their accounts. They accept the torso of earlier natural rights without the legs to support it.

It is curious, however, that Hamilton's theistic view of rights, namely that the entrance into civil society and government does not create rights, that rights existing in the state of nature remain undiminished in the new dispensation, was used by him to argue *against* the incorporation of a Bill of Rights into the Constitution. As he puts it in *The Federalist*, no. 84:

It has been several times truly remarked that bill of rights are, in their origins, stipulations between kings and their subjects, abridgements of prerogative in favor of privilege, reservations of rights not surrendered to the prince. Such was Magna Charta, obtained by the barons, sword in hand, from King John. Such were the subsequent confirmations of that charter by subsequent princes. Such was the Petition of Right assented to by Charles the First in the beginning of his reign. Such, also, was the Declaration of Right presented by the Lords and Commons to the Prince of Orange in 1688, and afterwards thrown into the form of an act of Parliament called the Bill of Rights. It is evident, therefore, that, according to their primitive signification, they have no application to constitutions, professedly founded upon the power of the people and executed by their immediate representatives and servants.[29]

The logic behind rights was unworthy of a free people. The government is not to be thought of as a sovereign to whom the citizen must give up rights in exchange for protection. For Hamilton, the freedom and dignity of the people depends upon a well-designed Constitution, "on public opinion, and on the general spirit of the people and of the government," not a Bill of Rights. Institutional structure and balance, and civic, republican temper and prudence, are "the only solid basis for all our rights."[30] Of course, even the Federalists came around to accepting the idea of a Bill of Rights. Nonetheless, the insight that what rights are meant to designate and protect can best be effectuated and safeguarded by an effective frame of government and a culture of self-rule also carried the day.

The assertion of rights also entails a project of constructing a limited government by design. As a *political* rather than a strictly theological-ethical matter, rights and constitutionalism are linked on the modern account. Regrettably, however, Novak is almost completely silent about this central matter of political theory. Why the silence? It begins, I think, with too easily eliding "community" into "polity."[31] In order to enable Jewish law to speak to political matters, Novak needs to view the various communal contexts in which Jewish law has always operated as if they were or could be political contexts of relevant scale, including, at least as a logical possibility, the scale of the modern state. Yet it is precisely this assumption that must be argued for. A contemporary Jewish ethicist has raised the issue of whether the medieval texts that modern Jews apply to issues such as euthanasia really do bear on those issues. That is, he problematizes the hermeneutic moves that moderns must make to get texts that speak of woodchoppers to address the problems of respirators.[32] The same criticism can be raised here. How should the admittedly rich store of Jewish law apply to problems of contemporary political thought? The conceptual device needed to mediate between text tradition and political reality must be more than a moral theory. It must be a constitutional theory.

Political theory ought to involve questions of constitutionalism, of the design of regimes. How would power, for example, be structured and divided in a Jewish commonwealth? What would the relative balance between popular consent and rabbinic authority be? Without some sense of the constitutional status of Jewish law and its interpreters within the polity, determinations of law are premature. These questions are largely overlooked in Novak's account of rights. In fairness, however, constitutional law is one of the least developed areas of Jewish law. Nonetheless, it seems odd in a book of political theory that so little emphasis should be given to so crucial a political matter. While Novak can describe what a good community, on the Jewish account, is, he cannot specify how a good community is to be politically organized.

Another issue must be confronted, namely, the reduced or highly problematic role that all three Jewish thinkers assigned to liberty in the Jewish polity. The Jewish emphasis on positive freedom, on the liberty to fulfill the terms of the covenant, surely presents an incompatibility between Judaism's liberty and the liberty of the American political tradition. In the American political tradition, liberty is an orienting good. Americans were to be a free people under the Constitution. Their liberty was to be both positive, that is, the liberty to participate as a nation in a great project of self-rule, and negative, that is, to pursue their own life projects with little interference. Liberty is a good in this tradition to a degree and with an emphasis that is not the case in Judaism. Rights are one of the tokens and warrants of that liberty. Redefining and "correcting" rights, as Novak does, that is, deepening their status as the authorized and grounded claims of persons, communities, and God, blurs the vast distance between the American vision of a free society and the conditioned, covenantal freedom of Judaism. The Founders, as republican thinkers, should not be confused with modern liberals, yet for all that, the *optima respublica* of the Founders remains far from Judaism's vision of a well-ordered society.

The Jewish understandings of rights depart significantly from both the liberal and the communitarian, as well as the older republican, accounts. From the liberal point of view, the Jewish thinkers remove the critical edge from the concept of rights. Their fideistic vantage points bar them from accepting as valid a critique of Jewish law from the perspective of rights. They believe that the law of the Torah is, in some sense, perfectly just and that the sort of critique and reform that taking rights seriously has enabled Western civilization to accomplish is simply not required. From a communitarian or republican point of view, the Jewish thinkers certainly have a high regard for community and civic virtue, but they do not emphasize self-rule and its internal connection to liberty as much as a republican would like. The entire business of governance and constitutional architecture is problematic. It is hard to see how the Jewish thinkers could agree with republican principles of self-governance and liberty. The God of Israel not only guarantees rights and prescribes duties, but he does so in a more intense and invasive way than a modern finds compatible with liberty. Hamilton thought that a constitution that "has the regulation of every species of personal and private concerns" was invidious to liberty.[33] Is this not prima facie a good description of Torah? Between rights, on whatever account, and Torah lies an uneasiness that cannot soon be dispelled.

Up until now, we have focused on the critical tensions between modern themes of consent and rights, and Jewish teachings. In the next chapter, we turn to the problem of political obligation and its Jewish parallels. We contrast modes of Jewish belonging to the Jewish polity with modern arguments for social solidarity and political commitment.

Notes

1. Alaisdair MacIntyre, *After Virtue* (Notre Dame: University of Notre Dame Press, 1984), ch. 16 passim; for MacIntyre's harsh critique of rights, see 68-70.

2. Hermann Cohen, *Religion der Vernunft aus den Quellen des Judentums*, Bruno Strauss, ed. (Wiesbaden: Fourier Verlag, 1978), 25, 219ff.

3. For a penetrating study of the shift from "natural right" to history, that is, to culture-bound conventions as the foundation for justice, see Leo Strauss, *Natural Right and History* (Chicago: University of Chicago Press, 1965). For Strauss's discussion of the right or just as that which is "according to nature," see especially ch. 4.

4. Abraham Irving Melden, *Rights and Persons* (Berkeley: University of California Press, 1977), 231.

5. It would have been more correct to trace the turn toward modern rights to Hobbes rather than to Locke. For Locke sees humans in the state of nature as still

subject to moral norms. Hobbes does not. Locke sustains a natural law position and does not "metaphysically disentangle" persons from their primal and prepolitical rights and duties.

6. Melden, *Rights and Persons*, 46.

7. Ibid., 25-26.

8. Michael Sandel traces the origins of this view of rights to the circumstances of American constitutionalism. The need to see constitutional law as fundamental law, that is, as law prior to the enactments of legislatures, led to the idea that the rights secured under constitutions were not conventional. Basic rights were not hereditary privileges or perennial features of a traditional polity but extracontextual, independent of political or juridical decisionmaking. See Michael Sandel, *Democracy's Discontent: America in Search of a Public Philosophy* (Cambridge, Mass.: Harvard University Press, 1996), 31-32.

9. Sol Roth, *Halakhah and Politics* (New York: Ktav Publishing House and Yeshiva University Press, 1988), 97.

10. Roth draws this thesis from the work of Roderick Chisholm. See Chisholm's *Theory of Knowledge* (Englewood Cliffs, N.J.: *Halakhah and Politics*, Prentice Hall, 1966), 11.

11. Roth, *Halakhah and Politics*, 118.

12. Ibid., 119.

13. Ibid., 120.

14. Ibid., 124.

15. "Murder and theft are prohibited; therefore, there are human rights to life and personal property." Ibid.

16. Sandel, *Democracy's Discontent*, Pt. 1.

17. Ibid., 34.

18. For a thorough treatment of these themes, see Alan L. Mittleman, *Between Kant and Kabbalah: An Introduction to Isaac Breuer's Philosophy of Judaism* (Albany: State University of New York Press, 1990) especially chapter 4.

19. Isaac Breuer, *Moriah* (Hebrew) (Jerusalem: Mossad Ha-Rav Kook, 1982), 3-7.

20. This essay is most readily available in its Hebrew translation, "Mishpat ha-Eshah, ha-Eved veha-Nokri," *Tsiyyunei Derekh* (Jerusalem: Mossad Ha-Rav Kook, 1982).

21. Kant's "Einleitung in die Rechtslehre," in *Metaphysik der Sitten, Werke*, VII, 30ff. quoted in Carl Joachim Friedrich, *The Philosophy of Law in Historical Perspective*, 2nd ed. (Chicago: University of Chicago Press, 1963), 127.

22. Isaac Breuer, *Die Welt als Schöpfung und Natur* (Frankfurt/Main: J. Kauffman Verlag, 1926), 19ff. See also Mittleman, *Between Kant and Kabbalah*, 158.

23. David Novak, *Covenantal Rights: A Study in Jewish Political Theory* (Princeton: Princeton University Press, 2000), 12.

24. Ibid., 9.

25. Ibid.,, ibid., 10.

26. Ibid., 12.

27. Ibid., 18-19.

28. Cited in Hadley Arkes, "A Word Unfitly Spoken: The Rejection of 'Contract' and the Argument over the Bill of Rights," in *The Judeo-Christian Tradition and the*

U.S. Constitution, Jewish Quarterly Review Supplement (Philadelphia: Annenberg Research Institute, 1989), 18.

29. Clinton Rossiter, ed., *The Federalist Papers* (New York: New American Library, 1961), 512-13.

30. Ibid., 514-15.

31. Novak, *Covenantal Rights*, ix.

32. Lewis Newman, "Woodchoppers and Respirators: The Problem of Interpretation in Contemporary Jewish Ethics," in *Modern Judaism* 10:2 (February 1990), 17-42.

33. Rossiter, *The Federalist Papers*, 513.

Chapter Six

The Dilemma of Modern Judaism As a Problem of Political Obligation

Leo Strauss, in his analysis of Thomas Hobbes, explicated a transformation that sheds light on the modern Jewish dilemma. Explaining how the concept of modern rights arose, he wrote:

> The tradition which Hobbes opposed had assumed that man could not reach the perfection of his nature except in and through civil society and, therefore, that civil society is prior to the individual. It was this assumption which led to the view that the primary moral fact is duty and not rights. One could not assert the primacy of natural rights without asserting that the individual is in every respect prior to civil society.[1]

Hobbes, on Strauss's account, founded political knowledge on what seemed to him the only bedrock: the individual's passionate fear of violent death and corresponding passion to stay alive by whatever means were requisite (*Leviathan*, Pt. I, ch.13). Hobbes eschewed as illusory or derivative such ideals as virtue and self-perfection. These values of traditional political theory could no longer serve as the legitimating foundation for politics in the new age of individualism.

The approach of Hobbes, an echo of the breakdown of medieval Catholic *universitas*, sets the stage for the dilemma, the theological-political crisis, of modern Judaism.[2] The background of the dilemma may be provisionally described as follows. Jews traditionally understood themselves to be humans who were, *ab ovo,* metaphysically and socially encumbered. Metaphysically, claims were made on them, which had little or nothing to do with commitments they as individuals had actually assumed. They were engaged by a God who told them, "You only have I known of all the families of the earth; therefore I will visit all your iniquities upon you" (Amos 3:2). The Jews had been claimed by God. True, the ancestors of the Jews had chosen to be chosen and, subsequently, both whole generations and individuals had the opportunity of reaffirming the voluntary, covenantal affirmation of the ancestors. But they did not really have the opportunity of repudiating the covenant. "Even though he sins," the Talmud rules, "he is still an Israelite" (B. Sanhedrin 44a). The individual Jew was thus metaphysically encumbered by or implicated in a scheme of retributive justice not of his or her own choosing.

Socially, the Jews understood themselves to belong to an ancient, unique nation the reality of which in every way preceded and exceeded the individual's own reality. In Strauss's terms, "civil society" was prior to the individual. Although the individual had to account for his or her sins before a righteous Judge (thus indicating the presence of a significant concept of individuality), the individual nonetheless stood before God wrapped in the merits of the heroic ancestors and supported by pleas that the whole community made for recognition of its corporate, or at least historic, fidelity.[3] The corporate structure of society as a whole gave plausibility to the symbolic picture of the Jews as a people that dwells apart, a people whose fate does not lie in its own hands. In the most mythic formulation of Judaism, kabbalah, this sociological situation expressed itself in the cosmizing symbol of an archetypal, transcendent Israel, a *knesset Israel* ontologically related to the divine. *Knesset Israel* mediated between the world of the divine emanations (*sefirot*) and the world of empirical Israel and the individual Jews that comprised it. This reified, supernal Israel became a channel for a flow of divine energy from the higher realms to the historical sphere.[4] Social and metaphysical identity were closely interrelated.

With the political, economic, and intellectual transformations of modernity, the individual was thrust forward to the front of the moral and ontological stage.[5] As such, the consciousness of being encumbered or claimed, that is, the belief that duty precedes rights, retreated. The society to which we have a duty still, of course, precedes us in time, but it does not exceed us in value. It cannot, as God claimed Jeremiah, claim us in the womb. It does not lay valid claims upon us in the above sense of a metaphysical or social encumbrance. Our relationship as individuals to our society is held to be ours to construct. The modern *homo faber* not only makes sense of social reality, he also makes (so it is often said) social reality. Social reality is socially constructed. Social reality no longer has naturalness. In a constructed world, the primary orientation is no longer one of natural piety toward all that which has brought one to life, that is, toward both God and a historic chain of ancestors from whom and because of whom one has received life. Rather, the primary orientation is toward the autonomous individual and his or her predicament. Relationships lost their primordiality, their naturalness. How to constitute them, that is, how to understand and weigh relationships toward parents, tribe, nation, and so on, has become an open-ended problem.

In traditional cultures, a thankfulness or gratitude toward those who have gone before, whose way has led to one's being, was morally self-evident. Saadia Gaon, following Muslim philosophical theology (*kalam*), simply states that it is a command of reason to return a kindness done to one or to render thanks to a benefactor. Humans have a natural and rational duty of gratitude toward those, living or dead, human or divine, who have conferred benefits upon them.[6] God has conferred the greatest benefit upon us, namely, existence. Therefore, if we owe gratitude to anyone, we certainly owe gratitude to God. The rationality of our gratitude toward God for having created us grounds, in Saadia's theory, the rationality of divine worship. By creating us, God encumbers us morally and metaphysically. Because he has given us being, we are obligated to him. The mere fact of our birth embeds us in a relationship with the divine that we did not choose. We did not have the freedom to choose or reject our own birth. Neither do we have the freedom to escape the duties that flow from it.

Modern consciousness, by contrast, understands the givenness of life against a background anthropology of the passional, precultural, biological self. It can do no other than start with the bare datum of life; the strange "thrownness" of the individual into life, rather than with the embeddedness of life into a way of life that precedes it. Philosophers took this precultural, biological self and designed for it an originary point, a "state of nature." Because the human being in the state of nature is not constituted by any attachments and has, as it were, no way of life, he need not have any gratitude for the way of life in which he finds himself. This is not to say that he routinely has no gratitude, but only that the moral self-evidence of gratitude is not urgent. Thus Hobbes treats gratitude in a purely utilitarian fashion. Gratitude is a means of maximizing one's social advantage. If one does not want to risk descending back into the state of nature and hence war with others, one had better acknowledge the friendship or gifts one receives from others. (*Leviathan* Pt. I, ch. 15). Gratitude does not flow from piety, that is, from awe at the mystery of one's being, but from prudence. It is a purely tactical move.

Insofar as the modern chooses a way of life, the prima facie claim of the ancestral, "natural" way of life on obligatory gratitude is all the weaker. For the way of life is not radically constitutive of one's being. One's being is conceivable without it, accident rather than substance. Existence precedes essence. One can have curiosity about one's ancestors, pride or interest in one's "roots," but gratitude seems out of place.

This order of priority inverts the traditional Jewish order. In the traditional order, the Jew is duty bound to acknowledge God as Creator and Sovereign and to affirm the Jewish community as the political space the Sovereign (and the Jews) have created so that divine sovereignty can become effective in this world.[7] That is, the Jew's political obligation to the Sovereign and to the Jewish polity has priority over the Jew's pursuit of life, liberty, property, and happiness. Duty to God and to God's way of life is a more fundamental category than the private project of eudaemonia. Nor is the sole or primary purpose of the polity to secure the conditions for eudaemonia. This is not to say that the fulfillment of duty is in principle antithetical to the pursuit of happiness, broadly conceived, but only that happiness is contingent upon existence in the polity and the polity is, at any rate, about purposes more comprehensive than its members' happiness. Private projects of happiness may be sacrificed if duty requires it. While both the individual Jew and the Jewish polity do not ignore the goal of survival, survival at any cost is not the highest goal. There are some conditions (the rule *yehareg ve'al ya'avor*—"Let him be killed rather than transgress"—B. Sanhedrin 74a.) under which survival, if sinful, is unacceptable. The polity is constantly requiring sacrifices from the individual. The individual understands that the polity per se cannot survive without making these demands. If it comes to a question of survival, the polity's survival, normatively speaking, outweighs the individual's survival. Insofar as the polity is the bearer of the historic chain of life that gave rise to the individual's life, gratitude requires that the needs of the polity be met, just as surely as gratitude requires that one's parents' needs be met.

These emphases are by no means uniquely Jewish. In Plato's early consideration of political obligation, the *Crito*, Socrates, speaking on behalf of the laws, argues that both he and his ancestors were "born and brought up and educated" as a "child and servant" of the laws (*Crito* 50e). To reject the punishment imposed by the laws is to reject the laws, and therefore to show ingratitude toward the way of life that made one what one is. Rejection of the laws is base and destructive: base toward oneself and destructive of the polity that nurtured one. The laws argue: "If you leave the city, Socrates, you shall return wrong for wrong and evil for evil, breaking your agreements and covenants with us, and injuring those whom you least ought to injure— yourself, your friends, your country, and us."[8] Socrates, who has lived by the laws, understands his obligation to include dying by the laws. The only possible alternative was to have abandoned the city long ago, before the troubles began and to have initiated a new way of life (52e). But this is actually an illusory alternative, for settling in any well-governed city would mean submitting to its laws, accepting its way of life or constitution as one's own. The problem of obligation, even if not grounded in so radical a degree of gratitude, would return. Socrates' individual well-being must be sacrificed if the common good, the maintenance of the laws, is to be upheld. Although this is not a very satisfying conclusion, what is remarkable about the *Crito* is that it is not the voice of some ham-fisted collectivism, but an elegant, rational argument designed to persuade a critical individual. That is, it is an argument designed to win an individual's consent. Socrates, who is already convinced, persuades Crito that they ought to be grateful to Athens and that this gratitude is correlated with an enormous duty. Their duty is to consent to what the laws require. They must not merely suffer the consequences of transgressing the laws, they must approve of the punishment the laws wreak upon them. They must, as rational individuals, accept rational arguments for sacrificing their own individuality when the polity requires it. Furthermore, they would not only be guilty were they to flee the laws, they should also feel shame. Their identification with the laws should run so deep as to signify that by betraying the laws, they betray themselves.

The modern Jew's dilemma vis-à-vis Judaism is not unlike Socrates', that is, he or she faces a problem of political obligation. The problem of political obligation arises when there is a conflict of goods. When there is a happy correspondence between the individual's happiness and the demands of the polity, that is, of civilized life, the problem of political obligation does not arise or, at least, is not urgent. The problem arises when the acceptance of authority conflicts in an urgent and painful way with one's own projects. It is at this point that the priority of duty, that is, of duty to the polity, over the exercise of one's own rights must be justified. Judaism, like Socrates' Athens, is constituted by its laws, its ancestral way of life. This way of life was sustained by the gratitude that the Jews showed it for having sustained them as a people. The way of life could and did conflict with one's own projects, with the desire of every man "to do what is right in his own eyes." Yet for the most part, the majority of the Jewish people were persuaded to maintain their "agreements and covenants" and hold to the priority of communal duty over personal right.

Judaism's theological-political dilemma is that, if it is to recognize itself as Judaism, it cannot help but think in terms of the priority of duty over right. It has to do this, however, in an age of eudaemonism, indeed, of hedonism, where its ordering of duty and right no longer seems credible. It cannot promise that the duty of belonging to the historic Jewish polity, the locus of God's sovereignty on earth, brings happiness or, in Hobbesian terms, peace. It can only promise that this is right for the Jew, indeed that it is, when all is said and done, the only thing that is right for the Jew. In fact, it can virtually promise that duty to this God and to this polity will bring sacrifice and suffering in excess of happiness or peace.

Now what is most disturbing about this consequence is that it is not merely an accident of Jewish history, lachrymose or not, but is built rather into the foundational stories of the biblical narrative. As Jon Levenson has argued, Israel's symbolic representation of itself to itself as a chosen people commits it to believe that its collective, historical life cannot be a matter of political or cultural normalcy.[9] To be Israel is to be implicated in a paradoxical destiny: whom God takes as his beloved son journeys toward exaltation only by way of humiliation. Chosenness is not a matter of the greatest good for the greatest number. It is a matter of test and trial, death and resurrection. Inclusion in the divine plan implies exclusion from the ordinary human mechanics of right or good.

Judaism's foundational narratives "encumber" the Jews with a God who has a standing claim on the firstborn or, alternately, on the most beloved son. For the Bible, that claim is expressed in the requirement that the firstborn of the herd be sacrificed to God and that the human firstborn be, if not actually sacrificed, then substituted for (Exod. 13:12-13; 22:28; 34:20). Levenson argues that, at an early stage of Israelite life, firstborn child sacrifice may well have been practiced. Later, the practice of redemption of the firstborn becomes normative. But the idea that it is a kind of supererogatory piety, of *middat hasidut*, to continue to actually sacrifice the firstborn is very slow to fade. As the practice declines, its lingering normative appeal is affirmed by biblical narratives that depict the "death and resurrection of the beloved son." The stories of Abel, Ishmael, Isaac, Joseph (and eventually, Jesus) depict archetypal firstborn or beloved sons who are marked for peculiar trial, exile, or death. All are linked in a dense intertextual mutuality, anticipating and reflecting the fate of chosen Israel. To be Israel is to be the beloved son whose life "is not his by right, but by gift."[10] The response to a gift, as Job ultimately learns, should only be gratitude, never a justified personal claim or demand.

Insofar as Israel's Bible presents Israel's life as God's possession to be returned to him whenever he wills, every modern notion of the primordiality and inalienability of the most fundamental right, the right to life, is undercut. A world in which an irrevocable right to life is understood as a revocable divine gift, a gift that, out of gratitude we have a duty to give back, is a world in which it is much easier to justify the priority of duty over right than is our world. The problem is that Judaism has to exist in our world.

In the political understanding basic to our world, the first function of a political society is to protect us from "continual fear and violent death" (*Leviathan* Pt. I, ch. 13). Humans leave the state of nature, according to Hobbes, and enter into a civil or political state only to secure their own interest. The most primordial interest is that of physical security, of cessation of the state of war. With the Hobbesian turn that signals the onset of modern political thought, civil society is not to be based on any vision higher than the establishment of the sort of peace that provides for security. The modern tradition of civil society, with its primacy of rights, foremost among them the right to life, eclipsed the older tradition of both the Bible and Greeks wherein the highest purpose of political society was to facilitate the collective achievement of virtue or the collective obedience to a divine law. Yet this very divine law seems to mandate that the best and most defenseless members of the society be subject to sudden and violent death. If this is so, then both the law and the society flunk the most basic test of what law and society are for on the modern account, that is, securing the right to life. Indeed, given the principle of *maaseh avot siman l'banim* (the story of the fathers is a sign for the children), the risk for Jews of being God's beloved offspring remains perpetual. Thus, the story of the binding of Isaac (*aqedah*) was appropriated generation by generation as an icon of martyrdom to which the Jews, duty-bound, consented.[11]

Historic Judaism, a polity of obedience and duty where the prime duty is to give a demanding God his due, is in deep tension with the community of rights, to the civil society founded on the principle of sanctified personal interests. To the extent, the very large extent, that Judaism remains a polity founded on obedience and duty, it remains in tension with the leading modern concept of ordered society. To the extent that Judaism must stress the enduring salience of God's claim on his people, our awareness of the incompatibility of the Jewish principle of order with the prevailing modern one grows acute. A eudaemonistic interpretation of being chosen, of being Israel, is ruled out. The modern ethos of security, of securing a space where persons can pursue private projects of life, liberty, and happiness, has a troubled relationship with Judaism.

The theological-political problem of modern Judaism is therefore somewhat more acute than the traditional problem of political obligation faced by Socrates or Hobbes. For Socrates, one ought to sacrifice one's private projects of life out of gratitude and noble loyalty to one's state. The very community that trained one in virtue and that made possible one's achievement of happiness may legitimately require one to sacrifice one's happiness. And one ought not resist, because this community is one's source and superior (otherwise it could not have trained or enabled one).

Yet Plato himself was evidently not satisfied with this, for in his later dialogues he redefines obligation in terms of obligation to the *best* regime.[12] Not any ordinary, flawed regime, but the regime of the philosopher-king or the regime that is open to the teachings of the philosopher is worthy of the loyalty of the best type of man. Indeed, the philosopher himself ought to feel and act upon obligation to the best regime (*Republic* 520b). This formulation significantly resituates the rational individual as the judge of what sort of regime deserves his loyalty. It weakens the sense of obligation based on natural, pre-critical ties. It makes obligation contingent upon whether the ideals of the polity correspond with one's own highest ideals. While Socrates' more pious view may accord better with ancient Judaism, Plato's revision was compatible with the philosophical Judaism of the Middle Ages largely inspired by his political teaching. Jewish philosophers such as Maimonides were convinced that the prophetic regime embodied by the Torah constitution was in fact the best regime and thus the one with an unimpeachable claim on the Jews' (and the philosopher's) loyalty.

The contrast with Hobbes, however, is striking. For Hobbes, one submits to a system of laws in order to secure a peace that makes private projects of life possible. The laws do not cover all aspects of life. They are not about ethics or virtues: they are about civil order. One enters into them because they offer a greater measure of insurance than life in the wild. Having tasted of the security that life under the law brings, one has a duty to give the law its due. If one wants to be treated equally by the law, one must abide by the law, that is, one must be as obedient to it as one's fellows. Having done this, one is left alone to pursue one's private project of happiness, noble or base as it might be (*Leviathan*, Pt. II, ch. 18).

Insofar as Hobbes wants conformity to the laws, but allows a considerable space for the private life, he would reject the implications of the Talmudic dictum: "When the community is in distress one should not say, I will go home, eat and drink, and peace will be upon my soul . . . . One should therefore afflict himself with the community."[13] All who retreat from the suffering of the nation into a sphere of private life will fail to experience the ultimate comforting of the nation. The *Mekhilta*, similarly, expresses the ideal of this complete and radical identification of the individual with the community as follows:

> It is said: *Israel is a scattered sheep* (Jeremiah 50:17). The people of Israel are compared to a lamb. What is the nature of a lamb? If it is hurt in one limb, all its limbs feel the pain. So also the people of Israel. One of them commits a sin and all of them suffer from the punishment.[14]

As in the first source, one has a duty to consider oneself an organic part of the nation. That duty requires not only the ordering of private life to the common good, but a keen sense of the consequences of one's private actions for the common good. Hobbes's teaching, thorough and demanding as it is with respect to obedience to the sovereign and conformity to the laws, does not penetrate to this personal depth. The depth of loyalty required is an echo of Jewish covenantal thought. The vassal, Israel, has to show loving fidelity (*hesed*) to the suzerain, God.

Even in those versions of modern political thought such as Rousseau's that stress a high level of consensus, a civil religion as a prerequisite for political life, the emphasis remains on social peace rather than collective virtue. Rousseau instrumentalizes religion: its worth, insofar as it has worth, is as an agent of social solidarity. Religion is about peace, not truth. That religion that is about truth, Christianity, is destructive of peace (*The Social Contract*, Bk. 3, chs. 9, 11; Bk. 4, ch. 8). This decoupling of political religion from truth plays into the overemphasis on political order as an end in itself that lends to Rousseau's thought a totalitarian inclination.

The modern communitarian (and totalitarian, for that matter) response to liberalism envisions an eclipse or invasion of the private sphere in the name of something allegedly higher than Hobbesian prudence. Yet this something higher that would command our loyalty and obligate us cannot free itself of eudaemonism or hedonism. Its argument always returns to the hypothetical: if you want to live well, then you will want to fully participate in a polity of thus and such a sort.

Judaism has always offered its own version of a eudaemonistic hypothetical. If you obey, Deuteronomy says in essence, you will be blessed; if you disobey, you will be appropriately cursed. But Judaism has also managed to contextualize the personal and collective search for a good life within a framework of duty that is oblivious to eudaemonistic consequences. It is fully conceivable (and, sadly, all too frequent) that someone who was born a Jew chooses a rich, satisfying, productive life at the cost of abandoning any tie to Judaism and Jewishness. If a good life were the only goal, there would be nothing to object to here. But for loyal Jews there is much to object to. Such a person, however satisfying a life he has managed to make for himself, has shown ingratitude and betrayed those who have gone before. This is ignoble and a dereliction of his duty.

Leo Strauss argued along these lines when he wrote:

> I repeat: it is impossible to get rid of one's past. It is necessary to accept one's past. That means that out of this undeniable necessity one must make a virtue. The virtue in question is fidelity, loyalty, piety in the old Latin sense of the word *pietas*. The necessity of taking this step appears from the disgraceful character of the only alternative, of denying one's origin, past or heritage.[15]

Perhaps Strauss, who was raised in an atmosphere of traditional piety, was influenced here by the arguments of nineteenth-century apologists for Orthodoxy, such as Samson Raphael Hirsch. Hirsch often made the point against his liberal, assimilationist opponents that only Orthodox Jews could become good Germans. This must have seemed a bizarre point to Hirsch's Reform opponents. How could traditionalists, clinging to the fullest measure (compatible with Emancipation) of an ancestral way of life become more German than those who tried hardest to resemble the Germans? Hirsch's answer was that a Jew who didn't keep his "agreements and covenants" with God and his ancestors could not be trusted to evince a noble loyalty to his state. Citizenship demanded precisely the sort of integrity and fidelity that Jewish traditionalists live by every day. This was, of course, an overly idealistic reading of the contemporary social situation.

The warrant in the preceding arguments for fidelity to the ancient way of life is nobility. Strauss's argument is essentially aristocratic. It appeals to the aristocratic virtue of honor, of the desire to avoid what is base or disgraceful. It assumes the power of the sense of shame. Insofar as abandonment of Judaism and Jewishness, the abandonment of deference to the ancestral, is ignoble, it is something of which a Jew should be ashamed. Jews, one might argue, should not promote Judaism on the eudaemonistic or hedonistic basis of how it can enhance or enrich one's life, as much as we might hope and believe that that is true. Jews should emphasize the debasing consequences of abandoning the way of life, of rejecting the nation, into which one has been born and reared.

Yet the power of the sense of shame is not what it used to be. Shame is a deflated currency. Appeals to nobility are likely to fall flat in as antielitist a culture as our own. Rather than emphasizing the avoidance of the base, we ought to try once again to cultivate a sense of gratitude. As Saadia, and even more extensively, the eleventh to twelfth-century moralist Bahya ibn Pakuda, affirmed, gratitude is a natural, and therefore universal, response. Humans are inclined, on the whole, to show thankfulness toward those who benefit them. "It is a known and accepted fact that our obligation to thank our benefactor should be according to his good intention toward us."[16] Bahya takes the universality of gratitude for granted. He goes on to argue that in all the ways in which humans benefit one another, self-interest is mixed with altruism. Nonetheless, the beneficiary is still bound to show gratitude toward the benefactor. Bahya's point is that only in the case of God's benefiting humans is no divine self-interest to be found. Therefore, one's duty to be grateful to God is all the more radical than one's duty to be grateful to other humans. We would probably be much less inclined than Bahya to ascribe universality and naturalness to the practice of gratitude. Nonetheless, if anthropologists such as Marcel Mauss are correct, the dynamics of gift-giving, of generosity and obligatedness, are embedded in every society, from the most archaic to the most advanced. Indebtedness is an ineluctable feature of the human condition insofar as it is the complement of sociality. To be a social being is to be indebted to all of those other social beings who make one's being possible.[17]

If universal indebtedness is the case, then the universal necessity for gratitude follows on the assumption that life is a good and that one ought to be grateful for goods received. One is principally indebted to one's parents for having given one life. The proper response to this radical indebtedness is gratitude. For Jews, there is an additional dimension. A Jew is not only, as all other humans, born, but a Jew is born as a Jew. (The case of the convert is special.) A Jew is born precisely because two other Jews linked their lives together. Judaism played a role in this linkage. Judaism was a factor in the process that led to a Jewish child's coming into being. The response of a Jewish child must therefore be not simply one of gratitude to one's parents for having given him or her life, but also gratitude to Judaism for being a factor or force in the parents' course of life. Were it not for Judaism as a shared faith and culture, my parents would not have found one another and I would not have been born. (Nor would they have been born, had their Jewish parents not found one another, an event once again credited to the shared world of Jewishness or

Judaism that they inhabited.) I must credit Judaism, the historic matrix of the lives of Jews, for my very existence. Recognizing *that I am* cannot be decoupled from recognizing *what I am*. Radical gratitude toward Judaism is the appropriate response to the fact of my existence.

Recognizing the existence-engendering and supporting role of Judaism and responding in gratitude to it is different for born Jews than for converts. Yet for converts, the issue of consent is much more straightforward. Choosing to be a Jew, like choosing to become an American citizen, obligates one to uphold the Torah just as it obligates one to uphold the Constitution. The convert's situation accords well with the modern affirmation of autonomy and consent. It is the anomalous situation of the born Jew, the one entangled by a net of indebtedness and constitutedness not of his or her own choosing, that needs to be explained and justified.

Obligation to the Jewish people, Judaism, or the Jewish polity based on a sense of radical gratitude toward the conditions that enabled one's own existence does not necessarily require nobility. It requires intelligence and realism. It requires an ability to transcend the illusion of radical individualism, to see the interconnectedness, through past and present, of persons. It requires that one gain a sense of one's own dependencies and constitutedness. To know oneself as a political animal means to know how much one is implicated in the lives of others and how much they are implicated in one's own life.

Notes

1. Leo Strauss, *Natural Right and History* (Chicago: University of Chicago Press, 1965), 183.

2. On the breakdown of medieval Catholic thought and its social order, see Karl Mannheim, *Ideology and Utopia*, Edward Shils and Louis Wirth, trans. (New York: Harcourt, Brace and World, 1936), 12.

3. The idea that ancient Israel's prophets discovered individuality is fundamental to Hermann Cohen's great work, *The Religion of Reason out of the Sources of Judaism*. That it needs to be fundamental to the work is symptomatic of its modernity. See *Religion der Vernunft aus den Quellen des Judentums* (Wiesbaden: Fourier Verlag, 1978), 22-23. For the concept of *zekhut avot*, the merit of the fathers, see Ephraim Urbach, *The Sages: The World and Wisdom of the Rabbis of the Talmud*, Israel Abrahams, trans. (Cambridge, Mass.: Harvard University Press, 1975), 496-508. Urbach explores the intergenerational interdependence of Jews on one another with respect to covenantal fidelity before God. Both the merits of the patriarchs and matriarchs, and the merits of their most virtuous descendants help the entire people. It is interesting to note that the word *zekhut*, the term for merit in this sense in rabbinic Hebrew, becomes the word for a "right" in modern Hebrew.

4. For a typical formulation of this doctrine, see Joseph ben Abraham Gikatilla, *Sha'are Orah*, Joseph ben Schlomo, ed. (Jerusalem: Mossad Bialik, 1970), 33.

5. A classic treatment of this theme is found in Hannah Arendt's *The Human Condition* (Chicago: University of Chicago Press, 1958), 299-300 and passim.

6. Saadia Gaon, *Sefer Ha-Emunot ve Ha-Deot*, Part III, Yehudah ibn Tibbon, trans. (New York: Om Publishing, 1947) 71.

7. In David Novak's work, briefly considered in the last chapter, rights and duties are simultaneous and always correlative. It is not true, in his view, that Jews have a duty to God, for example, that precedes their rights vis-à-vis God. For Novak, the principal right Jews have against God is the right to cry out to him, to pray. They do not have a right to expect him to be obliged to grant their individual requests (*baqashot*). Their right rather entails the valid claim that they have on him to be heard. He is not bound, however, to answer them in any specific way. Novak takes the ubiquitous correlation of rights and duties to stem from the covenantal reality of Judaism. Similarly, the individual person has significant duties toward community, and community has significant duties toward the persons who comprise it, such as the duty to assist them, to refrain from harming them, etc. Thus, the individual person's rights against the community are as primary as the community's claim on the individual's duty. Novak's stipulation of the correlation of rights and duties does not contradict my claim that, under the covenant, duty precedes right. Despite similarity of usage, we are not really talking on the same level of language. He is referring to the moral claims and responses of agents. I am using the word in a looser sense to refer to states of being. By using "duty" in Strauss's sense, I refer to the state of obligation and indebtedness one is in vis-à-vis the community that has nurtured one. Of course, on the level of agency, the individual does have rights against the community. As a Jew, however, one is in a state, a situation, of radical obligation to the community when it suffers. Personal claims lose meaning. Claims against God, as covenant partner, can be made, but what do these claims really amount to? Do individual and community really have rights against God? Novak has so qualified the idea of a primordial human right against God (rather than simply a duty toward God) as, arguably, to have emptied *right* of unequivocal content. Plainly, our putative right against God is unlike our rights against human persons. Given this equivocal meaning, I wonder whether it is cogent—absent negative theology—to speak of a right at all. David Novak, *Covenantal Rights* (Princeton: Princeton University Press, 1999), chs. 2, 6, 7.

8. Edith Hamilton and Huntington Cairns, eds. *Plato: The Collected Dialogues* (Princeton: Princeton University Press, 1973), 39.

9. Jon Levenson, *The Death and Resurrection of the Beloved Son* (New Haven: Yale University Press, 1993), passim.

10. Ibid., 59.

11. For the classic study of the repercussions of the *aqedah* in Jewish life and thought, see Shalom Spiegel, *The Last Trial*, Judah Goldin, trans. (New York: Pantheon Books, 1967).

12. Sheldon Wolin, *Politics and Vision* (Boston: Little, Brown, 1960), 53.

13. *B. Ta'anit* 11a, cited in Henry Malter, trans., *The Treatise Ta'anit* (Philadelphia: Jewish Publication Society, 1956), 148-50.

14. Jacob Z. Lauterbach, trans., *Mekilta de-Rabbi Ishmael*, Vol. II (Philadelphia: Jewish Publication Society, 1933), 205.

15. Leo Strauss, *Jewish Philosophy and the Crisis of Modernity: Essays and Lectures in Modern Jewish Thought*, Kenneth Hart Green, ed. (Albany: State University of New York Press, 1997), 320. For an illuminating comment on the limits of deference toward and "embrace of" the ancestral, see Hadley Arkes, "Athens and Jerusalem: The Legacy of Leo Strauss," in David Novak, ed., *Leo Strauss and Judaism: Jerusalem and Athens Critically Revisited* (Lanham, Md.: Rowman & Littlefield, 1996), 20.

16. Bahya Ben Joseph ibn Paquda, *The Book of Direction to the Duties of the Heart*, Menahem Mansoor, trans. (London: Routledge & Kegan Paul, 1973), 176.

17. It is interesting to note that Machiavelli, unlike Hobbes, laid out an important role for gratitude. Gratitude is the source of justice in the social order. He writes: "These variations of government amongst men are due to chance. For in the beginning of the world, when its inhabitants were few, they lived for a time scattered like the beasts. Then, with the multiplication of their offspring, they drew together and, in order the better to be able to defend themselves, began to look about for a man stronger and more courageous than the rest, made him their head, and obeyed him. It was thus that men learned what is honest and good from what is pernicious and wicked, for the sight of someone injuring his benefactor evoked in them hatred and sympathy and they blamed the ungrateful and respected those who showed gratitude, well aware that the same injuries might have been done to themselves. Hence to prevent evil of this kind they took to making laws and to assigning punishments to those who contravened them. The notion of justice then came into being." Niccolo Machiavelli, *The Discourses*, Leslie J. Walker, trans. (New Haven: Yale University Press, 1950), 212-13.

Chapter Seven

Individuals and the Common Good

The German scholar Georg Jellinek wrote, "To recognize the true boundaries between the individual and the community is the highest problem that thoughtful consideration of human society has to solve."[1]   At present, thoughtful Americans are considering this crucial and perennial issue under the headings of "liberalism" and "communitarianism." Both have deep roots in the American polity and its political thought and culture. Communitarianism is a late and fully secular version of our civic republican tradition, which itself is based on an older Reformed Protestant covenantal and communal tradition. Liberalism is rooted in the Enlightenment, particularly in the English and Scottish version. This chapter explores some of the issues that divide liberals and communitarians in order to situate traditional Judaism's "thoughtful consideration" of the problem.

Liberals and Communitarians

Democracy has been the most valued form of regime in the West for at least the past two centuries, and liberalism has been, increasingly, its normative orientation. While not identical, democracy and liberalism have often been paired. Democracy requires liberalism, or something like it, for democracy is only a means and does not by itself constitute a set of unambiguous values. Liberalism, however, does denote a set of substantive ethical and political values, held together by an underlying philosophical anthropology. While democracy answers the question "Who shall rule?" liberalism provides the values by which those in power shall rule. For although rule by the people goes some way toward alleviating the arbitrariness and unaccountability characteristic of nondemocratic regimes, it cannot alone provide the restraints on power or the equality before the law that liberals affirm are necessary for the requirements of justice to be satisfied. One can speak of a "totalitarian democracy" as a true democracy insofar as a majority or the representative of a majority exercises unrestrained power in the name of a collectivity. In such a democracy, people might choose to surrender their freedom to a common purpose or to oppress an ethnic or ideological minority in their midst. This is compatible with democracy in a formal sense (although not in the elevated, morally charged sense in which we often use the term). Yet this would certainly not be a liberal democracy.

What liberalism provides is a theory and practice of limits. Beginning with thinkers such as Locke, liberalism envisages the polity as a voluntary contract created by free, sovereign individuals who are endowed, prior to their political relationship, with natural rights. They enter into political association, in Locke's view, in order to secure a more effective defense of their natural rights. Indeed, although they were free before their association, true liberty is only possible in political community because liberty depends on the mutual restraint achievable only under a civil law. Insofar as the voluntarist creators of the political order intend it solely as a way of protecting their several natural rights and endow it with only as much of their alienated private sovereignty as it needs for that purpose, the emergent polity is strictly limited in its power over its members. Its function is prophylactic: it protects the members from one another better than they could have done singly in the state of nature. Thus the liberal principle is born: the chief public business is to make the world safe for private business. State interference in the lives and projects of individuals is justified only when it prevents wrongdoers from infringing the liberty of others. When Locke speaks in the *Second Treatise* of the common or public good (e.g., sect. IX, para. 131; sect. XI, para. 134), he conceives of it as a state wherein every private good (more accurately, every private right) is respected. The common good results when just institutions function to protect citizens' lives and property. Where procedural justice is satisfied, the common good, that is, the cumulative defense of every private good, is achieved.

Locke's doctrine of common good, as well as his conception of community, is remarkably thin. From an internal point of view, community is an agglomeration of autonomous individuals who voluntarily agree to respect the same laws and institutions. From an external point of view, that is, from the point of view of individuals in the state of nature or in other political entities, the community does appear to have a natural unity, to be "one body" (sect. XII, para. 145). This unity has, however, marginal implications for life "on the inside."

Locke's classical liberalism rests on a philosophical anthropology grounded in a post-teleological metaphysics. Seventeenth-century science no longer conceived of the law of nature as a grand hierarchical ordering of a cosmos that culminated in the perfection of the divine. Nature was conceived rather as an ensemble of discrete entities governed by impersonal, mechanical laws. The cosmos has no direction or goal that could be discovered by rational inquiry. Inquiry rather is directed toward uncovering the principles of its mechanics. Reason turns from the exploration of ends to that of causes. Nature so conceived does not deposit within human beings any imperatives regarding their development or ultimate purpose; that is, human life per se has no determinate telos.

Rather than a divine endowment uniquely suited to respond to divine presence, mind becomes a product of sensory experience. With materialism, the emphasis in anthropology turns from reason to will. Humanity is not discovered: it is self-made. Existence, as Sartre would eventually put it, precedes essence. Similarly, the design of the good society is not discovered in the nature of things by reason, but willed *ex nihilo* by human creators. Lacking any universal human good as the principle of the good society—owing to the demise of the old Aristotelian teleology with its metaphysical biology—the human good, that is, human ends, are to be infinitely diverse. The good society becomes one that acknowledges and facilitates that infinite localization of the good. Indeed, the good society is one that forswears any but the most narrow public discourse about the good, for the ends of life are as varied as persons. All the state may do is secure the conditions under which persons may pursue them.

This set of individualist liberal values meets a formidable critic in Jean-Jacques Rousseau. Although contractarian and ostensibly concerned with serving the freedom of man ("who is born free, yet everywhere in chains"), Rousseau's liberalism is heavily qualified. He rejects, at any rate, the thoroughgoing individualism of the British tradition and introduces an explicit doctrine of the common good. Rousseau gives the community, i.e., the political association born of contract by free men emerging from the state of nature, its own reality. More than an agglomeration of discrete individuals pursuing their own private interests, the community has a unique, simple nature. A mob of individuals expresses a sum of interests ("the will of all"), but a political community is grounded in an identity of interests, that is, a voluntary surrender of private desires to a universal desire to serve the whole. Rousseau terms this the "general will" and holds it to be the necessary condition for political association. This distinction between the will of all and the general will serves to justify the coercive power of the state. If the state were not grounded in an act of radical identification with a common purpose, then the exercise of its power over its subjects would simply be suppression of some private interests in the name of other (more powerful) private interests. Political association creates, as it were, a new man: one who finds his own felicity in the common purposes of his new civil state. Although using the language of natural rights in a Lockean sense, Rousseau contradicts this tradition (and himself) with his view that rights are really only the product of the political community's attribution. Only the citizen, not natural man, is the bearer of rights. Rousseau accordingly neglects the topic of institutional checks on the coercive power of the community.

For Rousseau, the community's rights take precedence over the individual's rights. The individual ought to believe (through the medium of "civil religion," a term first coined and advocated by Rousseau) that the general will can never err and that only by aligning his private will with the general will can he achieve freedom. For one who cannot so believe, his fellow citizens may "compel (him) to be free," which is to say compel him to conform to the general will (*Social Contract*, Bk. I, sect. VII). For those incapable of consummating this identification, the community

> can banish from the State all who fail . . . as lacking in social sense, and being incapable of sincerely loving the laws and justice, or of sacrificing, should the need arise, their lives to their duty. Any man who, after acknowledging these articles of faith [in the civil religion], proceeds to act as though he did not believe them, is deserving of the death penalty. (*Social Contract*, Bk. IV, sect.VIII)

In this doctrine of a common good "with teeth," liberalism finds its recurrent nightmare. Any adequate communitarian account of the common good will have to avoid the invitation to coercion provided by Rousseau. Thus one must be ambivalent toward Rousseau's legacy. His articulation of the almost mystical reality of a community distinct from its membership did support, on the one hand, those (at least comparatively) benign American concepts of republican or civic virtue whose decline has recently been studied by Robert Bellah and others. On the other hand, Rousseau lends support to an ominous collectivism. (The same ambivalence marks Hegel, whose formulation is even more extreme.) If Rousseau's darkest implications are totalitarian, the salvageable side of his thought, however, is communitarian. Far more pointedly than Locke (or Hume or Smith), Rousseau explores the anthropological, moral, and political implications of a framework in which the reality of human derivativeness and interrelatedness predominates.

The contemporary communitarian critique of liberalism, found in the works of Michael Sandel, Alisdaire MacIntyre, Barbara Rowland, and others asserts the philosophical implications of an anthropology of radical human interrelatedness. A familiar target of the communitarians, as Amitai Etzioni points out, is John Rawls. Rawls typifies modern liberalism's individualist tradition. "Each person possesses an inviolability founded on justice that even the welfare of society as a whole cannot override. For this reason justice denies that the loss of freedom for some is made right by a greater good shared by others."[2] For Rawls, the basic category is justice. Following Kant, the right is to take priority over the good. Justice is understood by Rawls in the sense of fairness. The institutions of society should be arranged in such a way that (a) everyone has liberty and (b) no one is hampered in his or her liberty by morally irrelevant disadvantages.

Rawls, basing his approach to some extent on Kant, affirms the priority of the atomistic rational subject vis-à-vis the community of subjects and vis-à-vis the rational subject's own accidental attributes. He draws the strongest possible distinction between the self and any set of empirical qualities a self may "possess." Rawls's analogue to the state of nature, the "original position," envisions these atomistic rational subjects separated by a "veil of ignorance" from their eventual attributes (being black, Jewish, female, blind, rich, poor, etc.). Owing to this ignorance and to the nonessential quality of their attributes (that is, nonessential vis-à-vis their rationality), the subjects would choose a social arrangement in which they would have a right to the highest degree of basic liberties compatible with a like degree for all. Their eventual attributes, the empirical situation of the self, should not matter from the point of view of procedural justice. But unlike classical liberals such as Locke, contemporary liberals, such as Rawls or Ronald Dworkin, go beyond a strictly procedural justice to a concept of distributive justice. They are concerned to justify both a high degree of personal rights-based liberty (through a procedural argument) and a welfare-oriented social policy (unlike traditional libertarians such as Hayek or Nozick, for example). In this scheme, the subject (conceived as a Kantian transcendental ego), precisely because it does not possess its attributes, cannot claim any merit or legitimate desert on account of them. The "merit" of such desirable attributes as being wealthy or smart ought to be entirely irrelevant to how society distributes its shares of goods, because the subject of hypothetical merit is not in fact the subject of possession of those putatively meritorious attributes. They have been distributed by nature and circumstance in an arbitrary and morally irrelevant fashion—any given self cannot base a claim of special treatment on them. They must be harnessed by the proper subject of possession for morally justifiable ends.

All of a sudden, a more determinative concept of community has emerged. Community claims to, in some sense, possess the subject's attributes and to judge how the value of such putatively common assets is to be divided. The problem, as Michael Sandel points out, is that this latter agenda requires a doctrine of both an interrelated and derivative self, and an empowered community at once fuller and thicker than individualist liberals want to affirm. If what is essential about the self is its preempirical radical autonomy (the so-called unsituated self), then any conjunction of such selves will remain logically and morally problematic. Community will appear, at best, a "necessary burden." Furthermore, how is a discourse about the good, particularly the common good, to find a secure footing in a language that emphasizes private right? Communitarians charge that even when liberals confront this problem directly their proneness to individualistic principles flaws their results. Rawls's answer to this problem is the "difference principle" and the notion of "common assets." He considers several ways in which differences in attributes that are socially salient may be justified. The one he prefers, "democratic equality," justifies differences only insofar as they work to the benefit of the most disadvantaged members of society. "Those who have been favored by nature, whoever they are, may gain from their good fortune only on terms that improve the situation of those who have lost out."[3] Since advantageous attributes belong to no one in particular, they belong to all in common. They are "common assets" that ought to serve common purposes. This is essentially a moral argument for a cooperative society.

An example of how this works can be found in Ronald Dworkin's argument for affirmative action. Dworkin argued that while discrimination is a real problem (you cannot enter law school because you are black), there is no such thing as reverse discrimination (we want this black to enter law school instead of this white). No one merits law school admission on the basis of any claim of "possession" of relevant attributes. "Reverse discrimination" is only society's selection of a worthy social goal (increased minority professionals). The attribute of minority status does not constitute a claim to special treatment any more than any other attribute. Society decides, in a utilitarian fashion, how to maximize the value of this "common asset." Of course, this process of distributing goods on the basis of socially constructed "merit" can only take place once basic procedural justice is secured.[4]

This sudden shift from a discourse of individual rights to a thesis about collective purposes depends upon the unexamined and unargued presupposition that the community (which community—the national one? a local one?) is the subject of possession of the self's attributes. But why? If individuals are autonomous, what justifies their being used as means rather than ends for some collective purpose? Rawls and Dworkin believe that once basic liberties are secured, differences in wealth and status can be justified only by their reconciliation with the common good. Yet, as Michael Sandel points out, an argument for a common good that relies on a fully individuated conception of the self always suggests the exploitation and compromise of such a self. The way out, communitarians like Sandel argue, is to reinvent a self that understands itself as constituted by its community in the first place. Community is not an option undertaken from a presocial original position. Community is the existence condition of the self as such.

Alisdaire MacIntyre argues this thesis in his critique of modern moral philosophy, *After Virtue*. MacIntyre believes that modern moral philosophy is an incoherent melange of inherited and invented concepts such as "rights," "utility," and "persons." Our moral debates are irresolvable and the various frameworks we subscribe to are incommensurable ever since the Aristotelian tradition fell into disrepute. MacIntyre contends that the Greek and medieval Christian traditions conceived of a human life as a "narrative unity," taking the form of a journey. The journey was made meaningful by the pursuit of virtues, discovered in the practice of communities. A "practice," in MacIntyre's technical sense, is a communally valued, shared activity that entails an internal good and supports the acquisition of a human excellence or virtue. For MacIntyre, our ancestors' life's work was to acquire the virtues esteemed by their communities through the pursuit of relevant practices. The key point is that private good was inconceivable without common good. Personal meaning necessarily participated in shared understandings of the ends of life.

> For if the conception of a good has to be expounded in terms of such notions as those of a practice, of the narrative unity of a human life, and of a moral tradition, then goods, and with them the only grounds for the authority of laws and virtues, can only be discovered by entering into those relationships which constitute communities whose central bond is a shared vision of an understanding of goods. To cut oneself off from shared activity in which one has initially to learn obediently as an apprentice learns, to isolate oneself from the communities which find their point and purpose in such activities, will be to debar oneself from finding any good outside of oneself.[5]

What education in the virtues teaches me is that my good as a man is one and the same as the good of those others with whom I am bound up in human community. There is no way of my pursuing my good that is necessarily antagonistic to you because good is neither mine peculiarly nor yours peculiarly—goods are not private property.[6]

MacIntyre thus rejects, in the strongest form, the tradition of individualist liberalism of the past three centuries. He affirms the radical interrelatedness and sociality of the self, and the axiological primacy of the common good. For the contemporary communitarians then, the chief issues include the critique of the autonomous, rational self of liberalism and its enlargement through constitutive attachments, the replacement of a rights-and-justice-oriented (i.e., deontological) discourse by a goods-oriented, teleological one, and an empowerment, both conceptual and practical, of community without a huge loss of those liberties made possible by liberalism.

Rabbinic Considerations

Many of these issues are reflected in Mishna, Baba Batra 1:5 and its gemara (Talmudic discussion), as well as in the laws Maimonides derives from them in *Mishneh Torah, Hilkhot Shkheinim*, ch. 6.[7] The concern of the mishna is with how citizens should live in community. The text adumbrates such questions as:

What do they owe to one another? What do they owe to the whole? What common purposes override the liberties of individuals and what justifies the primacy of common purpose over individual purpose?

The mishna begins with the case of a resident of a courtyard and then applies its principle of justified coercion to the resident of a city. Significantly, it draws no distinction between the quality of public obligation required of each. Both neighbors and citizens are related to one another by a thick net of mutual obligations.

> He [a resident of a courtyard] may be compelled [by the rest] to [contribute to] the building of a porter's lodge and a door for the courtyard. Rabban Simeon b. Gamliel, however, says that not all courtyards require a porter's lodge. He [a resident of a city] may be compelled to contribute to the building of a wall, folding doors and a crossbar. Rabban Simeon b. Gamliel says that not all towns require a wall. (Baba Batra 1:5)

Why should one be obligated to contribute to a "porter's lodge" or gatehouse? To understand the gemara's treatment of this mishna (B. Baba Batra 7b), we must step back into the context of the larger discussion of the chapter on capital improvements that owners of adjoining property can require each other to make if the custom of the community mandates it. The general principle is that "all is according to the custom of the country." Mishna and gemara assume that neighbors, following local tradition, can compel one another to participate in common projects such as building walls between their properties. The language of the mishna oscillates between pure voluntarism ("if joint owners *want* to make a division in their courtyard . . ." Baba Batra 1:1) and compulsion ("in a place where it is customary to fence off an orchard, either can be *compelled* to do so" [Baba Batra 1:2]. The mishna allows people not to participate only when it is not local custom to do so. Deference to local traditions, to MacIntyre's constitutive practices of the community, as it were, predominates.

This is not an ironfisted collectivism, however. The mishna is concerned to specify what an equitable contribution to, for example, the building of a wall should be so as to divide the neighbors' responsibility fairly and to ensure that they share equally in the benefit the capital improvement provides. Thus individual interests are assumed to identify with common interests. The scheme of responsibilities and benefits is so arranged that all gain and none loses.

To return to our mishna, the gemara considers whether a gatehouse is another case of customary capital improvement. It immediately raises the public implication of the increase in privacy that this modification of a structure would bring. Perhaps building a gatehouse is morally problematic. What if it prevents the poor from coming in to beg? The gemara presents the case of a pious man whom the prophet Elijah used to come and visit until he built a gatehouse. Yet if gatehouse construction is morally objectionable, why does the mishna seem to require it? The gemara's answer is to reconcile the apparent contradiction between the pious man's objectionable action and the mishna's rule that gatehouses are legitimate common projects by stipulating that the gatehouse must be built in such a way that it causes no problems for prospective beggars. Apparently, the pious man did not provide his gatehouse with a latch or handle such that the poor could simply open it and walk through it. Thus the gemara adduces another level of public obligation for the neighbors: they are not only obligated to one another for participating in capital improvements, but they are obligated to the local poor to not impede them as they come to claim *tsedakah*. Their resources are not only to be pooled in relevant respects within their courtyard, but are to be pooled for the sake of relevant strangers as well.

Just when we might think that the rabbis have no regard for those constraints on public coercion that are central to liberalism, the gemara shows a streak of "liberal" concern. The text moves to Rabban Shimon b. Gamliel's caution that not all courtyards require gatehouses. Rabban Gamliel would condition a resident's obligation not only on local custom but on architectural factors. The gemara introduces a *baraita* (an extramishnaic statement) that expands on Gamliel's mishnaic statement. Not all courtyards require gatehouses, only those that "abut on the public domain" because the privacy of the residents is most compromised in such cases. The rabbis disagree with Rabban Gamliel and add that even if the courtyard were set back from the street, a crowd of people could force their way in. Thus the rabbis allow the building of a gatehouse in all cases to minimize potential discomfort and intrusion. The "privacy rights" of the neighbors must be respected.

The neighborhood community thus reflects a delicate balance of private and public concerns. Turning from the gemara to Maimonides, we can see this balance in even higher relief. Maimonides is concerned to specify which commercial activities are permissible for residents of a courtyard (actually, an "alley"). Since in premodern times people worked in their homes, commercial and residential areas coincided. Most commercial activities will disturb the other residents, and criteria need to be developed (zoning laws, as it were) to balance the value of various enterprises against their negative "environmental impact." Maimonides ruled:

> If one of the residents of a blind alley wishes to become a blood letter or a weaver or a teacher of the children of heathen, the law is that residents of the alley can prevent him because he would increase the number of people coming in and going out. If there is a shop in a courtyard the neighbors can protest, saying, "We cannot sleep because of the noise of the people coming in and going out." The owner of the shop may however do his work in his shop, but he must sell in the market. In that case they cannot protest, saying, "We cannot sleep because of the noise of the hammer or of the mill," since

he has already established his right to have a workshop. (*Hilkhot Shkheinim* VI, 11-12)

Maimonides also defers to custom. If one wishes to become a certain kind of craftsman and the consequence of that is significant public disruption, one can be prohibited. However, if one is already a craftsman who has a workshop in the courtyard, one's right to be there is assumed by the absence of prior public protest, a sort of *argumentum e silentio*. Maimonides solves the problem of the disruptive but legitimate craftsman by differentiating between manufacture and commerce and requiring the latter to occur in the marketplace. If one already has a right, grounded in custom, to ply one's trade, then the private matter of how one earns one's living, even when it entails some unpleasant public consequences, is not a public concern. Yet although Maimonides would seem to protect "individual rights" in this case, he is not doing so for liberal reasons. His concern rather is with the common good. Commerce promotes the economic welfare of the courtyard. This is clear in the following ruling:

> If there is among the residents of an alley a craftsman and the other residents do not protest, or if there is a bathhouse or a shop or a mill and someone comes and makes another bathhouse opposite the first, or another mill, then the owner of the first cannot prevent him on the claim that the second cuts off his livelihood. Even if the second is from another alley they cannot prevent him, inasmuch as there is already that trade among them. (*Hilkhot Shkheinim* VI 8)

The assumption here is that commerce, indeed, competition, is a good thing. If the residents have agreed, at least tacitly, to allow it (and profit by competition), then those who are most likely to feel the negative effects (the monopolist who must now compete) cannot protest. The criterion for the zoning regulation is the public good. This is also clear from the following:

> Thus he [a resident of an alley] may also teach Jewish children in his house, and the partners cannot protest with the claim, "We cannot sleep because of the noise of the schoolchildren." (*Hilkhot Shkheinim* VI 12)

Here, even though the residents of the courtyard are disturbed, the public good of transmitting the tradition (*talmud torah*) outweighs the public good of tranquillity or any private inconvenience. If MacIntyre is correct, general agreement about the constitutive necessity of this practice would have prevailed and the residents would have agreed that their ultimate good did in fact reside in the studies of the noisy schoolchildren. It is important to note that Maimonides did not allow a Jew to establish a school for "heathen children," i.e., for secular studies. This is evidently not in the public interest.

To return to the mishna and gemara, we take up the case of the residents of a town compelling one another to contribute to the building of a wall. Rabban Shimon b. Gamliel introduces an identical problem: are walls suitable for all cities? Rabban Gamliel states in the gemara that only those cities adjacent to a frontier require a wall. The rabbis once again overrule him and state that all cities are liable to attack from roving bands. Having established that all cities need walls, and thus that all may be compelled to contribute to them, the gemara tries to fix how the tax for construction should be levied. Should it be a poll tax since arguably all benefit equally from a wall? Should it be an income tax since the rich arguably have more to lose in a robbery than the poor? Or should it be a service tax since those who live near the edge of town are more vulnerable than those who live in the center of town and so should pay more for the service the wall provides? The gemara records two opinions in the name of the same teacher, R. Johanan, that is, the tax should be both an income tax and a service tax. Medieval commentators (*tosaphot*) reconcile this in the following way: a poor man at the edge of town pays more than a poor man downtown, a rich man at the edge of town pays more than a rich man downtown, but a rich man, regardless of location, will always pay more than a poor man. This taxation scheme accommodates both the requirement of procedural justice—only those who profit from an institution should contribute to it—and of distributive justice (that is, Rawlsian justice as fairness)—discrepancies in advantage should benefit the disadvantaged. All are obligated to contribute to the common good and to find their own good within it.

The dual criterion of income tax and service tax has both moral presuppositions and consequences. The citizen is understood to be someone who benefits from life in community. Life in community is clearly reciprocal: community gives and receives, as does the citizen. For the situated or encumbered self, this giving and receiving sustains both human dignity and selfhood as such. Dignity inheres in the practice of fulfilling one's civic obligation. To take an analogous case, the poor have a right to collect ungleaned produce (*peah*), but they must pay a "price" for it insofar as they must wait until a designated hour when the farmer finishes his work to claim it. They must also harvest it themselves. This "workfare" system provides for their dignity by meeting their basic needs, but it also requires them to sustain their dignity by contributing to the practices of the community. Indeed, the poor must also give *tzedakah*.

The preceding discussions indicate that the Jewish tradition employs the concept of the common good as a regulative principle for political conduct. While pursuit of one's private ends has its place, the community constantly calls for the subordination of the private to the public when important common purposes are at stake. The sources presuppose and articulate a rich concept of community. Community is more than an agglomeration of private selves: it is an association of mutually obligated, interdependent selves who find their own good in common. Nonetheless, this system, while not liberal and not necessarily democratic, also embodies a serious concern for those enabling and restraining claims that liberal societies call "rights." Rights, however, cannot be entirely independent of the common good. Indeed, it is in terms of that framework that justice, the order of rules and rights, finds its point and purpose.

In the final chapter, we consider an attempt by a traditional Jewish thinker to articulate the constitutional requirements for a fully empowered community of the common good, an independent Jewish polity.

Notes

1. Cited in Barry Alan Shain, *The Myth of American Individualism: The Protestant Origins of American Political Thought* (Princeton: Princeton University Press, 1994), 23.

2. Rawls quoted in Amitai Etzioni, "Liberals and Communitarians," *Partisan Review* 57 (Spring 1990), 215.

3. Rawls quoted in Michael J. Sandel, *Liberalism and the Limits of Justice* (Cambridge: Cambridge University Press, 1982), 70.

4. Dworkin appears to be inconsistent. Why should discrimination be any more real than reverse discrimination on this account? His answer is that discrimination is based on the morally repugnant idea that one race is inherently inferior to another. "Reverse discrimination," however, is simply society's choice of how to distribute its assets. For Dworkin's argument and Sandel's critique of it, see Michael Sandel, *Liberalism and the Limits of Justice*, 135-47.

5. Alisdair MacIntyre, *After Virtue*, 2nd ed. (Notre Dame: University of Notre Dame Press, 1984), 258.

6. Ibid., 229.

7. All references to the mishna and gemara are taken from *The Babylonian Talmud, Seder Nezikin*, vol. 2, trans. I. Epstein (London: Soncino Press, 1935). All references to Maimonides are taken from *The Code of Maimonides*, Book XII, The Book of Acquistion, trans. I. Klein, Yale Judaica Series, vol. 5 (New Haven: Yale University Press, 1951).

Chapter Eight

The Constitution of a Jewish State: The Thought of R. Shimon Federbush

If a modern Jewish state were to be shaped in accordance with halakhic Judaism, what would it be like? Would such a state resemble the contemporary democracies with their tradition of constitutionally limited government and respect for fundamental freedoms, or would such a state resemble the authoritarian, hierocratic regime of Iran? Who would be the guiding philosopher of such a state, Plato or Locke? Is the tradition of modern republicanism, which informs the contemporary democracies, compatible with the ideal-typical political tendencies of Jewish tradition? If Torah, however broadly conceived, is thought to be the constitution of the Jewish people and polity, could it, a divinely given law, be comparable to any humanly constructed constitution? And if it is not comparable to any humanly constructed constitution, how could Jews living under its regime enjoy the benefits of constitutional government?

It seems useful to frame the issue of religion and state in constitutional terms, for there is an overlap between the characteristics and benefits of constitutional government and life under the Torah. As Charles McIlwain puts it, "in all its successive phases, constitutionalism has one essential quality: it is a legal limitation on government; it is the antithesis of arbitrary rule; its opposite is despotic government, the government of will instead of law."[1] Jewish sources were obviously concerned to limit government and to subject it to legal restraint and review. Thus, the category of constitutionalism is broad enough to describe and analyze both ancient and medieval Jewish examples of self-government, as well as the systems of the contemporary democracies. On the other hand, the idea of a constitution is also well suited to highlight the differences between Jewish polities and modern ones, especially insofar as moderns understand constitutions to be products of human deliberation and consent, whereas Jews understand the Torah as constitution to be God-given.

This chapter seeks to address these fundamental questions by investigating the work of a midcentury, halakhically oriented thinker, R. Shimon Federbush (1892-1969). Federbush, a leader in the Mizrachi movement, advocated a substantial incorporation of Jewish legal and political traditions into the polity and culture of Israel. Yet Federbush was also committed to the modern republican tradition that he encountered during his forty-year stay in the United States As a refugee from Nazi Europe, he had a fundamental commitment to a politics that safeguarded transcendent moral values such as equality before the law and freedom of thought and religion. He sought to square the Jewish political tradition, as he understood it, with democratic self-government and its culture of consent, dissent, and participation. Federbush's commitment to modern republicanism is particularly pronounced both in comparison with the leader of his movement, R. Fishman-Maimon, and with his older contemporary on the right, Isaac Breuer, who also advocated an incorporation of Jewish law in the incipient Jewish state. Federbush departs sharply from Fishman-Maimon's advocacy of a renewal of the Sanhedrin precisely because it would circumvent the democratic political process embodied in an elected legislature. And while, like Breuer, he embraces a certain conception of theocracy as the Jewish political norm, Federbush differed radically from Breuer insofar as his conception of Torah as constitution is dynamic and nationalistic. Breuer's is highly metaphysical and reificationist. In the case of Fishman-Maimon, the dividing issue is *by whom* and *how* public matters should be decided in a modern Jewish state. In the case of Breuer, the issue is *what* constitution is; specifically, what the Torah as constitution is. Before turning to an analysis of Federbush, however, let us briefly consider some of the theoretical issues that underlie inquiry in this field.

Torah-as-Constitution and Modern Constitutionalism

The problem of religion and state in the Jewish tradition, as a theoretical problem, involves the status of the Torah qua constitution. As in any constitutional inquiry, there is the question of *what* a constitution is. The issue here is not so much whether a constitution is a single text, a set of basic laws, or a collection of institutions as *what* makes a constitution authoritative. That is, why should a constitution obligate; what is the source of its authority? What grounds a constitutional order? Does a constitutional order derive its authority from an act, originary or ongoing or both, of a free people, or does such an order derive its legitimacy from its coherence with natural right or some other transcendent source? Is constitutional legitimacy conventional or transcendent? The divide in modern legal theory has been between positivism and natural law, in all their many varieties.[2] Jewish thinkers have sought to apply both of these frameworks to Torah. Construing Torah as a series of heteronomous divine commands, Marvin Fox or Alan Yuter, for example, reject any appeal to moral values that can be known by autonomous reason. Basing his approach on Hans Kelsen, Yuter substitutes a divine sovereign for Kelsen's state. David Novak, on the other hand, construes Torah as a positive law in harmony with a prior, epistemically available natural law.[3] Neither of these approaches seems to capture, however, the paradoxically hetero- or theonomic yet humanly consensual and articulated constitutionalism of the Torah. Can this be described in modern constitutional language?

One notable attempt to break through the positivist-natural law stalemate that might also shed light on Torah as constitution is that of the constitutional theorist Will Harris. Following the broadly Kantian approach of transcendental deduction, Harris argues that externally situated questions about the grounding of a constitutional order fundamentally misrepresent the reality of constitutionalism. Constitutions are texts that allow citizens to imagine and inhabit an interpretable social world. The interpretation of a constitutional reality must itself be situated within the constitutional order. The transcendental question about what grounds such an order must be posed and answered from within the order, taking the form of "What conditions make possible the way of life that we have together?"

> The enterprise of making an inhabitable world by writing a text requires a spaciousness and rigor of imagination, the capacity to project a workable image of an order not previously present. The central proposition begins to establish the position of *constitutionalism*—with its assertive world-making and restrictive text-binding character—as an independently theorized third term beyond *natural law* and *legal positivism*, which have in our discourse purported to exhaust the possibilities of political justification.[4]

Recalling the "internal realism" of Hilary Putnam, Harris refuses to reify any alleged metaphysical foundation for a constitutional order, yet he also refuses to abandon the practice of seeking the source of its authority. He locates the grounds of constitutional authority within the ongoing hermeneutic culture of a republican community of interpreters.

> In this crucially self-referential enterprise, a purposefully composed text creates its own normative author. It constructs the popular sovereign it needs to be authoritative, and it nurtures the political life of a People whose citizenship provides it with the only reality it can have or need. What they

have modeled is themselves, in public and realizable form. This People and these Citizens are not merely the analytical necessities for explaining the validity of the Constitution. Their persistent commitments and practices give the project its three-dimensionality as a meaningful world.[5]

The force of this theory, I take it, is to describe a constitutional order as a rich and self-sufficient form of life that produces its own knowledge, as well as its own canons for how to adjust that knowledge to political and social reality. A constitution produces a textually organized culture. The persistence of a community of interpreters within this culture "to go to the trouble" of understanding themselves and their social world by constant reference to the text ratifies the text as fundamental. The text becomes both a model of and a model for a world.

In some ways, this approach describes the world of Torah better than standard positivist or natural law philosophies. Only on the fringes of the Torah's world do philosophical interpreters worry about the fit or grounding of its social order with some imagined prior world of nature. The question of the actual coherence of the Torah order with the supervening will of God, while not irrelevant, is also secondary vis-à-vis the hermeneutic practices of the system. The Torah is not in heaven. Within the order, immanent standards of interpretation and decision making prevail. It is also the case that this model, with its rich discourse of a people imagining and enacting themselves in their hermeneutic practice, captures the lived thickness of Jewish existence more fully than the pale divine command theory of positivism. Nonetheless, on an ideal-typical level, it is clear that Harris's eminently modern model of a constitution and traditional Jewish views of Torah must diverge. Torah cannot ultimately be disentangled from its divine source. Recourse to the will of God, however irrelevant to the interpretation of halakha and the decision of the *posek*, cannot be jettisoned as a ground for the legitimacy of the system as a whole. The divine origin of the Torah must inevitably mean that the question, "What is a constitution?" will be answered differently by Jews (i.e. those Jews who would take Torah as their constitution) and by modern republicans. While late modern and postmodern thinkers are embarrassed by the scandal of foundationalism, Jewish thinkers cannot dispense with it. A ready example is Lenn Goodman's recent *On Justice,* which returns the question of ontology to the heart of ethics. Goodman advances a neo-Platonic account of being in order to reject conventionalist accounts of justice. Justice is founded on the deserts of beings, depending upon where they lie in a cosmic order of rank.[6] Between those committed to Torah as constitution and modern republicans, there is then a certain incommensurability in how the question "What is a constitution?" is to be settled.

In addition to the question of *what*, there are the questions of *who* and *how*. Who is fit to interpret the norms of common life, whatever their character and source? How are these norms to be implemented? If a constitution is primarily thought of as law (the *what* question), then expert legal interpreters such as judges and courts would be its primary interpreters (the *who* question). If a constitution is primarily the blueprint for and the ongoing actualization of a shared form of life, then its interpreters are the whole of its citizens.[7] How is the Torah as constitution to be conceived? If it is constructed primarily as a body of halakhic rules, then those with specialized expertise in the rules, i.e., rabbinic decisors, would figure as the leading class of interpreters. If Torah, however, is conceived as something broader and more fundamental than law, namely, as the basis for a morally oriented, politically organized collective life, then the class of qualified interpreters broadens to all of those who share in its moral orientation and in the commitment to its realization. (This latter move, as we shall see, is essentially the one taken by Federbush. He opens the interpretation of Torah up to all Jews who care about the common project of a Jewish polity.)

The question of *who* cannot be disentangled from the question of *how*. How is power effectively exercised in a constitutional order? Given that power cannot be arbitrary, where should it reside: in courts, legislatures, princes, or presidents? How should it be distributed? How should its holders come to exercise it or lose it? These questions are also acute for any Jewish polity. What role should rabbis (*which* rabbis?) have in decisions of public matters? Is there a secular sphere in which valid decisions can be made in spite of Torah guidelines if need be? How could such a sphere be constitutionally articulated and empowered?

The modern question about religion and state invariably comes down to the defense of such a sphere against the claims of religion to circumvent open-ended and rational deliberation. The value of deliberation rests on the presumed sovereignty of the people, which is juxtaposed to the presumptive claims of the clerical representatives of God. From Machiavelli on, the constitutionalized intrusion of official religion into the processes of governance has been rejected whether as an obstacle to civil peace or rational rule or, latterly, personal freedom.[8] What hope is there then for a Jewish theory that is committed both to the incorporation of Jewish law (with a constitutional status for its rabbinic interpreters) and to a modern republic with its endorsement of deliberation and popular sovereignty? That is the question Federbush hopes to answer.

Theocracy and Democracy

Federbush answers the question of *what* the Torah as constitution is by recourse to the idea of covenant. Covenant is the fundamental Jewish category. It represents the free, uncoerced choice of all the people for a way of life based on consent. The political order (*seder medini*) arises from consent. The consensual, covenant-making act precedes the giving of the Torah. Thus, law—

whatever its source—is predicated on consent. "There is no force to law (*tokef l'hukato*) without the consent of the people."[9] Consent looms large in Federbush's thought. Not only was the Sinai covenant contracted with popular consent, but the ongoing authority of public law requires consent. Only what the people accept and consent to has the force of law.[10] If the majority of the people, on their own or through their representatives, reject legislation, even after it has become law, it becomes void. Federbush sees an ongoing embodiment of popular consent in the fact that Joshua needed to recovenant with Israel at Shechem, even though his authority was accepted by them, in order for the Torah's law to have force. Kings needed to secure the consent of the people for their *mishpat ha-melukha*. In the same spirit, the Talmud (B. Berachot 55) lays down that a communal leader, a *parnas*, cannot be appointed over the public (*tzibur*) unless the public accepts him (*elah im kayn nimlakhim b'tzibur*).[11]

In proposing covenant as the fundamental category, Federbush is trying not only to underscore consent as the ground of authority, but also to articulate the unique circumstances of constitution-making. The constitution, although it contains law, precedes law. It arises prior to any law-making body, such as a legislature, which it authorizes. The constitution arises in the free will of an assembled people. Yet this people is not quite the people it wants to become. By accepting a constitution, Torah, the people is also making itself, imagining its own possibility. This possibility, the ideal type of a *medinat ha-torah*, is a state where moral ends are pursued in a moral way. In Federbush's view, the early states of antiquity were purely affairs of defense and aggression. Ethics pertained to the interpersonal, not the political realm. The ideal of a moral state, first mooted in Greece, is achieved, at least on an ideal level, in Israel. Israel's breakthough vis-à-vis Greece comes with the idea of human equality. In the ideal *medinat ha-torah*, both the Israelite and the resident alien have full equality of rights.[12] (Later, Federbush will argue for the moral and legal necessity of complete equality between citizens of different religions in the State of Israel, even to the extent that a non-Jew may be prime minister of the country if that is the will of the people!) The people can imagine themselves as a political people working toward a moral polity because the covenant—which precedes the state—has given them a utopian political vision (*hazon medini*).[13]

Israelite covenantalism, Federbush believes, has inspired both the polity building of the American puritans and the social contract tradition, which he evidently endorses. The latter is based on the early modern political philosophers' reading of Scripture. Unlike those moderns, however, Federbush wants to uphold the idea of theocracy and transvalue it for the sake of democracy. Unlike Hobbes, for example, Federbush believes that consenting, covenant-making humans, in this case Jews, did not alienate their rights to a human sovereign. "In the making of a covenant, the children of Israel did not give up their rights for the good of a human sovereign (*shilton enoshi*), rather, they gave their rights to God."[14] The consequence of this is that they retain a radical equality vis-à-vis one another. By making God their ruler, they deprive any presumptive human ruler of full legitimacy. Citing Spinoza with approval, Federbush endorses the idea of theocracy. The rule of God in theory made for a democratic order in practice.

> The Hebrews retained for themselves the right to govern themselves. They did not transmit this right to any ruler. The king was therefore only a public administrator (*menahel 'inyanei ha-am*) in terms of fixed, prior principles to which he was also subject.[15]

Theocracy, for Federbush, necessitates democracy. In this way, Federbush lays the ground for the legitimacy of the State of Israel, as an expression of popular political and legal—that is, constitutional—will.

Federbush's interpretation of the concept of theocracy is both realistic and republican, like Martin Buber's.[16] That is, he believes that early Israel was both descriptively and normatively theocratic. He rejects the later corruptions of the term into hierocracy as wholly out of keeping with the original character of the Torah constitution. This will come out more fully as we consider his construction of *mishpat ha-melukha* and *mishpat ha-torah* below. At this point, I want only to note that Federbush endorses another typical feature of modern republicanism: that religion should not have coercive power in the public realm.[17] Although he is not always consistent, Federbush generally follows Mendelssohn. Religion should exemplify, instruct, reform. It must not coerce. He shrewdly observes that in the United States, with its tradition of governmental non-involvement (*ayn ha-shilton ha-medini mit'arev b'inyanei ha-emunah*), religious institutions and practices are far more vital than in many European countries with long traditions of establishment. But beyond sociological observation and concession to the spirit of the times, Federbush posits that the division between religious authority and political authority is a matter of fundamental principle. This is in fact the major thrust of his entire work: that there is a categorical distinction between Torah law (*mishpat ha-torah*) and civil law (*mishpat ha-melukha)*. Each of these have their own proper sphere, their own *who* and *how*. The legitimacy of the modern republican project of the State of Israel, from a traditionalist point of view, rests on articulating the basis, scope, and powers of civil authority constituted under *mishpat ha-melukha*. Thus, as a provisional answer to the question of *what* the Torah as a constitution is, Federbush might answer: The Torah is a product of divine-human and human-human covenanting, based on consent, that allows for a principled yet dynamic relationship with political and historical reality.[18] The instrument for negotiating the relationship between the moral principles embedded in the practice of covenanting and political and historical reality is *mishpat ha-melukha*.

Mishpat ha-Torah and *Mishpat ha-Melukha*

The Torah as constitution engenders two broad spheres of legal and political creativity, a religious authority (*reshut ha-datit*) and a civil authority (*reshut ha-medinit*).[19] Federbush also uses the concept of "crowns," that is, *ketarim—keter kehuna* and *keter malkhut*—to designate these two spheres. The division was anticipated by the relative separation of roles between Moses and Aaron. This separation was constitutionalized by Moses, when he designated Joshua to be his successor in the domain of political leadership, while Elazar succeeded Aaron in the domain of religious leadership.[20] This Mosaic distinction is presupposed by Deuteronomy 17:9, when it counsels Israel to take its difficult questions to the "levitical priests or the magistrate in charge at the time." In Federbush's view, the principle of two *ketarim* was only breached during the later Hasmonean dynasty, when the priestly Hasmoneans assumed the royal title. He cites with approval Nachmanides' comment on Genesis 49 that the dynasty was punished due to this infringement on constitutional separation of authorities.

The Torah constitution frames a regime in which power is divided between authorities. Each of these authorities has its own legal framework, *mishpat ha-torah* (or *mishpat torani*) or *mishpat ha-melukha* (or *mishpat 'ivri* or *mishpat yisrael*). By using traditional language, Federbush tries to avoid importing an inappropriate, modernist distinction between religion and politics into ancient Judaism. The traditional language invokes a valid distinction. The distinction between two spheres can be maintained in an ancient context where kings and priests clearly had different functions. It is somewhat more difficult to sustain when leadership of the people passes to rabbis who incorporate both political and religious functions. Who represents *mishpat ha-torah*? Who represents *mishpat ha-melukha*? While civil leaders such as *parnasim* represent the latter, rabbis can represent both the latter and the former. Rabbis seem to wear two hats. Rabbis are as responsible for extending and developing *mishpat ha-melukha* as "laymen." The consequence of this is that, because rabbis are so involved in *mishpat ha-melukha*, it is hard to know from Federbush what is left of *mishpat ha-torah*.

Within the context of this (largely exilic) situation, Federbush seems to mean by *mishpat ha-torah* predominantly religious-cultic matters, that is, those matters most reminiscent of sacrificial procedures, as well as fixed halakhic rules. However, it is unclear from his text what, at the end of the day, really does fall into this category. Citing the *prosbul* as an example, he is convinced that the Torah gives sages broad power (indeed, gives them a duty) to innovate. One "fixed" part of Torah can be set aside to safeguard another and thereby preserve the whole.[21] So what actually counts as fixed halakha, settled *mishpat ha-torah*? Again, this is not quite clear. Federbush believes that much of the edifice of Jewish law, constructed over centuries in the diaspora, has now become questionable.[22] Statehood represents a fundamental shift. Rabbis must not avoid responsibility for making hard choices to preserve Torah under new conditions of national sovereignty.[23] Bold innovation requires the renewal and cultivation, in a systematic fashion, of *mishpat ha-melukha*. The force of his view is that, in a Jewish state, *mishpat ha-torah* is subordinated to *mishpat ha-melukha*. As the more dynamic, pragmatically oriented doman of the collective enterprise, *mishpat ha-melukha* rescues *mishpat ha-torah* from otherworldliness and irrelevancy. Similarly, those who represent *mishpat ha-torah* are subordinated to the representative, democratic institutions of the state. There is to be no clerical estate, no council of Torah sages, so to speak, with veto power over democratically formulated legislation. While there must be a chief rabbinate with a proper interest in promoting education about and commitment to Jewish law, it ought to have no coercive power.[24]

Before further elaborating his conception of *mishpat ha-melukha*, it is worth clarifying the conceptual framework of his discourse. As a religious Zionist, Federbush seems to have accepted the idea of "Hebrew law," *mishpat ivri*, as an organizing category for the study of the Jewish legal tradition. *Mishpat ivri* represented an attempt to construe the edifice of Jewish law as a product of historic, national creativity. German university-trained scholars such as Asher Gulak, influenced by the romanticist historian Friedrich Carl von Savigny, saw in Jewish law the unfolding of the Jewish nation's *Volksgeist*.[25] In Gulak's view, as David Myers puts it, Jewish law revealed a "uniquely ethical dimension: Jewish law entailed no segregation of law and morality; nor was it beholden to any single political leader or state organ, but rather to the ideal of social justice under God's dominion."[26]

Federbush's penchant for seeing Jewish law as a national enterprise informed by fundamental Hebraic social values such as equality or justice (*tzedek*), as well as his frequent use of the term *mishpat ivri*, indicates his adoption of this perspective. As such, halakha, or, as he puts it, *mishpat ha-torah*, seems to be a function of a more embracing paradigm. It emerges out of the covenantal, interpretive life of a constitutional people. It responds to the need of the constitutional people to constitute itself as a polity in history. Federbush is therefore in no sense a traditional halakhist. Indeed, he believes that many Jewish laws are outmoded products of the diaspora, toward which he has a quite ambivalent attitude. At any rate, Federbush believes that the true freedom offered now to Jews by the Jewish state must be accompanied by a true renewal of *mishpat ivri*. To avoid what the Hebrew essayist Ahad Ha-am called "slavery in the midst of freedom" and to effectively pursue redemption, law in Israel must return to its biblical, Talmudic, and subsequent sources. What saves this vision from reaction or antiquarianism is Federbush's frank admission that *mishpat ha-melukha*, although never abandoned, did shrivel in the diaspora and now needs bold and innovative advancement, as well as his buoyant confidence that it can be advanced in a consistently republican and humane direction. Rabbis, in Federbush's scheme, must be on the side of such advancement.

Strictly speaking, *mishpat ha-melukha*, a term deriving from I Samuel 10, designates the power given to properly constituted civil authority to frame the laws of the polity, including its civil (*ezrahi*) and criminal (*pelili*) laws, and especially to frame the duty of the citizen toward the state (*hovat ha-ezrah klapei ha-medina*).[27] Citing a responsum of Rav Kook, Federbush extends the category even further to include all matters of public policy and political decision bearing on the public welfare. Following Maimonides, R. Nissim, and others, Federbush endorses the view that civil authority can, indeed must, bypass or suspend Torah law when, in its judgment, that is required.

Mishpat ha-melukha is the golden thread uniting the Jewish political experience. Recalling nationalistically oriented historians such as Y. Baer, Federbush believes that properly constituted civil authority was present in every phase of historical Jewish existence. The entire Jewish communal experience, from antiquity to the present, took place under the constitutional umbrella of *mishpat ha-melukha*. This continuity implies that, although the State of Israel does represent a radical opportunity for renewal and fundamental shift in perspective, it does not represent a total break with the past. For Federbush, there is no return to history. The Jews never left it.

The continuous instantiation of properly constituted authority that characterizes the internal political history of the Jewish people derives from the people itself. In a time without a king, the powers of the king revert to the people who constitute whatever form of governance they find acceptable. For Federbush, the optimal regime is republican. Leaning heavily on Abravanel and his Talmudic antecedent, R. Nehorai, Federbush argues that appointing a king was an aberrancy that offended against the fundamental commitment of the Torah to the equality of all its citizens.[28] The law granting the appointment of a king was permissive rather than obligatory. Some laws, such as those relating to the beautiful captive or the blood avenger, were solely intended to restrain essentially pagan practices that had become prevalent in Israel. Kingship, on Federbush's view, was one of these. When the conditions that the law was intended to restrict become outmoded, then the law becomes outmoded as well. Thus the Talmud has made it impossible to restore kingship as there is no longer a Sanhedrin of seventy and a prophet to crown him.[29] There is no question that the State of Israel cannot be a monarchy but must be a republic.

Even in the days when there was a king, his power was limited by the constitution. The king's power to punish rebels, for example, was understood by the Talmud to derive from a consensual authorization by the people, given in the time of Joshua.[30] However, the people as a whole retain their right to rebel (indeed, they have a *duty* to rebel) should the king become a tyrant (*rodan*).

According to R. Nissim, a king (or those other forms of regime that are authorized to promulgate *mishpat ha-melukha*) must only be obeyed when his laws are righteous laws (*hukei tzedek*).[31]

Constitutionally limited secular governance is fully legitimated by the category of *mishpat ha-melukha*. In addition to matters of governance per se, Federbush also wants to legitimate "secular" forms of judgment and arbitration. He cites Talmudic evidence to show that secular courts, that is, courts that decided civil and even criminal matters on the basis of equity and prudence rather than positive halakha, existed in ancient Syria (*'arkhaot she-besurya*).[32] Their decisions are acceptable if accepted by the people. Agreeing with R. Menachem Meiri that the appointment of nonrabbinic judges is valid even if rabbinic experts are available, Federbush validates the courts of the State of Israel. He does so not to bow to necessity but to exalt the republican principle of popular sovereignty.

This principle leads Federbush to argue against those who, like the leader of his movement, R. Judah Fishman-Maimon, wanted to renew the Sanhedrin as a way of developing *mishpat ha-melukha* after its long latency in the diaspora. There are three positions, according to Federbush, in the debate on the renewal of the Sanhedrin. Some partisans want to give the "ruler's staff to the upholders of Torah," thus bringing the nation under the rule of Torah. All legislation would have to come out of the Sanhedrin. Others want to create an authoritative, universally recognized halakhic body that could settle questions and resolve disagreements within the Orthodox (*haredi*) world. Federbush does not give either of these much credence.[33] The third position accords much more with his outlook: the role of a renewed Sanhedrin would be one of sweeping advancement. It would not merely resuscitate unused halakhot, but comprehensively rework *mishpat ivri* under the new conditions of national sovereignty. This would be similar to R. Johanan ben Zakkai's making the court at Yavneh functionally equivalent to the Sanhedrin of Jerusalem.

After reviewing the nearly unlimited powers that sages assembled in a Sanhedrin would have, Federbush shrinks from the idea of renewal on halakhic, sociological, but also republican grounds. Halakhically, Federbush sides with what was apparently Maimonides' later position, that rabbinic ordination (*semikha*) cannot be restored.[34] Sociologically, Federbush observes that if R. Jacob Berab was unable to gather consent for a restoration of *semikha* in the sixteenth century, how much more impossible would it be today. Not only have most of the Jewish people, in Israel and elsewhere, abandoned Orthodoxy, but the Orthodox are badly divided among themselves. Furthermore, Judaism's historic tendency toward lenient rulings has been replaced by a culture of restriction. The contemporary rabbinate cannot even decree a fast day to commemorate the victims of the Shoah; how could a Sanhedrin boldly innovate in an Orthodox world dominated by an ethos of strictness (*humra*)? These conditions undermine the consent necessary for a

Sanhedrin to have authority. Restoring a Sanhedrin, even if possible, under conditions where its authority would not be recognized by society or state would be grievous for Torah. At any rate, the courts of the State of Israel, which do have the support and consent of the people of Israel, fill the role that a Sanhedrin and its subsidiary courts would have.[35] However, Federbush has not abandoned, as a theoretical possibility, the desirability of an eventual Sanhedrin. Until the time that society is ready for such an eventuality, the chief rabbinate should be strengthened and enhanced. Its authority should be broadened and "the best among us" should be appointed to it to judge according to Torah.[36] The precise sphere of its authority, however, is not defined by Federbush.

The lingering tension between republican and democratic principles on the one hand, and the range and scope of religious authority or influence on the other is an outstanding problem in Federbush's thought. This may be explored by reference to some concrete cases. Slightly less than half of Federbush's book is devoted to fundamental political-theoretical questions, with the remainder dedicated to specific domains of policy and law. An investigation of a few of these areas will give us some sense of what a politics of *mishpat ha-melukha* would be like.

Aspects of Life under *Mishpat ha-Melukha*

Ideally, there is a distinction between law and ethics: ethics does not require sanctions. Ethics flows from loving one's neighbor as oneself. The sages of Israel, however, introduced ethically-oriented commandments, backed by legal sanctions, in order to solidify moral awareness in their society. These moral commandments can serve as a basis for social legislation today. In fact, Federbush claims, the morally directed legislation of ancient Israel inspires the social legislation of the progressive societies today. By moral commandments or legislation, Federbush has in mind *mitzvot* such as burying the dead, dowering brides, welcoming guests, visiting the sick, and ransoming captives, all of which were derived, according to Maimonides, from the commandment to "love your neighbor as yourself."[37] Present legislation should be developed on the model, and in terms of the spirit, of this ancient *mishpat ivri*.

Federbush would involve the state in a primary cultural question. He argues that one of the first tasks of government is to secure Hebrew as a national language. He bases himself on a mishna that requires that public declarations be in Hebrew.[38] Citing other halakhic and aggadic sources, Federbush contends that using Hebrew as a daily language is both a social and political necessity and a redemptive spiritual duty (*hiyuv leumi v'mitzvah datit k'ehad*).[39]

Spreading Hebrew literacy depends, of course, on the larger project of spreading literacy. Federbush envisions an expansive state role in education.

Basing himself on a well-established Talmudic precedent whereby education became a public matter already in the Second Commonwealth, he extends the state's duty to the establishment of schools of all kinds.[40] The state has a duty to establish primary and secondary schools, vocational and technical schools, liberal arts and professional institutions. Girls and boys are to have equal access. Women's education is nonproblematic for him. Indeed, it is a positive value and a necessity. Indeed, women can hold high elective and judicial office in the republic if the people so will. Curricula should include not only the requisite academic subjects but sports, exercise, and self-defense. Just as the state is obligated, through ancient precedent, to support schools of Torah, it is also obligated to develop secular education through *mishpat ha-melukha*.

Federbush also considers areas of taxation, tariffs, and price fixing. The self-governing *kehilla* had much experience in the area of taxation. He notes that a long development of medieval *mishpat ha-melukha* worked to distribute tax burdens more equitably. A shift took place from a head tax toward an asset-based income tax. Nonetheless, while the past can instruct and the spirit of prior law can guide, the legislator must be aware of prevailing conditions and of fundamental changes in economic life over the centuries. Although the sources do not provide explicit support for a progressive income tax, Federbush believes that this is what social equity requires.[41] He also believes that government must take an activist role in breaking up monopolies, setting affordable prices for essential commodities, and ensuring competition. The Talmud and later sources present numerous examples of governmental intervention against price gouging and cartels.[42] Federbush rejects laissez-faire, although his optimal balance between markets and command is not clear.

It is clear that Federbush's state would have a somewhat paternalistic cast. Developing the ancient law of *ma'akeh* (Deut. 22), for example, Federbush would have the state intensively involved in guarding the health of its citizens. One area where it would do so is occupational safety. *Mishpat* would be developed to compel employers to minimize risk on factory floors.[43] The image that emerges from such social legislation is of an interventionist welfare state on a European social democratic model. The goal and ground of such legislation is the promotion and protection of the common good (*tovat ha-klal*). Federbush's assumption is that such laws are simply desirable and that an educated and enlightened populace would agree to them. But, to use a typical case, would a motorcycle rider who does not want to wear a helmet have a right to not wear one under Federbush's *mishpat ha-melukha*? It is not clear how he would deal with liberals of a Millian sort who reject paternalism on principle.

A more difficult example of the tension between a modern, secularized democracy and a paternal, religiously informed republicanism may be found in Federbush's consideration of issues bearing on the land of Israel. Here the tension between frameworks of normativity becomes acute. Federbush believes that the conquest of the land (*kivush ha-aretz*) is a mitzvah.[44] This seems to be an example of fixed halakha. He tries to balance his seemingly absolute commitment to the equality of all citizens, including national minorities, with what he takes to be a corollary of *kivush ha-aretz*, namely, that Jews must have sovereignty (*ribonut*) in the land. Whereas non-Jews can hold elected office, enjoy equality before the law, or operate their own courts if they so chose, Jewish sovereignty means Jewish control of the land. This means: (a) conquest of the land from foreigners is a commandment of the Torah incumbent on all generations; (b) it is forbidden to abandon the land and incumbent to develop it; (c) Jews are commanded to dwell in the land; (d) it is forbidden to divide the land and to alienate any portion of it within its historic boundaries; (e) it is forbidden to give control over the land to another people; (f) if the non-Jewish inhabitants of the land of Israel flee during a war (as was, he notes, actually the case), it is incumbent on Jews to settle the places they deserted; (g) it is forbidden to found another land as a homeland for Jews if all of the land of Israel is not in Jewish hands. This is the view of Nachmanides, which Federbush quotes with apparent approval. On their face, such absolutized laws would leave a Jewish government little room for policy making in the area of, for example, territorial concession. It is not clear how Federbush would balance his affirmation of representative government with these seemingly inflexible principles of the Torah.

We can get some indication of this balance from a related matter of policy. As a consequence of the commandment to dwell in the land of Israel (*yishuv b'eretz yisrael*), the right to leave the land of Israel is not absolute. The Torah imposes restrictions on who may leave and for what purposes.[45] Although there are some disagreements between commentators, Federbush concludes that the criteria for permission to leave are two: first, the trip abroad must be for a reason that ultimately is for the good of the land and its inhabitants (*l'tovat yishuv eretz yisrael*); second, the one who departs must have the intention to return.[46] If one does not have the intention to return, it would be forbidden even to leave for a necessary purpose such as Torah study or marriage. Federbush derives from this that, according to *mishpat ivri,* the state should restrict exit visas to those citizens who must travel either for acts such as Torah study or marriage, or whose business is for the good of the state. Additionally, the state should grant visas only for limited amounts of time and only to those citizens whose declared intention is to return. Should a citizen (*ezrah yisraeli*) intend to settle permanently in the diaspora, he or she should not be allowed to leave.

This remarkably illiberal policy recommendation brings into clear view the huge gulf between a republic with the Torah as its constitution and a modern constitutional republic. Although Federbush began his political analysis with a doctrine of rights reminiscent of contractarianism, he compromises, indeed repudiates, that doctrine when the Torah imposes a restriction that he cannot or will not undo. Of course, that Federbush is unwilling to loosen restrictions on what, in human rights terminology, is the "right to leave" does not mean that a properly constituted legislature operating under *mishpat ha-melukha* would agree. Federbush's system, after all, is remarkably flexible in its insistence that fixed Torah laws can be suspended in order to preserve other laws or principles. Federbush might agree that in 2000, unlike 1952, the Jewish population has reached a sufficiently critical mass so that citizens do not need to be prevented or discouraged from taking casual trips abroad. Nonetheless, it is at such junctures that the fundamental theoretical differences between Federbush's republic and the modern, secular republic appear.

Among the weaknesses of Federbush's political thought is, as we have seen, the lack of a clear-cut plan for separating spheres of authority. Although he has secured a theoretical separation between *mishpat ha-torah* and *mishpat ha-melukha*, he has not given us a well-articulated framework for institutionalizing these authorities. Furthermore, he has not devised a proper separation of powers within the *keter malkhut* itself. A separation and balance of powers among executive, legislative, and judicial branches seems to be presupposed, but it is not worked out in any adequate detail. Consequently, crucial matters in the design of government are unaddressed, which is to say that vital issues of freedom are unaddressed. These are serious weaknesses indeed.

But Federbush's strengths, while not exactly compensating for his weaknesses, are considerable. Perhaps his book should be viewed not as a fully developed theory of the Torah as constitution, but as an affirmation of republican politics searching for a Jewish expression. Federbush's contribution was to situate the modern political triumph of the Jewish people—the State of Israel—in an ancient and ongoing political tradition. Furthermore, he construed that tradition as basically republican in nature. Even though his project builds in areas of conflict between secularly and religiously oriented moral and political approaches, he also diminishes conflict at a fundamental level by validating the state and its institutions. His emphasis on the covenantal origins of the Jewish polity elegantly ties the modern republic to the Mosaic theocracy. In addition, his stress on consent as the ground of public authority as well as the flexibility of *mishpat ha-melukha* constantly work to offset the more unacceptable implications of theocracy. He has built a fertile tension into his own system.

The theoretical appeal of Federbush's system becomes clear in a brief comparison with Isaac Breuer. In Breuer's posthumously published Hebrew work *Nahaliel*, he describes his own *medinat ha-torah*.[47] Breuer's understanding of Torah as constitution is, unlike Federbush's, highly metaphysical. For Breuer, the Torah is a metahistorical "creation law," absolute, unnatural, and unchanging. It is in no sense a human artifact, a product of political reflection and judgment. Politics and history are enmeshed in a fallen cosmos over which the Sabbath veils of causality and individuation have been cast. To live according to Torah lifts one out of an ontic alienation, both personal and corporate, into a sphere of holiness. Yet this remarkably apolitical, contemplative vision has a thoroughly political cast. Breuer believes that Torah is in fact a constitution. Torah's full range is apparent only in a state where its laws rule. Jewish life, in its fullness and truth, is achievable only in such a state. *Nahaliel* sketches such a state, drawing almost entirely on Maimonides' *Mishneh Torah*. Because the Torah is an absolute law, a law exempt from transformation, growth, or decay, Breuer's political vision has a more purely utopian character than Federbush's. Although he has not fully worked out the constitutional mechanisms, it is clear that, in an important sense, the people rule in Federbush's republic. For Breuer, however, the law, not the people, rules. And the law is in no sense the expression of a general will. It is the expression purely and solely of the divine will. Breuer's book culminates in the laws of the rebuilt Temple, where the Shekhina will dwell in the Holy of Holies and history will reach its sought-for end. The concluding chapters of Federbush's work, in revealing contrast, deal with warfare, treaties, and the ethics of euthanasia. We can thus see a vast difference in scale between the two efforts. Despite its limitations, Federbush's work was intended as a contribution to an essentially practical and political discourse. Breuer's work remains embedded in a vision more unabashedly metaphysical than political. Both intend that the Torah be the constitution of the Jewish polity, yet their ideas of *what* that Torah is could not be more different. Nor could the matters of *who* or *how* be settled more differently. Of course, a radical secularist would be equally disinterested in both accounts, but that should not diminish the distance between them. What a modern state that embraces the Torah as its constitution would look like depends very much on what is meant by Torah and on who does the drafting.

Notes

1. Charles McIlwain, *Constitutionalism Ancient and Modern* (Ithaca: Cornell University Press, 1940), 24.

2. For a review of these issues, see Carl Joachim Friedrich, *The Philosophy of Law in Historical Perspective* (Chicago: University of Chicago Press, 1963), chs. 18-19. See also H. L. A. Hart, *The Concept of Law* (Oxford: Oxford University Press, 1978), ch. 9.

3. David Novak, *Jewish Social Ethics* (New York: Oxford University Press, 1992), 22-38.

4. William F. Harris II, *The Interpretable Constitution* (Baltimore: Johns Hopkins University Press, 1993), ix.

5. Ibid., xi.

6. Lenn E. Goodman, *On Justice: An Essay in Jewish Philosophy* (New Haven: Yale University Press, 1991), especially chs. 1, 4.

7. On the need to move constitutional theory away from dependence on legal and philosophy of law paradigms, see Harris, *The Interpretable Constitution*, 19-29.

8. For the views of the leading political philosophers of early modernity against religion, see Douglas Kries, ed. *Piety and Humanity: Essays on Religion and Early Modern Political Philosophy* (Lanham, Md.: Rowman & Littlefield, 1997).

9. Shimon Federbush, *Mishpat ha-Melukha b'Yisrael* (Jerusalem: Mosad Ha-Rav Kook, 1973), 34.

10. Ibid., 35. See Y. Shabbat 1:5; Y. Horayot 1:5

11. Ibid., 37.

12. Ibid., 15, 20-21.

13. By "utopian," I don't mean something fantastic and unreal, but rather intend Karl Mannheim's sense of the implicit ideal tendency of a political project. A utopia is an immanent and regulative norm.

14. Federbush, *Mishpat ha-Melukha*, 34.

15. Ibid.

16. For Buber's major statement on theocracy, see his *The Kingship of God*, Richard Scheimann, trans. (New York: Harper & Row, 1967).

17. Federbush, *Mishpat ha-Melukha*, 28.

18. It may perhaps be objected at this point that too little has been said about Torah as a divine-human covenant. Federbush actually says almost nothing on this point; he has no apparent doctrine of revelation. His discourse on covenant is almost exclusively framed in political terms. He goes against the grain of the rabbinic tradition of understanding covenant that we explored in chapter 3.

19. Federbush, *Mishpat ha-Melukha*, 27.

20. Ibid., 45.

21. Ibid., 9.

22. Ibid.

23. Ibid., 11.

24. Ibid., 28.

25. On Gulak and the construction of the discipline of *mishpat ivri* as an aspect of Zionist historiography, see David N. Myers, *Re-Inventing the Jewish Past: European Jewish Intellectuals and the Zionist Return to History* (New York: Oxford University Press, 1995), 88. On Savigny and the historical school, see Friedrich, *The Philosophy of Law*, 138-42.

26. Myers, *Re-Inventing the Jewish Past*, 89.

27. Federbush, *Mishpat ha-Melukha*, 49.

28. Ibid., 40.

29. Ibid., 42.

30. Ibid., 85. See Sanhedrin 49a.

31. Comment on Nedarim 28, cf. R. David b. Zimra; *Mishneh Torah*, Laws of Kings 3:8. See Federbush, *Mishpat ha-Melukha*, 87.

32. Ibid., 55. See B. Sanhedrin 23a.

33. Ibid., 92-93.

34. Ibid., 98.

35. Ibid., 100.

36. Ibid., 101.

37. *Mishneh Torah*, Laws of Mourning 14:1; Laws of Gifts to the Poor 8:10.

38. Mishnah Sotah ch 7.

39. Federbush, *Mishpat ha-Melukha*, 105.

40. B. Baba Batra 21a.

41. Federbush, *Mishpat ha-Melukha*, 108.

42. Ibid., 110.

43. Ibid., 112.

44. Ibid., 114.

45. *Mishneh Torah*, Laws of Kings, 5:9.

46. Federbush, *Mishpat ha-Melukha*, 118.

47. Isaac Breuer, *Nahaliel* (Jerusalem: Mossad Ha-Rav Kook, 1982). For a full treatment of Breuer's political philosophy, see Alan Mittleman, *Between Kant and Kabbalah* (Albany: State University of New York Press, 1991), ch. 4.

Afterword

In the context of an argument against Platonic political philosophy, Cicero wrote:

> There are some also who, either from zeal in attending to their own business or through some sort of aversion to their fellow-men, claim that they are occupied solely with their own affairs, without seeming to themselves to be doing anyone any injury. But while they steer clear of the one kind of injustice, they fall into the other: they are traitors to social life, for they contribute to it none of their interest, none of their effort, none of their means. (*De Officiis*, Book I:IX, 31)

Cicero is arguing against the philosopher king for whom public service is an unwelcome intrusion upon philosophical contemplation. For justice, Cicero believes, requires not only that one's fellows not be harmed, but that the common interests are served (*communi utilitati serviatur*). This sturdy republican sentiment translates well into the Jewish idiom. When the Talmud rules that "all Israel is responsible one for another" (B. Shevuot 39a), it too speaks of a common care for the polity and of the need to inculcate those virtues that make public-spiritedness possible. A much later source, the communal records, beginning in the 16th century, of the Jewish community of Cracow preserves the oath that the Polish magistrate imposed upon the newly elected Jewish communal leader. He is told to "preserve his Jewish republic in justice." No private interests, no favors to family or friends, no conspiracies should stand in the way of serving the common good (*tovat ha-klal*).[1]

Throughout these chapters, I have sought to bring out the republican strains within Jewish thought and political experience. Admittedly, this orientation is not the only one to be found in the Jewish sources. Medieval thinkers, such as Maimonides, developed a model of Jewish polity based on the Platonic philosopher-king. The republican strain is sidelined or suppressed by this model. Not surprisingly, Maimonides and some of his followers, such as Rabbenu Nissim, opt for a strong central leadership where the leader has wide discretion and can overturn the Torah constitution for the sake of political exigency. In this philosophically inclined expression of Judaism, as Leo Strauss made quite clear, Maimonides followed Plato rather than Aristotle in political theory. The philosopher-king, mediated by Islamic thinkers such as al-Farabi, better explained the archetype of the sacred lawgiver, Moses the prophet, than the Aristotelian mixed regime could, assuming that the Jews even knew of the *Politics*. Maimonides' Platonic political theory was linked to his neoplatonic theory of prophecy. But the idea of prophecy and the heavy dependence on charismatic leadership that it implies is, after a century of dictatorship, an unwelcome starting point for political reflection today. The ennobling capacity of persons to reach decisions in common in the absence of strong central leadership is more salient. For this reason, I have emphasized the republican dimensions of Jewish political teaching.

To say that the tradition has significant republican contours is not to say that the tradition is democratic, nor is it to deny that it is theocratic. It is not democratic in the modern sense because, although Jewish polities were often governed through direct elections, leadership had to do with more than the representation of the popular will. The polity as a whole was never considered a purely secular thing. It was a public thing, but the public to which it belonged was a "kingdom of priests and a holy nation." The ideal of divine rule, mediated through shared fidelity to a sacred law as interpreted by rabbinic elites, supervened upon a merely instrumental understanding of public life. But that too is compatible with republicanism, as the long tradition of civil religion in America obliquely illustrates. This republic once saw itself as a divine errand in the wilderness, its experiment in liberty being God's last, best, hope for mankind. If sentiments such as these are thought to be shamelessly self-serving nowadays it is not only because of increased secularity and cynicism. It is also because of decreased republicanism. The republican tradition, with its emphasis on community, was sensible about the need for public religion. Even those thinkers hostile to traditional religion, such as Spinoza or Locke, were convinced that republics required an "enlightened" religion, without which community—and hence polity—would be unsustainable.

What can Judaism, conceived to some degree as a republican project, bring to America? What can America, conceived as a republic in need of rediscovering that constitutive dimension of itself, bring to Judaism? Questions as large as these surely require a book of their own. But the outlines, at least, of an answer may be mooted. In the best American tradition, a serious, lively, and committed religious community is a place where persons learn to care about common purposes. They learn, as de Tocqueville taught, to acquire a heightened regard for concentric circles of society beyond their own group. Religion in America, at its best, contributed to a strong civic culture. At its worst, of course, it sanctified one or another morally defective status quo. But given the source of both Judaism and Christianity in the Bible, religion in America also brought the resources to undo its own complacency. It is not too late to believe that religion in America, and particularly Judaism with its republican proclivities, may yet contribute to a renewal of American public life and civic culture. It is to be hoped that American Jews find a compelling Jewish voice, nurtured by their own authentic sources, which they can add to the ecumenical political and moral conversation on which republican renewal depends.

This renewal, should it flourish, might also have salutary effects on Judaism. For Judaism as such has not had the opportunity to contribute to a common life engaging both Jews and non-Jews as true equals. Jews have had this opportunity in America, but Judaism, in a sense, has not. Its basic trope is still that of an adversarial relationship with Christianity and with the gentile world in particular. In a climate where Jews are accepted as equal participants in civic life rather than as a tolerated minority, we might expect that Judaism in America would recover and affirm its own civic traditions. It is my hope that this book will make a contribution, however small, to that recovery.

Notes

1. Meyer Balaban, "Der Kahal in Polen in XVI bis XVIII Jahrhundert, *Neue Jüdische Monatshefte* (Berlin: M. Goetz, 1916), 552-53.

Index

Abraham, 97, 98, 99
Abraham ibn Ezra, 99-100, 101
Abravanel, Isaac, 100, 101, 166
Adam and Eve, 98
Affirmative Action, 150
Althusius, Johannes, 50
antisemitism, 34
anxiety, 12, 13
apologetics, 2, 4, 8
aqedah, 137
Aristotle, 91, 93, 96, 109, 110, 150, 176
assimilation, 3, 59
authority, and autonomy, 108-09, 124; and charisma, 54, 65; and consent, 48, 49, 68n1, 127; and obligation, 135; sources of, 20-27, 79, 92-102, 159; of Torah constitution, 121, 166, 171
autonomy, Breuer's critique of, 117,121; and personhood, 15, 108-109, 113, 116, 141, 149; and rights, 114, 123

Baer, Yitzhak, 43n25
Bahya ben Asher, 90n33
Bahya ibn Pakuda, 140
Baron, Salo, 16n2
Belfer, Ella, 16n2
beliefs, evaluation of, 7
Biale, David, 16n2
Bible, political teaching of, 9, 21, 50; secular approaches to, 49, 50, 51
Bill of Rights, 116, 126
Blidstein, Gerald, 85, 90n27
Breuer, Isaac, 117-121, 158, 171-172
brit, 58, 62, 73-76, 81-85, 87, 88n3, 89n23
Buber, Martin, 163

Burke, Edmund, 79

ceremonial law, 28, 29, 30
charisma, 77, 96, 97, 101, 104n14
chosenness, 136
Christianity, 20, 28, 30, 57, 75, 138, 177
circumcision, 73, 74, 75, 83, 84, 88n3
civic republicanism. *See* republicanism civil religion, 30, 51, 55, 98, 101, 138, 148
civil society, 131, 132, 136, 137
Cohen, Hermann, 14, 34-35, 108
Cohen, Stuart, 16n, 103n8
commandments, 30, 31, 34. *See also mitzvot*
commerce, 154
commercial republic, 3, 51
common good, Jewish concepts of, 25, 138, 154-156, 169; modern concepts of, 125, 146-151; premodern concepts of, 109, 134
communal autonomy, 19, 20, 28, 29, 42n2, 47. *See also kehilla*
communal enactment, 24, 26, 27
communitarianism, 122, 125, 127,128, 138, 145, 148
community, and common good, 146, 148; as partnership, 25; and personhood, 122-123, 142n7, 149-151; and polity, 126, rabbinic views of, 152-153, 155
concepts, clarification of, 7, 10, 12
conscience, 51
consent, as basis of authority, 49, 68, 93-96, 127, 161-162, 167, 171; and covenant, 71-87, 102, 103n7, 163; and individual autonomy, 108,

179

71, 80, 102; and persons,
134-135; in Jewish thought,
72, 98, 137
political philosophy. *See*
philosophy, and politics
polity, founding of, 91-92
postmodernism, 14
power, abuse of, 100, 147; and
authority, 48,
institutionalization of, 95,
127, 146, 147, 161; and
rights, 114, 123
priests, 53, 56, 164
privacy, 153
prophecy, 23, 39, 51, 55, 56, 57
prophets. *See* prophecy
prudence, 133, 139
Puritanism, 60, 162
Putnam, Hilary, 159

Qumran. *See* Dead Sea Scrolls

rabbis, 27, 44n27, 90n31, 161,
164, 166
Raphael, David, 17n13
Rashi, 87, 89, 95, 99, 100, 103n9
rationalization, 59, 61
Rawls, John, 8, 148-150
rebellion, 97
Reform Judaism, 31, 32
relativism, 110, 116, 121, 126
religious language, 10, 11
representation, 27. *See also*
elections
Republic, 137
republicanism, and Judaism, 157,
163, 166, 169, 171; 176,
modern, 14, 15; and rights,
116-117
revelation, 49, 51, 109, 122,
173n18
rights, and common good, 154,
156; and duty, 131, 132, 135,
136, 137, 142n7; as grounds,
77, 82; in Jewish thought, 49,
162, 170; natural, 146, 148,;
and persons, 15, 107-128
Rosenzweig, Franz, 2, 8

Rotenstreich, Nathan, 45n48
Roth, Sol, 113-117, 121, 122
Rousseau, Jean-Jacques, 27, 93,
100, 138, 147, 148

Saadiah Gaon, 89n18, 133, 140
Sadducees, 39
Sandel, Michael, 7, 116, 128n8,
149, 150
Sanhedrin, 39, 158, 166, 167-168
Schiffman, Lawrence, 88n3
Schorsch, Ismar, 16n, 32, 45n52
Schwarzschild, Steven, 5, 12
science, 109-110, 147
Second Treatise of Government,
146
self, concepts of, 15, 108, 150,
151, 155
self-representation, 20, 31, 41. *See
also* self-understanding of
Jews
self-rule, 121, 128, 158. *See also*
communal autonomy
self-understanding, of Jews, 14,
15, 47, 67. *See also* self-
representation
separation of powers, 171
shame, 135, 139, 140
Shema, 74, 76
Shoah, 167
Social Contract, 148
social contract theory, and
consent, 72, 86, 93; and
covenant, 162; and
individuals, 108, 122-23,
124, 146
sociology of knowledge, 60; of
religion, 59
Socrates, 14, 98
sovereignty, Jewish, 28, 29, 170
Spinoza, excommunication of 28;
influence of, 30, 36, 49,
69n4, 176; political teaching
of, 21, 55
Stammler, Rudolph, 117-118
state, and biblical Israel, 54, 57;
Breuer's view of, 120;
Federbush's view of, 162,

About the Author

Alan Mittleman is Associate Professor of Religion at Muhlenberg College in Allentown, Pennsylvania, and Head of the Religion Department. The author of two prior books on Jewish thought and political life, he also serves as Co-Director of the project "American Jews and the American Public Square" funded by the Pew Charitable Trusts.